Reading the Ground

Brian John

Reading the Ground

The Poetry

of Thomas Kinsella

The Catholic University of
America Press • Washington, D.C.

Printed in the United States of America

The paper used in this publication meets the minimum requirements of American National Standards for Information Science—Permanence of Paper for Printed Library materials, ANSI Z39.48-1984.
∞

Library of Congress Cataloging-in-Publication Data

John, Brian, 1935–
Reading the ground : the poetry of Thomas Kinsella / by Brian John.
p. cm.
Includes bibliographical references (p.) and index.
1. Kinsella, Thomas—Criticism and interpretation.
2. Ireland—In literature. I. Title.
821'.914—dc20
95-17095
ISBN 0-8132-0837-8 (cl : alk. paper).—ISBN 0-8132-0838-6 (pa : alk. paper)

For Margaret

Contents

Acknowledgments

I wish to acknowledge first the poet, Thomas Kinsella, for his generous granting of permission to quote from his copyrighted work and for his patient and willing answers to my various queries. For any errors or failures of judgment, on the other hand, I am, of course, alone responsible. I am grateful also to McMaster University for granting me a research leave and to the McMaster Arts Research Board for a travel grant to the United Kingdom and Ireland. For their courtesy, helpfulness and enthusiasm I appreciate David J. McGonagle, Susan Needham and the staff at the Catholic University of America Press, and especially the invaluable contribution of Philip Holthaus, my copy editor. I particularly cherish the friendship of Eamonn and Rosemary Gunn, from whom I have learned much of Ireland and things Irish. Finally, my greatest debt, as always, is to my wife, Margaret, for her constant support and encouragement.

Abbreviations

AS	*Another September* (Dublin: Dolmen Press, 1958)
BF	*Blood and Family* (Oxford: Oxford University Press, 1988)
D	*Downstream* (Dublin: Dolmen Press; London: Oxford University Press, 1962)
Duanaire	*An Duanaire, 1600–1900: Poems of the Dispossessed*, sel. Seán Ó Tuama, trans. Thomas Kinsella (Dublin: Dolmen Press, 1981)
FCC	*From Centre City* (Oxford: Oxford University Press, 1994)
FD	*Fifteen Dead* (Dublin: Dolmen Press; London: Oxford University Press, 1979)
N	*Nightwalker and Other Poems* (Dublin: Dolmen Press, 1968)
NLD	*Notes from the Land of the Dead and Other Poems* (New York: Knopf, 1973)
NLD Cuala	*Notes from the Land of the Dead* (Dublin: Cuala Press, 1972)

One	*One and Other Poems* (Dublin: Dolmen Press; London: Oxford University Press, 1979)
Poems	*Poems* (Glenageary, Co. Dublin: Dolmen Press, 1956)
PP	*Personal Places*, Peppercanister 14 (Dublin: Dedalus Press, 1990)
SPsyche	*Songs of the Psyche*, Peppercanister 9 (Dublin: Dolmen Press, 1985)
Táin	*The Táin*, trans. Thomas Kinsella (1969; Dublin: Dolmen Press; London: Oxford University Press, 1970)
TNOBIV	*The New Oxford Book of Irish Verse*, ed. and trans. Thomas Kinsella (Oxford: Oxford University Press, 1986)

Introduction

Reviewing Richard Murphy's first volume, *The Archaeology of Love*, in December 1955, Thomas Kinsella welcomed the new poet but gloomily pronounced that "[a] volume from an Irish poet is a rarity in these desolate days."[1] It is a measure of the change—more appropriately, the transformation—poetry in Ireland has experienced in subsequent decades that Kinsella's pronouncement now seems excessive. Yet he could not have anticipated either the succession of major Irish poets—not just Murphy but John Montague, Seamus Heaney, Derek Mahon, and Michael Longley—or the remarkable regeneration of Austin Clarke. For Clarke revealed in the same year as Kinsella's pronouncement a new and strong satirical voice with the publication of *Ancient Lights*, a voice Kinsella defined twenty years later as of "sudden, full-fledged humanitarian rage."[2] Indeed, Kinsella's own slim first volume, *Poems* (1956), was only six months away. Clearly, the current state of Irish literature differs greatly from that in 1955, just as the country itself has undergone similarly far-reaching social, cultural, and economic changes.

1. Kinsella, *Irish Writing* 33 (December 1955): 62.

2. Kinsella, "Introduction" to *Selected Poems*, by Austin Clarke (Dublin: Dolmen Press, 1976), xiii.

Kinsella was not alone in experiencing "those flat years in Ireland at the beginning of the 1950s, depressed so thoroughly that one scarcely noticed it."[3] As "a marooned northerner," John Montague found that "what prevailed in the poetic world of Dublin was acrimony and insult: a poem was to be kicked, not examined; the begrudgers ruled"; he noted that "when I was starting out all Irish poets were in a state of stunned isolation, except for Louis MacNeice."[4] For Derek Mahon in Belfast the situation was no better: "The 1950s were a bleak time in Northern Ireland. The place was a cultural desert. There were one or two painters, but not a single writer of any consequence lived there."[5] Seamus Heaney has likewise described the Northern Ireland of the next decade, in the early sixties, as "being on the outside of things. . . . Belfast at that time had no literary publishers, no poetry readings, no sense of a literary identity."[6]

The problem was hardly new. "There has been little experimental work" among Irish poets for the previous fifteen years, Robert Greacen[7] complained in 1947. Certainly in the thirties the modernist movement had been opposed and Beckett ignored,[8] while the years after Yeats's death represented "pour les intellectuels irlandais des années de dépression—de régression même."[9] Ireland in 1955 continued to suffer from the cultural isolationism practiced by successive governments since the establishment of the Free State in 1922, an isolationism reinforced by its neutrality during World War II.[10] In

3. Kinsella, quoted in Hugh Kenner, "Thomas Kinsella: An Anecdote and Some Reflections," *The Genres of the Irish Literary Revival*, ed. Ronald Schliefer (Norman, Okla.: Pilgrim Books/Dublin: Wolfhound Press, 1980), 179.

4. Montague, *The Figure in the Cave and Other Essays*, ed. Antoinette Quinn (Syracuse: Syracuse University Press, 1989), x, 53–54. Cf. Dennis O'Driscoll, "An Interview with John Montague," *Irish University Review* 19 (Spring 1989): 71.

5. Mahon, "Poetry in Northern Ireland," *Twentieth-Century Studies* 4 (November 1970): 90.

6. Heaney, "The Placeless Heaven: Another Look at Kavanagh," in *The Government of the Tongue* (London: Faber and Faber, 1988), 6.

7. Greacen, "The Two Voices," *Irish Writing* 3 (November 1947): 89.

8. Terence Brown, *Ireland: A Social and Cultural History*, 1922–79 (Glasgow: Collins, 1981), 147, 168. F. S. L. Lyons noted that, while the 1930s produced three superb autobiographies—by Peig Sayers, Tomás Ó Criomhthain, and Muiris Ó Súilleabháin—all three "were essentially vehicles for nostalgia rather than harbingers of a modern literature." See Lyons, *Culture and Anarchy in Ireland*, 1890–1939 (1979; Oxford: Oxford University Press, 1982), 162.

9. Serge Fauchereau, "La génération d'après-guerre," *Les Lettres Nouvelles*, special issue, *Écrivains irlandais d'aujourd' hui*, edited by Serge Fauchereau (March 1973), 99.

10. Lyons, *Culture and Anarchy*, 147ff., 173–74.

Patrick Kavanagh's words, "All Ireland . . . froze for want of Europe."[11] Such weather forecasting applied not only to Irish experience during the 1939–1945 war but, with only minor modification, retroactively. From 1922 until the declaration of the Republic in 1949, various forces—political, cultural, and clerical—combined to create a society intrinsically insular, provincial, and cramped: an economy that remained steadfastly rural and underdeveloped; a culture in which its major writers, such as Joyce and Beckett, lived in voluntary exile; and a church hierarchy that rigidly exercised authority, imposed censorship, and banned authors, books, dramatic performances, paintings, and films in order to preserve "public morals." A record 1,034 books, for example, were banned in 1954 alone, and the Censorship Board was not reined in until the early 1960s.[12] Since independence, the founding fathers had been content to create "one of the most conservative states in Europe."[13] Such deliberate and deep conservatism could also prove claustrophobic[14]—hence the description of the period by one literary historian as "The Era of Inhibitions," and by another as rendering Ireland no longer "a mythological centre" but "a provincial backwater."[15]

Despite its isolationism, however, Ireland did not remain untouched by World War II nor the momentous changes that followed the peace. Commenting upon Seán Ó Riordáin and the postwar generation of poets writing in Irish, Seán Ó Tuama notes: "Post-Christian Europe with its doubts, moods and attitudes, began to really affect the traditional Irish mind from the mid-forties on."[16] In retrospect, it appears not entirely coincidental that the major cultural, social, political, and economic changes that accelerated in the decades after 1945 were matched by a transformed literary situation, the beginnings

11. Kavanagh, *Lough Derg: A Poem* (1942; London: Martin Brian and O'Keeffe, 1978), 16.

12. Brown, *Ireland*, 198. Kevin Boyle and Julia Carson note that "the machinery of literary censorship [the Censorship of Publications Act] is still in place." See *Banned in Ireland: Censorship and the Irish Writer*, ed. Julia Carson for Article 19 (Athens: University of Georgia Press, 1990), viii, 10.

13. F. S. L. Lyons, *Ireland since the Famine* (1971; London: Fontana, 1973), 103.

14. Cf. Eavan Boland, "Downstream," *Tracks* 7 (1987): 20.

15. Maurice Harmon, "The Era of Inhibitions: Irish Literature 1920–60," *Emory University Quarterly* 22 (Spring 1966): 18–28; Seamus Deane, "Irish Poetry and Irish Nationalism," in *Two Decades of Irish Writing: A Critical Survey*, ed. Douglas Dunn (Cheadle, U.K.: Carcanet, 1975), 11.

16. Seán Ó Tuama, "Seán Ó Ríordáin," in *The Pleasures of Gaelic Poetry*, ed. Seán Mac Réamoinn (London: Allen Lane, 1982), 131.

of which became evident in the late fifties. The most concrete evidence may be seen in the increasing international role of the new Republic, which participated in the equally new United Nations and contributed to important UN peacekeeping military forces; in the eventual relaxation of censorship in the 1960s; in the slowly changing place of the Catholic Church in Irish society; and, not least, in the Economic Programme drawn up in 1958 by T. K. Whitaker, to whom Kinsella was at one time private secretary in the Irish Civil Service. The result was a "delayed peaceful social revolution."[17] and the revived economy of the sixties. This is not to say that, overnight, liberalism ruled—in truth, between 1960 and 1965 some 1,900 books were banned—nor that censorship had gone unopposed in previous decades. To their great credit, figures like W. B. Yeats in the early years of the Free State and Sean O'Faolain and Frank O'Connor in the thirties and forties led a constant battle in Ireland for artistic freedom. Yet the combined forces of de Valera nationalism and clerical conservatism prevailed, and it was only in the mid-sixties that John Montague could celebrate their passing in ironic parody of Yeats's refrain: "*Puritan Ireland's dead and gone, / A myth of O'Connor and O'Faolain.*"[18]

Kinsella's gloomy 1955 pronouncement, however, was founded upon literary as well as nonliterary grounds. The young poet starting out, like Murphy or Kinsella himself, was faced with other, more explicitly aesthetic problems. The most crucial was the absence of a satisfactory exemplar or poetic guide, an issue that goes beyond mere imitation to touch upon subject matter, perspective, language, tone, tradition, and the individual talent. In Ireland, where political and linguistic histories complicate the situation, these are no simple matters. The Irish poet writing in English cannot fail to recognize the powerful gravitational pull of the English literary tradition while at the same time wishing to uphold an Irish identity. Stephen Dedalus's musing at the speech of his dean of studies, "a countryman of Ben Jonson," remains relevant: "The language in which we are speaking is his before it is mine. How different are the words, *home, Christ,*

17. David Thornley, "Ireland: The End of an Era?" (1965), quoted in Brown, *Ireland*, 245.

18. Montague, "The Siege of Mullingar," in *A Chosen Light* (London: MacGibbon and Kee, 1967), 60. Censorship and clerical intervention continued, however, causing needless suffering for writers like John McGahern. See *Banned in Ireland*, ed. Carson, 56.

ale, master, on his lips and on mine!"[19] Ireland's Michael Hartnett, who came "with meagre voice / to court the language of [his] people" and in 1975 declared his "Farewell to English" and his intention to write thereafter in Irish only, is a rare exception (and, more recently, has begun writing again in English).[20]

Yet for the writer possessing no Irish or for whom the Gaelic tradition might be at best remote, at worst totally alien, to which literary heritage might he or she look? Individual choice reflected in turn not just language but the particular political and cultural, and in many cases also the religious, tribe with which one aligned oneself. Richard Murphy, through Anglo-Irish ancestry and English education and upbringing, could rely upon either the English or the Anglo-Irish traditions. Nevertheless, one motif, in his early volumes at least, is an acute sense of division within himself, for he was brought up in one world but wanted to belong to another, and was caught between his English and his Irish roots.[21] For Kinsella, brought up in a working-class Catholic family in Dublin, neither the English nor the Anglo-Irish tradition was ultimately satisfactory, because both were intrinsically alien. Although poets like Murphy might remain conscious of and participate in the Anglo-Irish tradition, it was a tradition that, for Kinsella at least, had died with Yeats. "I am not sure that an Anglo-Irish poetry survives," he declared in 1958, "apart from Yeats and his personal reign over two generations. Good poetry by Irishmen is quickly absorbed into the English system and is only vaguely differentiated there."[22] Clearly a more useful model was needed, one that reflected the contemporary Irish mind and one free of what Kinsella then recognized as "the gravitic force of English writing." Austin Clarke, on the other hand, had appeared committed to a Celtic romanesque which in its neomedievalism contributed little to relieving the poet's predicament. Clarke's major achievement was yet to come;

19. James Joyce, *A Portrait of the Artist as a Young Man* (1916; New York: Viking, 1960), 189.

20. Hartnett, *A Farewell to English*, ed. Peter Fallon (1975; Dublin: Gallery Books, 1978), 67. He returned to English with *Inchicore in Haiku* (Dublin: Raven Arts Press, 1985).

21. Writing of his childhood sense of the "truly Irish," Murphy declared: "They seemed sharper, freer, more cunning than we were. Stones, salmon-falls, rain-clouds and drownings had entered and shaped their minds, loaded with ancestral bias"; quoted in Brown, *Ireland*, 191. Cf. Lyons on "the diversity of cultures in Ireland" [English, Gaelic, Anglo-Irish, and Ulster Protestant] in *Culture and Anarchy*, ch. 1.

22. Kinsella, *Poetry Book Society Bulletin* 17 (March 1958).

his previous work seemed more to illustrate problems to be avoided than to provide models to emulate. Patrick Kavanagh was either technically uneven or irrelevant to the concerns of an emerging urban poet—a "memorable and uneven long poem," Kinsella described *The Great Hunger* in 1959, as he welcomed Kavanagh's turning his back on "unconquerable meanness, misunderstanding and injustice."[23]

Above all, however, the ghost of W. B. Yeats proved all-powerful and absorbing. It is not at all coincidental that a recent critic (Dillon Johnston) should focus upon Irish poetry "after Joyce," since Joyce rather than Yeats has proved, for Kinsella and others, the more seminal and liberating exemplar. In Kinsella's case that preference also involved a shared Catholic, urban, and economically depressed upbringing. Moreover, Joyce's achievement was in a different genre and so was less immediately intimidating. Yeats, on the other hand, merely added to the numerous claustrophobic influences closing in upon the emerging Irish poet. As Austin Clarke testified in 1949, "So far as the younger generation of poets are concerned here in Ireland, Yeats was rather like an enormous oak-tree which, of course, kept us in the shade."[24] The English poet Donald Davie, a contemporary of Kinsella and, like him, beginning to publish in the mid-fifties, has argued similarly: "When a poet so great as Yeats is born in a country as small as Ireland, this is a wonderful windfall for everyone in that country *except the poets*. For them it is a disaster."[25] Indeed, for other young English poets Yeats constituted a persistently powerful and overwhelming voice. Philip Larkin acknowledged as an Oxford undergraduate having been "swamped . . . with Yeats" through the influence of Vernon Watkins:

> As a result I spent the next three years [1943–1945] trying to write like Yeats, not because I liked his personality or understood his ideas but out of infatuation with his music (to use the word I think Vernon used). In fairness to myself it must be admitted it is a particularly potent music, pervasive as garlic, and has ruined many a better talent.[26]

23. Kinsella, "Song at Fifty," rev. of *Come Dance with Kitty Stobling*, by Patrick Kavanagh, *Irish Times*, 9 July 1959, p. 8.

24. Clarke, quoted in Dillon Johnston, *Irish Poetry after Joyce* (Notre Dame, Ind.: University of Notre Dame Press/Mountrath: Dolmen Press, 1985), 24. Cf. Patrick Kavanagh, for whom "Yeats dominates the landscape," *Envoy*, June 1950, p. 85.

25. Donald Davie, "Austin Clarke and Padraic Fallon," in *Two Decades of Irish Writing*, ed. Dunn, 41.

26. Larkin, Introduction to *The North Ship* (1945; London: Faber and Faber, 1966), 9.

Consequently, reviewing Austin Clarke's *Ancient Lights* and intensifying Clarke's earlier oak-tree shade imagery, Kinsella saw in the older man "an Irish poet labouring in the double shadow of Yeats and English verse."[27] Yet, as John Jordan later recognized, "The effect of *Ancient Lights* on young poets of the decade was electric,"[28] and, while Clarke's usefulness to Kinsella might not prove extensive, his liberation from beneath that "double shadow" was an important example. The Irish literary landscape in the mid-fifties was in fact in the process of drastic change.

"Yeats's shadow," Kinsella has recently declared, "certainly fell very heavily on Austin Clarke and his generation. But by the time we were growing up, in the nineteen-fifties, Yeats was a poet of the past, no more present, or 'threatening,' than Joyce or anyone else."[29] Yet, as this study will show, Yeats's influence, for all Kinsella's disclaimers, was not so easily overcome nor so finally rejected. Moreover, if Yeats proved either too potent or too superannuated a voice to the emerging Irish poet, the alternative English poetic tradition implied abandonment of one's national origin and identity. Furthermore, the influence of the British publishing houses and recognition by London's literary circles was considerable and seductive. Consequently, the establishment in 1951 of Liam Miller's Dolmen Press, which published Kinsella's work from the very beginning, is an important factor in the development of Irish literature and taste, not to say publishing, in subsequent decades. Even as early as 1958 Kinsella could thus legitimately describe Miller as restocking "a country lean in poetry after recent greatness,"[30] for the Dolmen Press served vitally to redress the balance with British publishing. Twenty-one years later, Kinsella

27. Kinsella, "Art of Austin Clarke," *Irish Press*, 10 March, 1956, p. 6. *Ancient Lights* was printed by Dolmen and issued under Clarke's own imprint of Bridges Press. See Liam Miller, *Dolmen XXV: An Illustrated Bibliography of the Dolmen Press, 1951–1976* (Dublin: Dolmen Press, 1976), 19.

28. Jordan, "Irish Poetry 1939–1972," *Irish Poetry Now*, Project Arts Centre Exhibition Catalogue (29 February–11 March 1972), with preface by Eiléan Ní Chuilleanáin, 7. Cf. Denis Donoghue, for whom Clarke was "the best poet writing in Ireland today"; see "Irish Writing," *Month* n.s., 17 (March 1957): 184.

29. Dennis O'Driscoll, "Interview with Thomas Kinsella," *Poetry Ireland Review* 25 (Spring 1989): 58.

30. Kinsella, *Poetry Book Society Bulletin* 17 (March 1958). Cf. Macdara Woods's view that "[t]here were very few publishers of verse in Ireland in the fifties," in *Poetry Ireland Review* 25 (Spring 1989): 19; and John Montague, "Against the Grain," in *Bitter Harvest: An Anthology of Contemporary Irish Verse* (New York: Charles Scribner's Sons, 1989), xvii.

could speak no less emphatically: "The notion of primary publication in Ireland always seemed important to me—not to look for an English publisher as if that were the only real publication."[31]

Nevertheless, early Kinsella—for all his commitment from the outset to translation from early Irish literature and his publication by Dolmen—shows few obvious signs of distinctively Irish origins. In subject matter, perspective, voice, tone, or diction—all features in the mature Kinsella that are recognizably his and recognizably Irish—he may be readily accommodated as an English poet of the mid-fifties. While this accommodation is, with hindsight, misleading, even such a quintessential Irish element as commitment to place is lacking: the vast majority of his early poems take place against a backdrop of night skies, moon, and stars but only rarely in an explicitly Irish setting. Not surprisingly, then, in the early years of his career, Kinsella was warmly received in Britain, often "placed" among the regional poets of Scotland, Wales, and Ireland, and so incorporated within the broad English tradition. A similar fate has overtaken other Irish poets, especially from the North, in the case of Seamus Heaney as recently as 1982.[32] Moreover, the formal controlled voice and structure of Kinsella's early poetry coincided with the emerging Movement poetry in Britain. He was praised by Donald Davie and Robert Conquest and included in the latter's anthology, *New Lines—II* (1963).[33] Further recognition came through his inclusion in the prestigious Guinness Books of Poetry: "Midsummer" appeared in the 1956–1957 volume (1958) and "Thinking of Mr. D." was the Guinness Award–winning poem the following year. Both *Another September* (1958) and *Downstream* (1962) were made "Choices" of the British Poetry Book Society, and *Nightwalker* (1968) was made a "Recommendation." By 1962 Kinsella could thus be described by even the

31. O'Driscoll, "Interview," 59.

32. Both G. S. Fraser, ed., in *Poetry Now* (London: Faber and Faber, 1956), and Anthony Thwaite, in *Poetry Today, 1960–1973* (Harlow, U.K.: Longman and the British Council, 1973), 81–82, grouped Irish poets, including Kinsella, as British. For reaction to his inclusion in *The Penguin Book of Contemporary British Poetry*, eds. Blake Morrison and Andrew Motion, see Seamus Heaney, *An Open Letter* (Derry: Field Day Theatre Company, 1983).

33. Kinsella himself reviewed Davie, Conquest, Elizabeth Jennings, and *New Lines* (1956). See *Irish Press*, 5 November and 19 November 1955; 16 June and 1 December 1956; and 22 February 1958.

unsympathetic critic as "well known in England and becoming known in America."[34]

The emergence in Britain of works as diverse as Philip Larkin's *The Less Deceived* (1955), Charles Tomlinson's *The Necklace* (1955), and Ted Hughes's *The Hawk in the Rain* (1957), together with Robert Conquest's manifesto anthology, *New Lines* (1956), suggests in retrospect perceptible shifts in taste and the practice of poetry. In Ireland, comparable shifts were still a few more years away and, in Kinsella's own development, may be seen occurring in 1963–1964 and coinciding with his first visit to the United States, his retirement from the Civil Service, and his full-time commitment to a writing career. Indeed, one might suggest a correlation between the rapid social, economic, and cultural changes in the Ireland of the sixties and Kinsella's own poetic development. Coinciding with the increasingly liberal attitudes prevalent in Irish society, Kinsella consciously examined and rejected "received forms and rhyme" in favor of "free forms" and poems with "unique shape."[35] There may be critics, such as Edna Longley, who continue to prefer "the mellifluous cadences that grace Kinsella's first few volumes."[36] Others, however, are likely to share Seamus Heaney's view that "he [Kinsella] has strenuously punished the lyricist in himself who carried off such stylish performances in the early books" in order to pursue "a denser, more laconic, more indigenous way with the poetic line."[37] Certainly, for Kinsella, the mature style more precisely reveals the nature of his experience and of what he calls "the data":

> It is not so much that I'm looking for anything laconic or lapidary; it's just that the notion of decorative language, of poetry as linguistic entertainment, seems to me a trivial exercise. I'm not talking about something necessarily elaborate, as with Rilke. What I mean is facile rhetoric, or "music" or mimesis for its own sake.
>
> I am looking for totality of imaginative response with the merely lin-

34. Edna Broderick, review of *AS* and *D*, in *Icarus* 38 (December 1962): 40. Broderick later married the Northern poet Michael Longley.

35. Kinsella, in *Viewpoints: Poets in Conversation*, ed. John Haffenden (London: Faber and Faber, 1981), 108.

36. Longley, "Spinning through the Void," (London) *Times Literary Supplement*, 19 December 1980, p. 1446.

37. Heaney, "The Poems of the Dispossessed Repossessed," in *The Government of the Tongue*, 32.

> guistic characteristics deleted so that one is brought closer and closer to the data and to the form and unity embodied in the data.[38]

Not ideas about the thing, then, but the thing itself. To arrive at his mature style and vision Kinsella has pursued a rigorous discipline that has replaced early mellifluousness with a distinctive, dynamic lyricism, reinforced in turn by his involvement in both the Gaelic and English of Ireland's dual tradition.

This study seeks to define the nature of Thomas Kinsella's poetic achievement; to trace the poet's development through to the most recent volume, *From Centre City* (1994); to recognize the various strategies enabling that development; to appreciate its distinctive concerns, subject matter, and voice; and above all, to "see how the whole thing / works" (*One* 33). Previous critics have increasingly recognized that Kinsella has produced a substantial and significant body of work over the past four decades. The true nature of his achievement, on the other hand, remains largely undervalued, not the least within Ireland itself. He has been misunderstood, misrepresented, and misread: he has been praised for his early formal lyrics at the expense of his later work; he has been regarded as obscure, as offering little to the reader beyond gloom and bleakness; and, in his use of the Irish Gaelic tradition, he has been accused of promoting a distinctly partisan line that proves unhelpful, even belligerently antithetical, to the writer in the North.[39] A dispassionate examination of these issues will reveal otherwise.

That Kinsella has evolved as a poet is indisputable: he has shown increasing awareness of the complexities of his recurrent concerns and greater assurance in handling his material or "instruments." The reader is not likely to confuse an early for a late poem; both form and tone are recognizably different. The tight formal forms, lyrical tone,

38. O'Driscoll, "Interview," 65.

39. John Hewitt, in a mixed review of AS, criticized Kinsella's obscurity; see "Recent Verse by Irish Poets," *Threshold* 2 (Summer 1958): 70–75. Cf. Kinsella's response to John F. Deane's question about the obscurity of late Peppercanisters, in "A Conversation: Dublin, September 1986," *Tracks* 7 (1987): 88. Also see James Simmons's review of *TNOBIV* (*Linen Hall Review* 3 [Autumn 1986]: 7–9); he found Kinsella's work "impenetrable" and objected to his union of Gaelic and English in the Irish tradition: "In the back of his mind he feels we all ought to read Irish"; "we can't pronounce the names or know where the places are. We feel wantonly excluded." For Edna Longley, Kinsella is "A brooding presence"; see Longley, "Spinning through the Void," 1446.

and language of the early volumes give way by the early seventies to experimentalism, to interior landscapes, and to freer, more fragmented, and fragmentary structures that cohere in turn in larger embracing sequences. In the last resort, the sequences form, as he himself has described, "a totality that is happening, with the individual poem a contribution to something accumulating."[40] The several stages in Kinsella's development are relatively distinct and hardly debatable. At the same time, however, too strict and neat a division of the total work risks not just oversimplification but distortion. There are no sharp about-turns, for all his thematic and technical advances; the poetry remains intrinsically all of a piece. In Seamus Deane's appropriate Joycean parallel, it is "Work in Progress which will some day be visible to its readers in a coherent and complex whole."[41] Above all, what will become clear is a formidable accomplishment: of a poet who has produced a substantial body of work over four decades, both reflecting and contributing to the development of contemporary Irish poetry, writing now at the height of his powers, and warranting comparison with the grand masters of twentieth-century literature in English—with Yeats, Joyce, and Beckett. These are the terms by which the poetry of Thomas Kinsella demands to be judged and the major nature of his achievement recognized.

40. O'Driscoll, "Interview," 59.

41. Deane, "The Music of Kinsella's Poetry," *Irish Literary Supplement* 7 (Fall 1988): 34.

one

The Double Shadow

Like the work of many poets at the outset of their careers, Kinsella's first volumes—*Poems* (1956), *Another September* (1958), and *Downstream* (1962)—reflect his search for a style and an enabling voice. In Kinsella's case, that search is complicated further by his laboring, for all his disclaimer that Yeats's potent influence no longer applied, under the same "double shadow of Yeats and English verse" that he recognized as affecting the work of Austin Clarke. Early Kinsella persistently reveals his indebtedness to the older man and also to the English poetic tradition, and particularly to W. H. Auden. Indeed, as we shall see, Kinsella's later work indicates less a repudiation than an assimilation of Yeats in a larger Irish poetic ancestry. In these first volumes, however, Kinsella's recurrent preoccupations—time, mortality and death, love, and the poetic process—show little sign of Irish origins. Furthermore, such themes are expressed within traditional English forms, employing tightly controlled stanza units, regular rhyme schemes, and a formal, dignified, controlled tone. The poetry, as Kinsella later acknowledged, appears rooted more in literature than in experience and lacks that contact with "the data" that he came to regard as essential to the artistic act.[1]

I

In 1958 Kinsella admitted that the several "voices" in his poetry "have not yet succeeded in uttering the kind of poetry" he most admired.[2] His voices still bear the accents of influential past masters—more often of W. B. Yeats and W. H. Auden, but also occasionally of Dylan Thomas and John Keats. *Poems* (1956), his first book, provides ten of its thirteen poems to *Another September* (1958) and constitutes over a third of that first major volume.[3] While the poems retained strike the recognizable early Kinsella note, even the opening "Per Imaginem," later omitted from the 1958 volume, addresses central Kinsella questions. "Alone we make symbols of love," the volume begins, thus pointing to two fundamental concerns: the lonely separateness or alienation humanity must endure, set not so much against as in conjunction with the equally human desire for love, a union of selves that brings not just comfort and security but fulfillment and understanding. The poems' action takes place in what are quickly to become Kinsella's characteristic settings, nighttime, and more precisely at a moment of heightened uncertainty, of transition from the darkness of night to the light of day: "Stars ticked uncontrollably down / The night-face" (*Poems* 10); "In the deep reaches of the night / The ticking stars keep order" (18). The reader is thus made uneasy, is displaced in time and space, is led through experiences that either threaten or suggest threat, certainly frustrate and deny, but also posit a more desirable, satisfying state, like a transcendent world with which contact is occasionally achieved. The units of "Per Imaginem" are traditional seven-line stanzas that, like the vast majority of poems in this first book, possess a regular and well-managed rhyme scheme. The subject matter likewise is not exceptional: love, death, time,

1. For Kinsella's comment upon his early poetry, see *Viewpoints*, ed. Haffenden, 104; for his comment upon his later work, see O'Driscoll, "Interview," 65.

2. Kinsella, *Poetry Book Society Bulletin* 17 (March 1958).

3. *Poems* (1956) did not collect two pamphlet poems, *The Starlit Eye* (Dublin: Dolmen Press, 1952) and *Three Legendary Sonnets* (Dublin: Dolmen Press, 1952), or the two translations from the Irish, *Longes Mac nUsnig: Being the Exile and Death of the Sons of Usnech* (Dublin: Dolmen Press, 1954) and *Thirty-three Triads* (Dublin: Dolmen Press, 1955). The first two titles have not been reprinted; the last two were included in *Poems and Translations* (New York: Athenaeum, 1961).

mortality, art. But the focus upon the nature of the experience and upon the poet's grappling to analyze it provides the interior drama that constitutes the matter of the poems. The landscapes described or the narratives pursued bear upon the interior experience and owe their existence to the experiencing self.

The result is an intensely personal, lyrical poetry in which the experiences of poetry and love become intrinsically fused. However, the formal language and tone and the emblematic metaphor establish distance, enabling the poet to avoid narcissism or confessionalism, but at the same time, in reflecting a more distinctly English taste, suggest the gravitational pull of the English poetic tradition. That said, several of the *Poems*—"Soft to Your Places," "Midsummer," "Dusk Music" (later retitled "A Lady of Quality"), "Who Is My Proper Art"—continue to impress as central works in *Another September*.

It is a measure of Kinsella's early achievement that even less obviously substantial poems, such as the two "Night Songs," display a mastery of touch, albeit in a lyricism and elegant formality later dispensed with. The curiously inverted syntax, in which verbs often precede their subject, increases the formality, suggesting an archaic English practice, while Kinsella conveys a sense of completion accompanying the emergence of "the sunken dawn" through ingenious use of half-rhymes to complete the circle of opening and closing two lines: "sleep" / "step," "down" / "dawn."

> Now, before I sleep,
> My heart is cut down
> Like poplar trees, nothing
> —Poetry nor love—achieving.
>
> Turns again in my room,
> Alas, the crippled leopard.
> Paw-pad, configured
> Yellow light of his eyes,
> Pass, repass, repass.
>
> Quiet, my hand; he is tame.
>
> Soon, while I lie, will step
> And stir the sunken dawn.
>
> (11)

The persona's "heart is cut down"; the leopard turning in his room is "crippled" and nothing, whether of poetry or love, is achieved. Like many twentieth-century poets, Kinsella has written a lovely lyric on his inability to write a poem.

The "Second Night Song," however, serves as a pendant or contrary to the first, in which a vision of "A woman with a golden skin" appears, bringing inspiration and satisfaction to the persona. The woman, who is to prove a central Kinsella figure, is the night-woman, lover, muse, or *spéirbhean* (sky- or vision-woman) of the Irish vision poem, the *aisling*.[4] Poetry and love here fuse to offer illumination to the sleeping poet. It may be part of the "double shadow" that, despite the Irish *aisling* figure, Kinsella's imagery is reminiscent of both Yeats and the English romanticism of Coleridge's "Kubla Khan" ("For he on honey-dew hath fed, / And drunk the milk of Paradise"). On the other hand, throughout his work Kinsella is to pursue the theme of appetite, its instinctive drive within the self and within the external world. Hence, while Seamus Deane's commentary on the poet's later imagery of eating and tasting is exact and just—he remarks that "Eating is the act of survival, but it is never far removed from disgust"[5] —here appetite, not at all disgusting, leads to vision and consciousness. The imagery fuses the ideal ("golden") and the threatening ("Darkness"), and the compound epithet "apple-tasted," while reminiscent of the innocent world of Dylan Thomas's "Fern Hill," includes also in its describing darkness the suggestion of Adam's apple and the Fall into Original Sin. Nevertheless, sleep "breaks" open to reveal the visionary golden woman or muse figure. As if to affirm the second song's positive nature, the poet employs a firm masculine full end-rhyme, a succession of couplets with a unifying single rhyme (light / midnight / appetite), and at every third line a delicate shift from four to three stresses:

> Before I woke there entered in
> A woman with a golden skin
>   That tangled with the light.
> A tang of orchards climbed the stair
> And dwindled in the waxen air,
>   Crisping the midnight.

4. For the *aisling* figure, see John Jordan, "Aogán Ó Rathaille," in *The Pleasures of Gaelic Poetry*, ed. Mac Réamoinn, 86; also see Liam de Paor, *The Peoples of Ireland: From Prehistory to Modern Times* (London: Hutchinson/Notre Dame, Ind.: University of Notre Dame Press, 1986), 175; and Kinsella, *Duanaire*, xxvii.

5. Deane, "Thomas Kinsella: 'Nursed Out of Wreckage,' " in *Celtic Revivals: Essays in Modern Irish Literature*, 1880–1980 (London: Faber and Faber, 1985), 137.

And the white pillows of my bed
On apple-tasted darkness fed.
    Weakened with appetite
Sleep broke like a dish wherein
A woman lay with golden skin.
(11)

The shorter line in each instance is crucial, whether it notes the intricate, antithetical ("tangled") nature of the woman's beauty, the heightening of the moment ("Crisping"), or the effect of appetite ("Weakened").

There are occasions, however, when individual lines impress but the poem as a whole fails. "Love I consider a difficult, scrupulous art" is a worthy conclusion to the opening stanza of "Per Imaginem" and, like much of the poem, is heavily indebted to Yeats. Yet the stanza remains for the most part stilted and prosaic:

Alone we make symbols of love
Out of echoes its lack makes in an empty word.
Inaccessible softness of breast or voice in the dove
Or high gull grace are what we are thinking of,
The poise in quality of a bird.
Time must pare such images to the heart.
Love I consider a difficult, scrupulous art.[6]
(9)

The subsequent imagery of lake and swan, "flaming throat" and "composite hearts," proves too Yeatsian to be acceptable: the poet may have been brought to the attainment such imagery suggests but, unlike his performance in the two "Night Songs," his dependence upon the older poet serves to undermine the reader's confidence in the sincerity of the expression. The same is true of the conclusion to "First Light."[7]

On the other hand, both Yeats and Auden contribute to the success of "Soft to Your Places" (12), where, while the manner may be imita-

6. The poem's first publication, as a wedding present in a limited edition of twenty-five copies, had for line 5 "the poised canticle of a bird." Kinsella's habit of revising had already begun.

7. Arthur E. McGuinness noted the poem's various appearances in *Poems* (1956) and AS (1958), as quoted above, but revised in *Wormwood* (1966) and again in N (1968) to become a radically different poem. See " 'Bright Quincunx Newly Risen': Thomas Kinsella's Inward 'I,' " *Eire-Ireland* 15 (Winter 1980): 110.

tive, the poet's handling of that inheritance is elegant and sure. The reader is led convincingly through the poem's dialectic—from love's luck to "love's difficulty"; from the "mighty work" of the primrose to beauty, the "easy thing"; from the inevitable passage of time to the equally inevitable ravaging of beauty—a dialectic transcended, if only temporarily, by the speaker's affirmation of love. The first refrain—"*And yet we have seen that all's / A fiction that is heard of love's difficulty*"—both echoes and contradicts Yeats, but each refrain operates in turn in distinctly Yeatsian fashion as a counterpoint to the rest of the stanza. For the italicized refrain serves to offer an alternative view, a perspective undercutting that which is posed in the body of the stanza. The speaker calls upon the animals to perform their "legendary duty," to bring good fortune to the lovers, only to pursue a different tack by denying the "fiction . . . of love's difficulty." The fact that the animals have "places" suggests a formal order in contrast to the intervention of luck. Such imagery of "places" or "stations," like the aspiration toward an ideal rational order, persists throughout the poet's early work. Yet at each stage here in the speaker's progress the querying voice posing doubt, difficulty, and uncertainty is overcome by the affirming alternative voice of the refrain. The language, tone, imagery, even the practice of posing questions—all suggest Yeats. Yet the dialectic pursued is used to evidence less the tragedy and more the positive nature of love, the existence of which is affirmed simply:

> Soft, to your places, love; I kiss
> Because it is, because it is.
>
> (12)

As Robin Skelton has rightly commented, "It is the first of Kinsella's poems in which the acceptance of man's mortality and imperfect understanding is seen as a necessary attribute, and part cause of human endeavour."[8] That acceptance constitutes a significant qualification of Kinsella's response to humanity's imperfect state.

The reliance upon the instinctive life and love of the animal parallels that of another major early influence, W. H. Auden, to whom Kinsella is much indebted in his first volumes. Auden—more specifically the Auden of the 1930s—proved a useful counterbalance to the influence of Yeats. The English poet also provided a political and

8. Skelton, "The Poetry of Thomas Kinsella," *Eire-Ireland* 4 (Spring 1969): 89.

social perspective with which Kinsella could more readily identify. Moreover, Auden's technical accomplishment in various traditional forms—ballad, sonnet, lyric, narrative—together with his particular imagery, often calculatedly shocking and iconoclastic, even its urban nature, all proved attractive to Kinsella. Both men shared too a more than passing interest in the sciences. Indeed, in Padraic Fallon's reproving eyes, Kinsella was "more influenced by Auden than by the Irish sagas in translation."[9] However, "Auden was not an escape," Kinsella has declared in justification of his influence, "but an entry into poetry. Reading Auden it occurred to me that there was a need in myself, and that I could write poetry. For a while I wrote only imitations of Auden."[10] The English poet showed the young Irish poet new potentialities for verse. Nor was Kinsella alone in this regard: for John Montague too Auden was "the liberating example," while for Seamus Heaney Auden "broke through" "with a kind of poem which carried the English lyric well beyond the domestic securities of the first person singular. Carried it, in fact, towards that kind of impersonal, eschatological poetry of post-war Europe of which contemporary English poetry is just now [1986] beginning to take proper cognizance."[11] In Kinsella's words, Auden, like Ezra Pound or William Carlos Williams later, was "an enabling voice."[12] The term is crucial and recurs in Kinsella's statements about those writers whose influence has meant most to him. Auden enabled poetry to be opened up to increased potentiality, enabled poetry to cover ground hitherto unexplored, indeed regarded as beneath or beyond a poet's purview. Kinsella was himself striving to find the proper voice by which to pursue his analysis of human nature and society. Auden's technique, more than his specific analyses, made him Kinsella's enabling voice, and in its formal, traditional structure and tone, in its symbolic land-

9. Fallon, "Synge to Kinsella: Half-a-century of Poetic Change," review of AS (1962) and *D*, *Irish Times* 20 October 1962, p. 9.

10. O'Driscoll, "Interview," 58.

11. Montague, "The Impact of International Modern Poetry on Irish Writing," in *The Figure in the Cave*, ed. Quinn, 217; Heaney, "Sounding Auden," in *The Government of the Tongue*, 116.

12. Kinsella, conversation with Brian John, Dublin, 3 May 1982. For Kinsella's early reviews of Auden, see "New Found Land," *Irish Writing* 36 (Autumn–Winter, 1956–1957): 184–86, and "Auden and Achilles," *Irish Press*, 18 February 1956, p. 4. Cf. his later acknowledgment of Auden's influence, in *Viewpoints*, ed. Haffenden, 101; Deane, "A Conversation," 86; O'Driscoll, "Interview," 58.

scapes, in its abstractions, "Mid-Summer" reflects the Irish poet's indebtedness.

The poem continues the affirmation of love expressed in the preceding poem, "Soft to Your Places"; both poems were written during his years of courtship in the early fifties, and the volume was published within the first year of the poet's marriage. ("Per Imaginem," for example, was first published separately in 1953 and "Soft to Your Places" in 1955.) Like "Soft to Your Places," "Mid-Summer" describes a natural instinctive world in happy coincidence with the lovers' "art" and "dear reason," so transforming the protective arching glade into "An endless tabernacle":

> Hereabouts the signs are good.
> Propitious creatures of the wood
>   After their fashion
> Have pitied and blessed before our eyes.
> All unpremeditated lies
>   Our scattered passion.
>
> Flowers whose names I do not know
> Make happy signals to us. O
>   Did ever bees
> Stumble on such a quiet before!
> (12–13)

Despite the apparently negative Audenesque image—"The evening is a huge closed door"—and the lovers' exclusive self-absorption, even to their "locking" themselves "inside one heart," no obvious criticism is implied. Rather, the imagery suggests some magical enclosure, like the poet's several glades, where the lovers, safe from harm, can practice their art. "Art" and "heart," appropriately enough, here form a rhyming couplet: instinctive life and achieved order marry in what might legitimately be conceived as a Yeatsian synthesis. The speaker may not "know" the flowers' names but such ignorance, rather than proving an impediment, merely reflects the same reliance upon instinct practiced by both lover and world. Hence, once more love is celebrated and, while by his conclusion the poet acknowledges the human potential for loneliness and alienation, such potential poses no threat here.

Unlike "Soft to Your Places," where the speaker is subject to contrary voices, the poet-lover in "Mid-Summer" remains convinced that for this year at least no impediment has interfered with this marriage of true minds. Such untainted love is delicately portrayed in imagery reminiscent of another contemporary English poet, Philip Larkin.[13]

> Something that for this long year
> Had hid and halted like a deer
> Turned marvellous,
> Parted the tragic grasses, tame,
> Lifted its perfect head and came
> To welcome us.
>
> (13)

Even the recognition that the human condition *can* also resemble—indeed, more normally for Kinsella, *is* most likely to resemble—a "desert" is not allowed to diminish the speaker's certainty. The "tabernacle" remains "endless":

> We have, dear reason, of this glade
> An endless tabernacle made,
> An origin.
> Well for whatever lonely one
> Will find this right place to lay down
> His desert in.
>
> (13)

One might normally object that terms like "Something" and "marvellous" are imprecise, vague, clichéd, but here they underline the magical process of love which replaces tragedy with perfection and supplies the regenerative "well" to transform the lonely one's "desert" by way of its healing, reviving waters, to bring about another kind of "well": well-being. Kinsella's tribute to the power of love and its relationship to his art reaches a climax only in the more substantial poem, "Phoenix Park" *(N)*, published at least a decade later, yet the sheer lyricism and technical accomplishment of these early love poems are for a first volume impressive.

More in character is "Dusk Music," retitled "A Lady of Quality" in *Another September*: another love poem, it is, through its experience of sickness, mortality, and the threat of death, both less ecstatic and

13. ". . . beyond the glass / The colourless vial of day painlessly spilled / My world back after a year, my lost lost world / Like a cropping deer strayed near my path again, / Bewaring the mind's least clutch. Turning, I kissed her, / Easily for sheer joy tipping the balance to love," from Larkin, "Waiting for Breakfast," *The North Ship* (1966), 48.

more touching. The poem remains with only minor revision, if in different sequence, in the next volume. Rooted in autobiography as well as being "specifically modelled, as an exercise, on a poem of Auden's,"[14] the poem describes the speaker's visit to his love recovering in the hospital from a serious illness. One is reminded of Kinsella's description of the contemporary Irish painter Louis Le Brocquy: "The humanity he paints has a hospital smell."[15] Although Kinsella has written only a handful of hospital poems, his work has a similar quality, in which sickness, like time, threatens love and harmony, and protagonists suffer as the heart becomes the ground over which battles are continually fought. Blood, bloodshed, heartbeat, pulse, bloodlines, and inheritance—all proceed to play their essential parts.

Here the rational life practiced by the lovers in "Mid-Summer" is reflected in the order of the hospital, its "airy architecture," "air . . . like a laundered sheet," and "hygienic ceiling." That order is reinforced further by the 1958 revision of stanza 9 where the plainly inadequate "limping ardour" of the poet's pen is replaced by the more fortuitous "Recovered order." For the poet is acutely conscious of the needs to maintain order, to regain health, and to protect their love in a world destructive of all such positives. In such a world the different arts of both poet and woman will be required. For despite the arrangement of "Books and flowers at her head" or "the nonsense said" by the two lovers, nicely imaged (in an echo of the *Táin* 52ff.) as "our pillow-chat," they are conscious of the need "To bless the room from present dread / Just for a brittle while." Instead of the expected phrase, "a little while," Kinsella's substitution is Audenesque in its ironic effect: the distinctive adjective "brittle" highlights the lovers' inadequacy before the superior forces of time and mortality. It may be that the natural world beyond the room, with its "leaping season" of bird, beast, and flower, reflects an alternative existence; it may also be that the healing provided by the hospital signifies one's attempt to counter the human condition. What both man and woman know, however, is the irrevocable and destructive passage of time, thus enabling "Tiny terrors" to multiply like runaway cells. Not for the last time, as becomes clear in subsequent volumes, the woman proves the superior

14. Kinsella, in *Viewpoints*, ed. Haffenden, 101.

15. Kinsella, "A Background to Modern Irish Painting," *National Student*, n.s., 110 (January 1951): 22.

partner, her awareness matched by a wish to conceal and so protect the man. The latter's knowledge is qualified by a significant "perhaps": "her care is spent concealing / What, perhaps, I know." Such knowledge, then, however imperfectly grasped, is of time itself, the process of which is described in imagery reminiscent of Auden—the ever-present "crack in time" that separates last summer's flourishing landscape from "this year's mountains"; the very polarity itself with the implied ascent and the struggle and suffering such mountainous ascent will require; the playful irony in juxtaposing the "crack" (suggesting fracture, separation, and imperfection) and the constancy of "ever-present"; the "Wild geese" (with their Irish historical relevance) released by the heart shot down ruthlessly by "sorrow's fowling-pieces."[16]

The lesson learnt is one Kinsella's readers will recognize as central to later poems: the need to endure suffering and gain understanding through purgation:[17] "We may regret, and must abide." But as further consequence in a poem that ends with increasing dark, with time announced by "sundry / Clocks about the building," with reminders also of journeys to be undertaken and the two lovers touching fingers in their parting, we are reminded also of the separate, if also complementary, roles the two must now play. Just as the poet seeks order through the shaping spirit of the imagination, so woman's art is to marry "beauty" and "human hungers," love and mind, the intuitive and the rational. The synthesis is Kinsella's version of the Yeatsian myth, of man led to composite blessedness through beautiful woman, Solomon made wise by dalliance with his queen. At the same time, the English poetic tradition may not be too distant: while "country ladies" may be a private acknowledgment of Eleanor Kinsella's rural upbringing in New Ross, Co. Wexford, the possibility of the Elizabethan erotic pun upon "country" should not, in the circumstances, be excluded:

16. Maurice Harmon noted the source of Kinsella's imagery: the self-imposed exile of the Irish aristocracy (the "Wild Geese") after 1691 and the archaic "fowling pieces." See *The Poetry of Thomas Kinsella: "With darkness for a nest"* (Dublin: Wolfhound Press, 1974), 22. This historical context is supported by my identification of the *Táin* echo ("pillow chat").

17. Cf. Kinsella's praise of Louis MacNeice: "This poet has found that, if anything is to be gained, problems must be lived through, not solved, and so his pen homes constantly on the place where the heart is" (review of *Autumn Sequel*, *Irish Writing* 29 [December 1954]: 66).

Our trophied love must now divide
  Into its separate parts,

And you go down with womankind
Who in her beauty has combined
  And focused human hungers,
With country ladies who could wind
A nation's love-affair with mind
  Around their little fingers,

And I communicate again
A limping ardour to my pen
  To find a further answer . . .

(15)

Woman plays a crucial role in the remaining poems of this first volume, whether as Penelope in "Ulysses" or the moon in "An Ancient Ballet" or the muse figure in "Who Is My Proper Art." And because the poetry moves away from autobiographical parallels, the reader discerns what in fact Kinsella has been pursuing all along: the path by which love and art fuse to bring enlightenment and direction to a life. Woman, whether as lover, wife, moon, or muse, epitomizes a powerful force on the path to understanding. The marriage of man and woman represents the synthesis of contraries, whether within the self or in the world at large—blood and moon, self and soul, body and mind, mystery and order, instinct and reason—the inchoate mass of life which, if it is to be understood and endured, requires the shaping spirit of the imagination.

Both "Ulysses" and "An Ancient Ballet" remind us that this is no modern phenomenon: it is a timeless process at the heart of which is the inevitable passage of time itself, with its potential for both growth and decay, blossoming and destruction, a process reflected in man's ancient myths and in the night sky, moon, and stars. Indeed, the former poem is an elaborate allegory in which the return of Ulysses to Penelope in Ithaca parallels the progression from summer to autumn, with the whole serving to comment upon the interaction of love and time, order and disorder, and the manner by which reintegration might be achieved. The parallels, however, as Donald Davie has argued, are not made "all along the line as in allegory" but through structural interweaving.[18] It is a technique Kinsella will develop to

18. Davie, "First Fruits: The Poetry of Thomas Kinsella," *Irish Writing* 37 (Autumn 1957): 47–49.

much greater effect in his later work of the seventies and eighties, but it is worth noting the use of such a technique at the outset of his career.

The poem's difficulty may be traced in part to Kinsella's own immaturity. More likely, however, is his own explanation for those poems in *Another September* that are "clouded and possibly obscure": such poems are the product of "a compulsion to arrange rather than to communicate."[19] It might reasonably be argued that every poet's duty is "to communicate" and therefore Kinsella is being cavalier and derelict. On the contrary, he notes another "voice" in the volume whose "poems are comparatively clear" because that voice is "reasonable." In seeking "to arrange rather than to communicate," Kinsella is already preoccupied with the distinctive form his later poetry will successfully adopt, a form that reflects "a world [that] is not completely closed." For these are experiences that are better understood when "arranged" rather than "communicated," whose reality is more precisely expressed and known not through logical reasoning, but through imaginative coalescing. The images come together in creative interaction, a structural interweaving, in which their total meaning is gained through accumulation. The most proficient and striking proponent of this technique in modern literature is James Joyce. While his successful absorption of Joyce does not surface until the next decade, with *Nightwalker* (1968), such a process is implicit, aptly enough, given Joyce's own use of the Greek myth, in Kinsella's poem, "Ulysses."

Although individual stanzas impress and Kinsella's writing clearly gains in tautness and complexity, Penelope's tragic vision is not wholly convincing:

> *Love is a long death*
> *And burial in this closet*
> *And I am being tampered with*
> *By Time! Again it is ghosts!*
> *An elegant laughter is faded . . .*
> *Harpsichord in the desert—*
>
> (18)

More convincing is the contrast between the dead suitors, ironically transcending time yet gaining no fulfillment, and Penelope's subjec-

19. Kinsella, *Poetry Book Society Bulletin* 17 (March 1958).

tion to time, facing its "unpitying shoals" with her own "unpitiable image." Hence the suitors die,

> Their everlasting impress
> Fixed in dusts of the sky,
> A-fever, their stars a morass
> That trembles when she goes by,
> Or eyes troubling her face
>
> Until it lifts, and her heels
> Are rock-still under the stroke
> And collapse of sails,
> Waiting for a tide to break
> And brush through unpitying shoals
> Her unpitiable image back.

The timeless process, as depicted in "An Ancient Ballet," is made more personal by involving the poem's protagonist in a moment of illumination or epiphany imaged by the moon's radiance. While the night sky with its "ticking stars" reflects a timeless order, life below is fraught with desire, and the ancient ballet of the poem's title is a Yeatsian dance performed by the stars but made possible in turn by temporal longing. The moon-muse figure pouring radiant light upon the protagonist also enlightens him as to their relationship: "We know her power is our longing // And I think that her stare discovers / Only what we pretend . . ." (19). It is a mark of Kinsella's early poetry that such enlightenment comes by way of a descent from on high, most likely because the poet is relying, as in the second "Night Song" earlier, upon the ancient Irish *aisling* or sky-woman figure, "gentler sister of Robert Graves's White Goddess," as John Montague rightly pointed out.[20] "O that mastering huge sky—/ Stare, downstreaming, witnessed!" as Kinsella puts it (20). In the later work his protagonists will likewise experience light by way of darkness, but the descent will involve movement into the interior of the self, into the unconscious, rather than this experience of an apparently external grace. The *aisling* figure thus gives way to the more ominous and threatening Hecate, the dark face of the White Goddess. At the same time the dichotomy of starlit night sky or crystalline coherent structure and the

20. Montague, reviewing AS in "Strife in Darkness," *Irish Times*, 26 April 1958, p. 6.

shambles of appetite, blood, heart, and time proves increasingly less a cause for longing for timeless order and more a source of the poet's acceptance of the world and the necessary dialectic of contraries. The poem is less successful than "Ulysses" and, despite its clearer narrative line, is handicapped by its debts to both Yeats and Dylan Thomas and by the prosaically expressed correspondence of time and longing, watch and wrist, night, moon, and tide.

The last in this series from *Poems* (1956) is, however, the most successful: "Who Is My Proper Art" brings together the themes of art and love, with the muse stationed appropriately "near the heart," and the poem is shaped into a satisfying commentary upon the poetic process. The structure is a narrative of forty-two lines, organized around a six-line rhyme scheme of *aabccb* that is maintained throughout by way of full and half rhymes. Even more impressive, however, is Kinsella's handling of the imagery, in which the enigmatic muse-woman, the poet working at his "still-white" papers, the two horses "penned / In a still-white field," and the inevitable conjunction of imagination, heart, and "calamities" all coincide with nice irony in the poet's eventual vision.

From the outset the reader is made aware of the internal character of the action:

> Much as calamities do, she took
> Her station near the heart; the crook
>   (That works the hand I steady
> This still-white leaf with) worked her voice
> To upper levels:
>
> (20)

Such a "station" emulates the Stations of the Cross[21] and relates suffering with regeneration; "the crook," however, is like a later Kinsella "instrument" or "probe," conducting the muse, as if with a shepherd's crook or bishop's crozier, from the heart to the "upper levels" of consciousness and reason. The familiar connection of "crook" with deceit, dishonesty, even evil, provides perhaps an unintentional irony, although the fact that the same crook proves necessary to the poet at work on his as yet unwritten poem suggests also the

21. The imagery of "stations" and "places" recurs; see *Poems* (1956) 12, 18–20; *D* 20–21, 45, 56; *One* 40; *BF* 61.

fabrication at the heart of the poetic process. Indeed, the poem, like other subsequent Kinsella poems, explores the nature of the poetic process and, in so doing, the poem gets written.

The muse is made more concrete in subsequent vivid imagery, appearing like some great queen-charioteer; the Irish parallel, given her connection with calamity, might be Deirdre, although the Platonic myth in the *Phaedrus* and Keats's charioteer in "Sleep and Poetry" are not too distant. Whatever the source, she brings "order and sanguinity" to the poet:

> White horses, twice
> Glimpsed, she made already
> A legend in a glade, pounding
> Harnessed in a green dream, rounding
> With manes streaming side
> By side a field she travelled past
> To come here that day. I kissed
> The effort in her wide
> Eyes and crowned the breasts where I
> Find order and sanguinity
> Beyond hope's finest-drawn
> Proposals, . . .
>
> (20–21)

The horses of the muse-queen had appeared "three / Springs ago"—a clear reference to Kinsella's own poetic career—like "Two grounded loves (penned / In a still-white field)" and "pastured in our sight." The sheer physicality of Kinsella's description captures the poet's ecstatic illumination on confronting the imagination, with the horses' galloping suitably taking "the shape of the heart-beat." For we are reminded constantly here how closely both heart and imagination and suffering are conjoined, and how the poetic process brings opposites together in a visionary experience. The poet will take "That latest / Look she drew from the world's sweetest / Well," a scene which the poet proceeds to qualify as "lying" but with a "true stare." The qualification may derive from Plato and his description of poetry as, at best, at a third remove from truth (*The Republic*, book 10), or, at worst, lying (books 2–3), but the poet's eyes are now both "clearer" and "blinder," just as "fashioner" and "finder" unite in the one being:

That latest
Look she drew from the world's sweetest
Well, that scene lying
Imagery for her, I will make
Fix its true stare for her sake
Into my clearer, blinder
Eyes. Who is my proper art,
Who rested here her soaring heart,
The fashioner, the finder.

(21)

II

"Who Is My Proper Art" is a fitting climax to an impressive introductory volume and an indication of how far and how quickly Kinsella developed. As the poet himself has stated, "I wrote my first poem, when I was eighteen, out of curiosity; my second, at twenty, as a joke. The third was written soon after with a faint foreboding. When I write now, it is with feelings like those of the Redemptorist preacher's sparrow, which so foolishly devoted itself to the task of transporting to an unknown destination, grain by grain, and for a reason it could scarcely grasp, the sands of the sea."[22] *Another September*, which was the Poetry Book Society spring 1958 "Choice," confirmed the emergence of an important new poet. Incorporating most of the poems from the introductory volume, *Another September* pursues the same thematic concerns with even greater technical assurance and complexity. Containing "most of what I have written in the last five years" and "printed in the order in which they were finished," the volume possesses a distinctive thematic unity:

> They are preoccupied largely with love, death and the artistic act, but I think that generally their effect is to make real, in whatever terms, the passing of time, the frightening exposure of all relationships and feeling to erosion.
>
> An instinct which dramatizes events against such an alien background is both the source my poems come from at present and the reason for any lack of public concern which may be found in them. I find in practice that social or political matters, for example, or any motifs characteristic of a group, never arise; little is relevant but the dignity of the isolated person,

22. Kinsella, *Poetry Book Society Bulletin* 17 (March 1958).

whose conscious or unconscious bargainings with time insist, like those of a condemned or dying man, that they be respected.[23]

He concedes that his work is not "especially Irish," rejecting the label of "Anglo-Irish" and acknowledging his awareness of the double shadow of Yeats and English verse:

In fact, I am not sure an Anglo-Irish poetry survives, apart from Yeats and his personal reign over two generations. Good poetry by Irishmen is quickly absorbed into the English system and is only vaguely differentiated there. Much of what is called Anglo-Irish is either a sophisticated imitation of Gaelic modes or else regional verse: these are the retreats most favoured by those who cannot otherwise resist, or keep their balance in, the gravitic force of English writing.

Clarke and Kavanagh, then, as well as Yeats, are firmly dispensed with and a wary eye cast on an English scene already offering him early tempting recognition.

Kinsella's summary of thematic concerns certainly touches upon the central poems of both *Poems* and *Another September*. Yet in describing his poems as "not . . . especially 'Irish' except, here and there, in certain habits of conception or expression which would be foreign to a writer in the English tradition," Kinsella is being somewhat misleading. It is true that his muse figure is only partly derived from the Irish *aislingi* and that his settings (for example, "night-face," "wood," and "hospital") are more often general than singularly Irish. But even the latter distinction is more applicable to *Poems* than to *Another September*: in the second volume the settings include Baggot Street, Dublin; Luttrell's Glen, Co. Dublin; King John's Castle, Co. Meath; and Vinegar Hill and the River Slaney, Co. Wexford. In none of these cases does Kinsella write a topographical poem, yet the explicitly Irish location of each is a new development, and John Montague's reproach "that the poems were not sufficiently anchored in time and place"[24] is only partly valid. Kinsella's underestimation of

23. This and subsequent quotations are from Kinsella, *Poetry Book Society Bulletin* 17 (March 1958). The order of the poems was revised in the final stages of publication as was the title. An advance proof copy in the Freyer Collection at Trinity College, Dublin, is entitled *Baggot Street Deserta* and includes a nine-line poem, "Triumph," omitted from *AS* and not collected since. Some revisions, particularly of "The Travelling Companion," occurred between the proofs stage and publication.

24. Montague, in *Contemporary Writers of the English Language: Contemporary Poets*, 2d. ed., ed. James Vinson (London: St. James Press, 1975), 835.

his Irish connections is less intentionally misleading than calculated to show him moving away from Yeats's shadow and to avoid, not wholly successfully as it turned out, being classified as a "regional" poet. Moreover, the action in the volume's opening poem, "Death of a Queen," becomes fully intelligible only when the reader appreciates that Kinsella is working with one of the most famous Irish tales, that of Deirdre and Naoise. He had in fact already translated that episode from the Irish sagas—*Longes Mac nUsnig: Being the Exile and Death of the Sons of Usnech* (1954)[25]—and while his two activities, his original work and his translations from the Irish, remain relatively distinct until the next decade, there are occasions when the Irish proves a significant source. The *aisling* sky-woman figure who merges with the muse is one instance; Deirdre in "Death of a Queen" is another. Both, however, go, like all good myth, beyond mere local habitation, so that Kinsella in the latter poem can reveal the queen's larger significance.

"Death of a Queen" describes a woman who suffers heartbreak within an emblematic landscape that reflects her own tragedy: her heart falls "among boulders" and her distinct separateness is caught movingly as "the promontory of her grief." Because of the loss of her beloved, her antagonists are memory, reality, grief, anger, and finally despair. External and internal landscapes fuse strikingly to establish Kinsella's allegory: "Wherever her heart turned / It fell among boulders . . ."; or "Every seventh wave / Dismembered further the nerves / Of her face and hands . . ." and, in fitting climax, "Her death and her lover utterly mated" as the queen shapes her lover's body, Isis-like, out of his scattered fragments. The process of reintegration includes both lover and queen, and is vividly depicted in imagery drawn from chess—more particularly from Yeats's play, *Deirdre*,[26] than from the original myth—and also from the distinctive Irish passage-grave or dolmen. At the same time the focus upon arrangement parallels Kinsella's own need as a poet to arrange experiences. The fragments so arranged confine the queen also:

25. James Liddy claimed (excessively) that Kinsella " 'lifted' " the poem from his translation of *Longes Mac nUsnig*. See "A Difficult, Scrupulous Art," *Kilkenny Magazine* 8 (Autumn–Winter 1962): 47. Liam Miller noted that *Longes Mac nUsnig* was the first in the Miller-Kinsella plan to translate the *Táin*; see *Dolmen* XXV, 8

26. W. B. Yeats, *Collected Plays* (London: Macmillan, 1953), 189–92.

And she set the fragments under
And among and up to the boulders' waists
And watched them fuse,

Forming a body gradually out of the dead.
The two final agonies were his eyes,
A knight and a queen.
One she kissed and checked with, one
She shuddered over and loved and at last put in place:
Her death and her lover utterly mated.

(*AS* 2)

Yet the final stanza undercuts the heroic tragedy, and the poet has his queen die not for lover or kingdom or palace, "But that life, late or soon, / Suddenly becomes, on the face, a jaded rouge." Death is sought out of an awareness of life's finiteness, of her own mortality, and of her beauty's ultimate decline. The poem may have originated in the Deirdre legend but Kinsella's poem has gone beyond the Irish tragic heroine to comment upon the effect of mutability upon love and art.

"Love and death have not a little to do with one another," Jung pronounced.[27] Their conjunction occurs again in "In the Ringwood" (*AS* 37–39) where Kinsella depends not upon Jung, a later exemplar, but once more upon Yeats and the traditional English ballad form. While the poem continues to impress, it might legitimately be argued that there are times when the "double shadow" falls too heavily. Kinsella's reliance upon the ballad form, however, should not surprise us: as he told Peter Orr in 1962, of the poetry he most enjoyed his "favourite poet is in fact Anon.—all songs of all time, and also Robert Burns."[28] Equally, the parallel with Keats and "La Belle Dame Sans Merci" and the intrusive echoes of Yeats in stanzas 5 and 6 are also predictable. On the same occasion he told Orr that "the poems which I really admire most are of another kind. They are the conscious, constructed real fabrications of the human intellect and spirit like Dante and Keats, and the later Yeats."[29]

27. C. G. Jung, *Symbols of Transformation: An Analysis of the Prelude to a Case of Schizophrenia*, trans. R. F. C. Hull, in *The Collected Works of* C. G. *Jung*, 20 vols., 2d ed., ed. Sir Herbert Read et al. (Princeton, N.J.: Princeton University Press, 1956), 5:285.

28. Kinsella, *The Poet Speaks: Interviews with Contemporary Poets*, ed. Peter Orr (London: Routledge and Kegan Paul, 1966), 108. He proceeded to distinguish between those poets he respected ("the formal constructors of poems"), those he enjoyed, and those he most admired.

29. Ibid.

"In the Ringwood," however, is given a distinctive and significant Irish setting: a particularly beautiful part of Co. Wexford, it is the area from which the poet's wife comes and a place where "many valuable things happened" to him.[30] It is also an area rich in associations with the 1798 Rebellion of United Irishmen defeated by the British in the Battle of Vinegar Hill. As ancestor of the place, then, the poet's wife has inherited the wisdom gained from such continuity. Indeed, Kinsella at a later date described the poem as an *aisling* in the manner of Aogán Ó Rathaille.[31] For such "ancient slaughter" overtakes the two lovers, husband and wife, to transform the poet's bride into "Sorrow's daughter," a change that enables her to speak of the inevitable decline of love into destruction. The woman-bride becomes a muse figure initiating her poet-husband into the tragedy of temporal existence, into the fearful appetitive "Dread, a grey devourer" or "dark that dogs our feet." "The human turns awry / The poles of the firmament," Kinsella writes, establishing his familiar antitheses of starlit sky and human existence. The woman's "Ravenhair" particularly is the first of several instances in Kinsella's poetry where temptation is experienced through hair.[32] At other times in the poem the imagery, rhetoric, and rhythms are heavily indebted to Yeats, particularly his Crazy Jane poems:

> "Many times the civil lover
> Climbed that pleasant place,
> Many times despairing
> Died in his love's face,
> His spittle turned to vinegar,
> Blood in his embrace.
>
> Love that is every miracle
> Is torn apart and rent.
> The human turns awry
> The poles of the firmament.
> The fish's bright side is pierced
> And good again is spent."
>
> (38)

30. Kinsella poetry reading, Project Arts Theatre, Dublin, 15 March 1982.

31. Ibid.

32. Cf. Peggy Broder for Kinsella's recurrent hair motif; see her "Images of the Feminine in the Poetry of Thomas Kinsella," *Canadian Journal of Irish Studies* 5 (June 1979): 94–95.

The conclusion's balladlike numerology underlines an age-old appetite in which poet, lover, and the natural world (the heron) participate:

> I kissed three times her shivering lips.
> I drank their naked chill.
> I watched the river shining
> Where the heron wiped his bill.
> I took my love in my icy arms
> In the Spring on Ringwood Hill.
>
> (39)

The same awareness of an ancient dark process is present in "Lead" (*AS* 44–45). The setting is Luttrell's Glen, Co. Dublin, but the literary, classical allusions to Zephyr, Vulcan, Chaos, and Gea serve to place the experience within a larger, more universal context. For within this setting the persona is led to increased awareness: Luttrell's Glen constitutes one more enclosure, like Kinsella's several glades where enlightenment is granted. In "Baggot Street Deserta" and in subsequent volumes, the glade, with its literary associations, gives way to the urban, almost Beckettian room. The setting of a glade, however, is not incidental: the enclosure suggests parallels with traditional archetypal holy places, where contraries meet in heightened synthesis, where epiphanies occur in some intersection of the timeless with time.

Here the persona comes across disused forges and in their midst "Two dull dice of lead." With fine irony the persona comments of the dice, "When time blew harder / Vulcan knew them blazing in a heap." Time proves both creative and destructive, bringing both order and chaos, and time's winds, like Vulcan's bellows, make dull lead blaze and so become malleable. Although later in the poem the recollection shifts to "leather-vizored workmen" who "in their time / Roofed many a teeming manor / With sheeted calms no violence could dispel," we are reminded, nevertheless, of lead used for more violent purpose. Of the dice we are told "Each weighed so deadly small," just as we recognize that the estate where the forges now lie idle was once owned by an English Ascendancy family. It is in fact Luttrellstown House, a distinguished Georgian residence, owned at one time by Luttrell, traitor to the "patriot" side after St. Ruth was killed at the Battle of Aughrim in 1691.[33] The deathly implications

33. For "Luttrell the Traitor," see Julian Moynahan, "*The Battle of Aughrim:* A Commentary," *Irish University Review* 13 (Spring 1983): 107–8, 111–12.

are thus most pertinent: as Richard Murphy has written in his own *Battle of Aughrim*, "The past is happening today."[34] Despite the historical setting, however, Kinsella meditates less upon violent Irish history than upon the ancient process in which the shaping spirit of the imagination proves central. For it is "Flame-breathing Vulcan in a maker's rage" upon which he concentrates, shaping "A bit to bridle Chaos," in which the maker's rage to order hammers space and time into an ordered, meaningful artifact. "The mind leaped towards the clash of the real," as Kinsella says. However, the process continues to evolve, and "Craft and craftsman, risen out of nothing, / Sank to a jackdaw chatter in the head" while "The road to Dublin churned back into mud."

For all Kinsella's preoccupation with the conjunction of love, art, and death, what distinguishes his work from the outset is his persistent self-examination: he seeks to know himself. A poem like "Clarence Mangan" shows him prepared to adopt a persona—here of the nineteenth-century Irish poet—[35] and to speak dramatically through the other. Both the dramatic projection and the distinctive imagery of knife and surgery reappear at a later date in Kinsella's poetry, although the beginnings are there at the outset of his career, in the uncollected *Three Legendary Sonnets* (1952) and their anatomical imagery defining Oedipus, Prometheus, and Orestes. What is remarkable about "Clarence Mangan" is the accomplished handling of ruthless self-examination caught in the distinctive, fearful tone that marks off the later work. For Mangan shares Kinsella's nocturnal experiences and confronts a similar "faceless destroyer":

> Long I waited to know what naked meeting would come
> With what was moving behind my eyes and desolating
> What I touched.
>
> Over a glass, or caught in lamplight, caught on the edge
> Of act, my hand is suddenly stopped and fills with waiting.

34. Murphy, *The Battle of Aughrim* (New York: Knopf, 1968), 24.

35. "With Mangan we are in touch with serious poetry, an art which from time to time, in its investigation of life, sounds the profoundest personal depths in a language that comes to life in organic textures and rhythms"; see Kinsella, "Irish Poetry and the Nineteenth Century" (1968); W. B. Yeats and Thomas Kinsella, *Davis, Mangan, Ferguson?: Tradition and the Irish Writer* (Chester Springs, Pa.: Dufour Editions, 1970), 67. Kinsella's interest in Mangan was shared by two of his major ancestors, Yeats and Joyce.

> Out of the shadows behind my laughter surgical fingers
> Come and I am strapped to a table.
>
> Ultimate, pitiless, again I ply the knife.
>
> (AS 24)

The same tone and imagery are not to become prominent until much later, in *Notes from the Land of the Dead* (1973) and *A Technical Supplement* (1976). More significantly, however, the same dramatic projection, with a few exceptions ("The Serving Maid," "Soft Toy," and, to a lesser extent, "The Poet Egan O Rahilly, Homesick in Old Age," in *Nightwalker* [1968]), does not resurface until the increased attention to psychic journeys and dramas that distinguish the poetry from *Notes from the Land of the Dead* onward. The shift is away from the more static portraiture of the early volumes to more dynamic expression from within the experiential self.[36]

Kinsella's handling of appetitive vision is equally effective in "The Travelling Companion," where the "two starved jaws of the will," light and dark, pursue their ravening path across an allegorical landscape. The image of "a fertile tension" as predatory animal is convincingly developed—"Naturally ravenous," as Kinsella puts it with wry ironic tone, the adverb suggesting both the natural and the expected. Moreover, the beast is seen as the driving force behind war and invasion, forcefully conveyed by a barrage of verbs and anticipating the assertion of multifarious experience and multiple existences by the Milesian Amergin in *Notes from the Land of the Dead*, who as an invader also "surfs ashore":

> Yet balanced, snarling, on claws, a fertile tension
> Stretched its brightening muscles, sniffed and made
> Off in a carnal wonder, prowled with the hungry,
> Panicked with alert deer, preyed in the sky,
> Skittered brilliantly across a still glade,
>
> Marched over murderous plains to the ocean with savages,
> Beat with a thousand hearts on a crowded headland,
> Knotted in fear of the narrow boats at its foot,

36. Edna Longley commented early on Kinsella's preoccupation in *AS* with portraiture; see her "The Heroic Agenda: The Poetry of Thomas Kinsella," *Dublin Magazine* 5 (Summer 1966): 73. Thomas Dillon Redshaw saw Kinsella's Mangan poem as anticipating his "imminent step from portraiture to confessionalism"; see "The Wormwood Revisions," *Eire-Ireland* 6 (Summer 1971): 113.

Came through the shrill distress of disturbed ledges
With stern invaders, surfing ashore for good.
(*AS* 5)

Kinsella's humor, black or ironic as it may be, should not be underestimated: the "good" toward which the invaders surf embraces permanence ("for good" meaning "forever") and an ethical goal (goodness), although they achieve neither. Their traveling companion of the will is engaged in a journey that both begins and ends with fumbling in the dark. Yet, like characters out of Beckett, their lack of success does not cancel out their willed compulsion: "you must go on, I can't go on, I'll go on."[37]

The single most significant poem in *Another September*, one also preoccupied with the will, is "Baggot Street Deserta"; it is, arguably, one of Kinsella's most significant poems within this first stage of his career and originally provided the volume's title. At the same time such achievement was not gained lightly. Like Yeats, Kinsella has spoken[38] of how laborious and slow his writing is; he has indicated that a poem can take years to gestate in notes and then months to be shaped into publishable form. What "Baggot Street Deserta" reveals also is the meticulous nature of Kinsella's craftsmanship, for he subjected the poem to wholesale revision between magazine publication and collection in a volume.[39] While some Kinsella poems remain virtually unchanged, others undergo extensive surgery. Of the latter kind "Downstream," the title poem of the 1962 volume, is one; "Baggot Street Deserta" is another; and both poems, it must be said, benefit immeasurably from their revision to become major statements in Kinsella's total work and landmarks in his poetic development.[40]

37. Samuel Beckett, *The Unnamable*, in *Three Novels: "Molloy," "Malone Dies," "The Unnamable"* (New York: Grove Press, 1965), 414.

38. As Kinsella told Dennis O'Driscoll, the method of composition, while remaining the same, "*is* getting more and more difficult, but also better"; "the technical demands of writing have increased. It has become more and more difficult"; see O'Driscoll, "Interview," 59, 63. Like Yeats, Kinsella is drawn by "the fascination of what's difficult."

39. Kinsella revised his translations in similar fashion: *Longes Mac nUsnig* (November 1954) underwent revision by the time of *Poems and Translations* (1961) but most drastically before its final appearance in the *Táin* (1969), with the language each time made tauter and more colloquial.

40. Cf. Edna Longley who, in contrast, sees "Baggot Street Deserta" as flawed by Kinsella's failure to absorb his influences, T. S. Eliot and Robert Lowell; see "The Heroic Agenda," 61.

"Baggot Street Deserta" was first published under the title "Unfinished Business," in *Irish Writing* (Spring 1956); it appeared in revised form under its final title in *Poetry Now*, edited by G. S. Fraser in the same year; and achieved its final form in *Another September* two years later.[41] For clarity's sake, the three versions will be designated A *(Irish Writing)*, B *(Poetry Now)*, and C *(AS)*; it must be admitted, however, that what follows is not an exhaustive comparison of the versions, for which greater space would be needed. The versions vary considerably in organization of paragraphs, individual phrasing, and length. C contains 81 lines; A, which runs to 156 lines, is almost twice as long; and B, which shows no sign of being an extract, has 142 lines. The scheme of rhyming alternate lines *(abab)* with the occasional couplet remains more or less unchanged throughout all three versions. Clearly the first and longest version, A, required the most drastic cutting and is the most prosaic in both writing and argument.

What comparison of all three versions indicates is that the poet's revisions involved sustained effort to shape and order his work into its most effective form. The opening paragraph remains virtually intact: by version C Kinsella has removed distracting, forced, or absurd imagery such as "a pelvic arch of stars" (l. 5) and "a wee / Belch of waters in the gorse" (ll. 13–14), although both instances had survived in versions A and B. The "tussle of syllables in the lilac" (a pastiche of T. S. Eliot's *Four Quartets*) gives way to C's "The breaking-cry, the strain of the rack" (imagery more akin to Dante's *Inferno*), while the first paragraph's concluding line in A, retained in B, disturbs by suggesting the callow fun Kinsella and Ó Riada enjoyed while intoning Wordsworth's "Upon Westminster Bridge" in BBC accents (*FD* 65): "A medium heart is lying still." If the line is meant as parody, it contradicts the poem's meditative nature; if read straight, it encourages laughter. Indeed, the self-analysis in C is offered at a distance by the cold, objective, impersonal tone, in keeping with the "sigh of educated boredom" the persona expresses. In version A the persona utters that same sigh but proceeds to unburden himself in irritating chatter:

> What,
> Dear world, is the matter? What's to be thought?

41. *AS* was reset in September 1962 when Kinsella made a few minor changes but none to "Baggot Street Deserta." Some poems were revised further in *Selected Poems, 1956–1968* (Dublin: Dolmen Press, 1973), although "Baggot Street Deserta" remained unchanged.

What's to be done? Something I
Have left undone, a friendly letter
To someone in another city,
Raises encouraging flags: (Dear debtor,
You owe me narrative; be witty.
Read good books and fall in love . . .
Assemble all the values; shun
All wasters and the pomps thereof . . .
Are Dublin's britches falling down?)

(A, ll. 19–30)

While the last line suggests a Joycean parody of "London Bridge is falling down, falling down," the persona's confusion and loss of direction read like bad Eliot; version B retains only the first three lines, while version C drops the whole passage.

Even punctuation needs revision: the removal of periods (versions A and B) and their substitution with more natural commas in C eliminates portentousness: "A cigarette. The moon. A sigh / Of educated boredom." And while at least one critic[42] has objected to the clichéd nature of version C's curlew with its "lingering, *threadbare* cry" (my italics), versions A and B, which vary marginally here, reveal slackness in desperate need of the poet's subsequent tightening:

That curlew-call of exile, half-
Buried longing, half-serious
Anger and the rueful laugh—
Dangerously near the spurious,
Commonplace, played out, as dry
A dose for the discriminating
As that lonely bird's threadbare cry,
As wild, as lost, as desolating.

(A, ll. 31–38)

Version A undergoes drastic revision in which entire paragraphs are omitted, with only occasional phrases and images retained. Its divisions into an introduction and two numbered sections are quickly dropped. A major change, however, is that in version A the protagonist addresses his predicament to another: "My curious friend, I turn to you / For having had a will to do"; "Allowing, Brendan, absence makes / A virtuoso of the heart. . . ." And instead of the "quarter-inch of cigarette," which since version C has continued its symbolic

42. Douglas Dunn, " 'Baggot Street Deserta,' " *Tracks* 7 (1987): 15.

flare down to Baggot Street, version A has for a concluding paragraph what the persona himself concedes is "our strident adolescence." The lines evidence the distance Kinsella traveled in the two years separating versions A and C:

> "I *will* count." "What is fact!" How we
> Stormed and plied the coffee-pot
> Until we teased the small hours out
> Like sheets we could not spare the time
> To sleep in! These rooms, where I put
> A self to the question now, redeem,
> A little because you have tinkered here,
> The murderous intracordal cutting
> Under the stubborn quick, the queer
> Uprooting, burying, prying, shutting
> Of sudden stares like holes in the sane
> Membrane of sight, the playing with taste
> Of words on the tongue like vintage, like rain,
> Until they speak what I can trust; . . .
> (A, ll. 134–47)

Version B concludes with the poet's "goddess who had light for thighs" and who "takes to bed / . . . / The marsh bird that children dread"; the final version proceeds for at least a further third of the poem.

While version B was in good company in G. S. Fraser's *Poetry Now*, an anthology that included works by most of the significant poets of the day, one wonders what Kinsella made of the editorial rationale: "The poets represented in this anthology are all British, and are mainly those British poets who either began to write, or who first properly discovered themselves, during or after the Second World War."[43] It might be noted that Maurice James Craig, Ewart Milne, and Richard Murphy join Kinsella among Fraser's "regionalists" (Scots, Irish, and Welsh). The shadow of English verse takes several forms, not the least a Home Counties centralism and political insensitivity.

"Baggot Street Deserta" in its final version emerges not only in tauter, more effective form but with its focus clarified. The persona certainly suffers from some existential angst but the whole is now clearly related to his practice as a poet. In Douglas Dunn's words, rather than "a topographical poem, it is a poem of the nocturnal

43. "Preface," *Poetry Now*, ed. Fraser, 15.

window, a poem of the room and of solitude, of the writer's past haunting his creative mind, the pain of the present teasing dilemmas with a ruminative lyricism."[44] At the same time Dublin, only barely perceptible in this poem, is to prove increasingly the distinctive Kinsella landscape: urban, nocturnal, at times numinous, frequently a land of the dead, always a setting for spiritual pilgrimage. The room, on the other hand, reflects both the security and the isolation of the enclosed self. The room signifies the womb where initiation takes place, but, like its corresponding image of the cell, can lead to illumination or darkness, growth or stasis. Both room and cell belong with the garden as metaphors for the self in its struggle to understand and be whole. But as the poetry becomes increasingly preoccupied with psychological and biological states, room and garden are frequently replaced by cell, embryo, and dark forces known along the blood.

With fine irony, the final version of "Baggot Street Deserta" (*AS* 29–31) begins, as did the first two versions, with the persona putting aside the poem on which he has been working: "Lulled, at silence, the spent attack. / The will to work is laid aside." And while "will" gives way to "educated boredom," what is evident is that Kinsella is again at work writing that characteristically modernist poem on the difficulty of writing a poem. In the meantime he draws upon several literary echoes to define his present place as a writer in the context of his Irish past. The "double shadow" in the process is overcome and Kinsella emerges very much his own man. We are meant, then, to recognize the echo of Joyce's Anna Livia Plurabelle, as described by the washers at the ford (*FW* 202–4),[45] in the poet's pursuit of the Liffey to its source in the Wicklow mountains, just as we identify, with help from *Nightwalker* (66–67) later, the "curlew's lingering threadbare cry / Of common loss" with Amergin, the first Irish poet. The reader readily discerns Joyce in the urban setting, but a more powerful early influence who showed Kinsella how the urban could exemplify the contemporary spiritual wasteland was T. S. Eliot. "He has been an inescapable influence for some time," Kinsella said in

44. Dunn, " 'Baggot Street Deserta,' " 14. Seamus Deane comments less favorably, in *Celtic Revivals*, 138. Denis Donoghue, who early found Kinsella "the most interesting of young Irish poets," criticized version A and the poet's "tendency to luxuriate in gestures of romantic isolation"; see "Irish Writing," 185.

45. This and subsequent citations are to James Joyce, *Finnegans Wake* (London: Faber and Faber, 1950), abbreviated as *FW*, followed by page and line number.

1962,[46] while also insisting that, except in his "very, very adolescent stage," he had not wanted to write in Eliot's manner. Kinsella's meditations and intellectual concern, his diction and symbolic landscapes, owe not a little, nevertheless, to Eliot's example, and "Baggot Street Deserta," like the later "Nightwalker," is not devoid of the older poet's influence. Moreover, in a poem using the paragraphing and four-stressed line of "Easter 1916," it is hardly surprising that Yeats ("Too long a sacrifice / Can make a stone of the heart") should surface, as a ghost to be exorcised in parody: "Versing, like an exile, makes / A virtuoso of the heart." Yet the poem focuses not upon public political events, like the Rising, but upon the persona's spiritual and aesthetic predicament as affected by that past. Again, the large Auden abstractions—Art, the One, Truth, Youth—appear also, but the "voice" that clarifies and puts all in their place is distinctively Kinsella, relying upon the endurance of suffering in his accommodation with time:

> A voice clarifies when the tingle
> Dies out of the nerves of time:
> *Endure and let the present punish.*
> Looking backward, all is lost;
> The Past becomes a fairy bog
> Alive with fancies, double crossed
> By pad of owl and hoot of dog.
> (*AS* 30)

The punishment of the present proves more positive to the self's development than any lingering backward look. Neither "the Celtic Twilight" nor Corkery's "Hidden Ireland" is an adequate alternative to the lessons to be learned from enduring time. The earlier adolescence too is firmly rejected, in lines impressive for their honesty and moving in their acceptance of time, personal culpability, and responsibility:

> I nonetheless inflict, endure,
> Tedium, intracordal hurt,
> The sting of memory's quick, the drear
> Uprooting, burying, prising apart
> Of loves a strident adolescent
> Spent in doubt and vanity.

46. *The Poet Speaks*, ed. Orr, 108. Cf. Heaney, "Reading T. S. Eliot and reading about T. S. Eliot were equally formative experiences for my generation"; see *The Government of the Tongue*, 91.

All feed a single stream, impassioned
Now with obsessed honesty,
A tugging scruple that can keep
Clear eyes staring down the mile,
The thousand fathoms, into sleep.
(31)

These lines, with their near-incantatory effect, serve in the manner of a poetic testament, an ethic and aesthetic by which his own fulfillment as a self and a poet can be attained. Moreover, while the backward look is renounced—Frank O'Connor's title is surely echoed in line 38, "Looking backward, all is lost"—the poet remains aware, through the imagery of the Pale in the poem's concluding paragraph, of the predicament of the Irish poet writing in English. It is a theme to which Kinsella will devote more time and thought in subsequent decades. As the poet leans out of his window and confronts the night—a suitable and recurrent Kinsella situation—he is made aware both of his "poet's cramp" and "The slow implosion" of his pulse. In versions A and B, the image was of "explosion": Kinsella was correct to invert the blood beat and reinforce the effect with the alliteration on the "mp" and "p" sounds in subsequent lines. But it is the Pale that dominates, in imagery both distinctively Irish and Audenesque, of frontiers, garrisons, threatening dark forces, and the heroic struggle toward light. Indeed, in a poem that established early his development into a significant Irish poet, Kinsella's "Chilly points of light" owe rather too much to Auden's "Ironic points of light" ("September 1, 1939"):

Fingers cold against the sill
Feel, below the stress of flight,
The slow implosion of my pulse
In a wrist with poet's cramp, a tight
Beat tapping out endless calls
Into the dark, as the alien
Garrison in my own blood
Keeps constant contact with the main
Mystery, not to be understood.
Out where imagination arches
Chilly points of light transact
The business of the border-marches
Of the Real, . . .
(31)

Douglas Dunn has rightly praised these lines for "their mixture of the audible, the tactile and the visible, the whole sensation tied to the intimate rhythm of blood."[47] Indeed, the lines nicely balance the abstract against the physical and immediate, and refute the charge against Kinsella of excessive and dry intellectualism. Yet the dominant feature of these lines is their several paradoxes: the poet's "pulse / In a wrist with poet's cramp" sends out its Morse code into the darkness, making "contact with the main / Mystery," which nevertheless remains incomprehensible, just as the imagination is envisaged as an "alien garrison." The artistic act may be completed, as the poem itself proves, but it is not understood. The imagination may connect with "the Real" in "Chilly points of light" but their coldness reflects their ultimate privacy from which the poet-protagonist remains cut off. Even that experience of the mystery of the creative process is at one and the same time "a fact / That may be countered or may not." The vividly actual cigarette butt thrown on to the street below thus takes on symbolic status, as evidencing the poet's return to the arduous business of composition, but also as a signal not of rejection, but of challenge, in the manner of a gauntlet. The participle, after all, is "flaring," a fit conclusion to a poem where illumination has seemed most blocked. Yet when illumination comes, as befits "the main / Mystery," in a manner "not to be understood," it requires effort, discipline, endurance, suffering, and will, the distinctive Kinsella attributes.

The volume ends bleakly with "Thinking of Mr. D." (46–47), a portrait of "A minding man whose body frays is forced / Into an abstract wrecking humour," and one who appears like "A barren Dante leaving us for hell." In that respect the poem provides entry into the subsequent volume, *Downstream* (1962). Kinsella's concern, however, is directed at the figure's bitter view of the world, a bitterness and anger to which he himself has been prone and against which he warned later (*A Technical Supplement*, Poem XXI, *One* 49–50).

More satisfying, instead, is the title poem, "Another September" (41), with the by-now familiar Kinsella setting: a nocturnal scene, a room, the time at that uncertain hour between the borders of night and day, like the season of autumn, a temporal frontier to be successfully traversed and, like the crossroads, posing threat and requiring choice. Kinsella has described it as a dream poem operating on the

47. Dunn, " 'Baggot Street Deserta,' " 16.

margin of consciousness, in which lover and beloved fall asleep and their union is maintained in the dream world.[48]

Once more the double shadow appears, here in the presence of an early favorite, Keats, and his ode "To Autumn." Yet the romantic poet's presence is not intrusive; rather, he serves as a sounding board against which the Irish poet plays. Certainly Keats's sensual awareness of the physical world, especially in the autumnal month of September, is recaptured by Kinsella, who was drawn also to the romantic's focus upon the synthesis of contraries, the disparities of birth and death, growth and decay, shaped together to culminate in the harvest season but also to act as prelude to the onset of winter. For all its apparent restfulness and ripeness, Kinsella's poem includes these antitheses to show the necessary dialectic running through all things.

The opening stanza describes such a "country bedroom," possessed of "a minor peace," surrounded by images of fullness and sweetness. Similarly, the season—not quite Keats's ruddy country girl—is imaged as some farm animal:

> Domestic Autumn, like an animal
> Long used to handling by these countrymen,
> Rubs her kind hide against the bedroom wall
> Sensing a fragrant child come back again . . .
>
> (41)

But within the idyllic scene of stanza 1 are "Long pitch black breaths" drawn by the garden, breathing which returns to trouble in the concluding stanza. The imagery of femalelike threatening figures appearing out of "the lampless darkness" must nevertheless be seen in perspective. Like the moths drawn to the window, all things progress toward the dark, toward death, but also toward rebirth. And, appropriately enough, given Kinsella's treatment of women, the figures move like women and take recognized archetypal forms like Justice and Truth. The poem's persona has been brought, like the persona in Keats's ode, to an awareness of life's dialectic, of the pattern by which things grow through birth, life, and maturity, to death but also to regeneration. Rather than being threatening figures, these women symbolize that awareness of darkness that we all must acquire if understanding is to be achieved.

Through his reliance upon Keats, Kinsella shows how much he

48. O'Driscoll, "Interview," 63.

must depend upon a foreign model to express the vision of the world he is in the process of developing. Such reliance reflects an inherited weakness in the early poetry, as he later conceded: "[A]t the beginning my poems were influenced by literature more than by fact."[49] In subsequent volumes Kinsella not only turns to distinctively Irish exemplars but gives his literary sources increased substance and force by rooting them in experience and fact.

49. *Viewpoints*, ed. Haffenden, 104.

two

Initiation into Experience

Downstream (1962)—or, more precisely, Kinsella's revision in 1964 of the title poem—represents the watershed beyond which he proceeds to formulate his own myth and to draw upon more indigenous material. The volume, in John Montague's words, marks "Kinsella's change of gear from lyric to meditative."[1] *Downstream*'s transitional character, however, is reflected in matters other than form, as Montague acknowledges. This third book also reflects the poet's increasing complexity and accomplishment: the vision darkens, the scope extends to encompass social and political life, the settings are now more recognizably Irish. Indeed, with hindsight, one can see the final section of the volume already anticipating its successor, *Nightwalker*, and the establishment of a new and important phase in Kinsella's development.

The "Prologue," on the other hand, striking a deliberately ironic stance, reads like many a Movement poem of the time (by, for instance, Kingsley Amis). The parallel should not entirely surprise us: among Kinsella's warmest early admirers, as we have seen, were Don-

1. Montague, in *Contemporary Writers of the English Language: Contemporary Poets*, ed. Vinson, 835.

ald Davie and Robert Conquest, while he appeared in the company of other Movement poets like Larkin, Davie, Conquest, and Amis in Conquest's anthology, *New Lines—II* (1963). Moreover, like Larkin, Kinsella admired the poet who also had a full-time job, and he regarded writing as not incompatible with his first career. Writing, rather than being his "occupation," was for him "an intense hobby. I'm a civil servant and was actually a civil servant before I wrote any poetry. I never found any clash between the two. In fact, I've found that my mental state when composing a particularly difficult minute is not unlike the process of writing a poem."[2] While such views proved compatible with Movement principles, Kinsella—in a very un-Movement choice—went on to single out for praise poets like Wallace Stevens and William Carlos Williams. The parallel with the Movement, more fortuitous than planned, thus needs qualification; already Kinsella was looking for more compatible exemplars elsewhere. Nevertheless, as their critical reception in Britain indicates, these early volumes proved acceptable within contemporary English practice.

Deliberately antiromantic and deflationary, the "Prologue" relies for its effect upon the play of wit and irony within rhyming couplets, and employs figures not out of place in an Augustan satire to personify human attributes, mostly frailties (Energy, Laziness, Discipline, Jaws-of-Death, Error, Routine, Futility). Moreover, the irony is directed also against the speaker, in part refuting the recurrent but misleading charge against Kinsella of unrelenting grimness. Indeed, critics have not always appreciated his extensive irony and mordant wit. The poem begins:

I wonder whether one expects
Flowing tie or expert sex
Or even absent-mindedness
Of poets any longer. Less
Candour than the average,
Less confidence, a ready rage,
Alertness when it comes to beer,
An affectation that their ear
For music is a little weak.
These are the attributes we seek;
But surely not the morning train,
The office lunch, the look of pain

2. *The Poet Speaks*, ed. Orr, 109. Cf. O'Driscoll, "Interview," 60.

Down the blotched suburban grass,
Not the weekly trance at Mass . . .
Drawing on my sober dress
These, alas, I must confess.
(D 9)

Such irony and wit serve Kinsella's moral purpose, but, in his deliberate echo of Yeats's circus animals, they serve also to indicate the distance he now feels confident in establishing between himself and the older poet. For the "double shadow" of Yeats and English verse is here played off against itself:

And so my bored menagerie
Once more emerges: Energy,
Blinking, only half awake,
Gives its tiny frame a shake;
Fouling itself, a giantess,
The bloodshot bulk of Laziness
Obscures the vision; Discipline
Limps after them with jutting chin,
Bleeding badly from the calf:
Old Jaws-of-Death gives laugh for laugh
With Error as they amble past,
And there as usual, lying last,
Helped along by blind Routine,
Futility flogs a tambourine . . .
(10)

In the later poetry Kinsella's menagerie animals take their place less in allegory and more in archetypal myth. He uses the term "allegory" in connection with generalization, as something that provides a structure by which experience can be ordered and known. Experience thus needs allegory.[3] But as he came increasingly to recognize the essentially organic nature of experience, allegory gave way to myth as the more appropriate aesthetic embodiment of experience.

Kinsella has noted that the volume's four sections group four different kinds of poems: the first consists of miscellaneous lyrics, the second offers "a formal sequence of epigrammatic poems" ("Moralities"),

3. "The obsession with fact, with specific individual data, wouldn't seem to me to make much sense unless it had some allegorical drive behind it. Experience by itself, however significant, won't do"; see *Viewpoints*, ed. Haffenden, 104. At times in the interview Kinsella remarked upon "the allegorical nature of the datum" (108–9, 112).

the third contains three longer allegorical poems, and the final section looks forward to "future work."[4] Thanks to the example of Yeats, among others, Kinsella saw that a book of poems might profit from being shaped into a formal unity. He described the poems in *Another September* as "printed in the order in which they were finished";[5] *Downstream* and subsequent volumes follow thematic rather than chronological lines.

I

The opening section provides considerable variety of theme and treatment, and, due to several unsuccessful poems ("Charlie," "Scylla and Charybdis," "Wedding Morning," "A Portrait of the Engineer"), uneven achievement. But the opening poem, "The Laundress," succeeds brilliantly, revealing certainty of touch, extended scope, and relevance, and constitutes one of the volume's major achievements.

"The Laundress" is based on a painting[6] of a pregnant woman mending a sheet, and whom Kinsella places in the context of August 1914, at the onset of World War I:

> Her chair drawn to the door,
> A basket at her feet,
> She sat against the sun
> And stitched a linen sheet.
> Over harrowed Flanders
> August moved the wheat.
>
> (13)

Individual and universal merge through the several parallels. The approaching full term of the laundress's pregnancy is matched by the contrapuntal harvest of wheat and soldiers, with corresponding imagery of grain and shell (as protecting the unborn in the womb, the grain in the husk, and the explosive in the artillery shell). The harvest to be reaped encompasses child, wheat, and soldier; the sheet is both bedsheet and winding sheet; and Yeats's image from "Adam's Curse" of stitching and unstitching is employed here to symbolize the dialec-

4. Kinsella, *Poetry Book Society Bulletin* 34 (September 1962); *D* was the fall choice.

5. Kinsella, *Poetry Book Society Bulletin* 17 (March 1958).

6. Kinsella, *Poetry Book Society Bulletin* 34 (September 1962).

tical forces at work in all things. What Kinsella catches is the ironic conjunction of war and peace, creation and destruction, innocence and culpability, life and death contained in this particular moment. Criticism is neither offered nor implied, not because the poet is indifferent but because he understands that such conjunction of opposites is both inevitable and necessary. Moreover, the woman belongs to a long and important line of female figures in Kinsella's poetry, women like his own wife or, later, his grandmother or others in the poet's family and upbringing, who represent an ancient intuitive wisdom and from whom the male might learn. The moment is full of movement and yet also held in temporary suspension; it is indeed an epiphany, and its regenerative nature is clarified further by another shell image, here only implied, of a chicken: "A cluck in the cobbled yard: / A shadow changed its stance." (The image anticipates a similar scene given more explicit significance in "Hen Woman," in *Notes from the Land of the Dead.*)

The woman becomes the means by which continuity and regeneration are achieved, and, appropriately enough, it is her heart's experience that makes the process possible. She knows through suffering as well as through love, by experiencing the contraries in the most immediate of ways. "The heels of ripeness" of the unborn kicking in her womb reappear much later, as the mercurial heels of the poet's father as he sets off on his own life's journey (*BF* 14), while the Audenesque animal imagery symbolizes instinctive life:

> As a fish disturbs the pond
> And sinks without a stain
> The heels of ripeness fluttered
> Under her apron. Then
> Her heart grew strained and light
> As the shell that shields the grain.
>
> (*D* 13)

By the time of the final stanza whatever movement taking place acquires an inevitability, reinforced by the succession of verbs ("plumps," "turns," "winnow," "grind," "searched," "fixed"), by the rhythm and end-stopping, by the alliteration on "w," and by the biblical imagery of winnowing and grinding. At the same time the woman is more than a passive agent in the face of such inevitability: she both endures and actively participates in this process, searching in her basket and fixing "her ruffled sheet":

> The sower plumps his acre,
> Flanders turns to the heat,
> The winds of Heaven winnow
> And the wheels grind the wheat.
> She searched in her basket
> And fixed her ruffled sheet.
>
> (13)

"Dick King" focuses upon another figure, this time from the poet's own past, a friend and neighbour whose characteristic silence nevertheless masks both kindness and sensitivity. Language proves central here, whether in the form of the wife's prayers and whispering or in the Gaeltacht the man leaves to seek work in Dublin, or, most significantly, in his "phantom vowels" and "low voice in a stubbled throat." For Dick King serves as one more, albeit this time male, instructor about the world's true nature. Not coincidentally, Kinsella describes him as "Bemused," for the man's contact with the sources of inspiration, the Muses, may be seen to contribute to the embryonic poet's own journey. Moreover, while the poet calls up his childhood experiences of the now-dead man, death as much as life brings increased awareness and love. Love and death once more come together, and the lines are made effective through paradox and oxymoron: the man's "Kind plague" fouls the poet's thoughts and yet brings love, with his "phantom vowels" speaking no less clearly than when alive:

> In your ghost, Dick King, in your phantom vowels I read
> That death roves our memories igniting
> Love. Kind plague, low voice in a stubbled throat,
> You haunt with the taint of age and of vanished good,
> Fouling my thought with losses.
>
> (20)

The man's death provokes not only memories of love but awareness of loss; as the first half of the poem develops, that loss includes the young boy's own childhood and innocence, the man's suffering in later life, and certainly the passing of time and of "vanished good." The neighborhood—of Basin Lane, Bow Lane, the Fountain, James and Thomas Streets—is rich in both personal and historical associations—of Kinsella's grandmother but also of Robert Emmet and the 1803 uprising, and of Jonathan Swift whose St. Patrick's Hospital is nearby. The neighborhood is the setting later for an entire sequence,

St. Catherine's Clock (1987). And it may be that Swift and Emmet, present in that later sequence, are among the dead named by Dick King, although the poem is silent on this score. The young boy's experience, however, is also reminiscent of similar initiations in *Dubliners*, and the poem possesses a Joycean immediacy and particularity, as the following lines indicate:

> Clearly now I remember rain on the cobbles,
> Ripples in the iron trough, and the horses' dipped
> Faces under the Fountain in James's Street,
> When I sheltered my nine years against your buttons
> And your own dread years were to come;
>
> And your voice, in a pause of softness, named the dead,
> Hushed as though the city had died by fire,
> Bemused . . . discovering, discovering
> A gate to enter temperate ghosthood by;
> And I squeezed your fingers till you found again
> My hand hidden in yours.
>
> (20)

The change to the ballad stanza and rhythm in the poem's second half, however, is not entirely successful. The reader must remain convinced that Dick King deserves to belong to that critical category of people whom Kinsella will distinguish in subsequent volumes with imagery of vertical man: "Dick King was an upright man." The problem lies partly in the singsong rhythm of the ballad form itself, but also in the reader's inability to accept the mundane details of the dead man's life as capable of carrying his symbolic status:[7]

> By the Southern Railway he increased:
> His second soul was born
> In the clangour of the iron sheds,
> The hush of the late horn.
>
> (21)

The reader's confidence is thus undermined, despite the poet's deep and sincere feelings.[8]

7. In the version published in *University Review* (2, no. 12 [1961]: 10–11) the poem offers minor variants but also two extra stanzas in the second part. Once more the later revisions improve the collected version.

8. Robin Skelton views the poem's structure more positively, seeing the two parts as set off antiphonally and reflecting "Kinsella's sense of divided man"; see "The Poetry of Thomas Kinsella," 99.

Death and initiation into pain are central to the third poem, "Cover Her Face," which describes the sudden death of a young woman, Maura, and how the poet and Maura's family come to terms with that fact. The poem is made effective by balancing distance and involvement. While touched by the woman's premature death, the poet assumes the role of observer ("Standing by the door . . ."; "I watch her drift . . ."). Such "apartness" enables him to place both life and death in the context of suffering and heartbreak and the need for acceptance. That acceptance is reinforced by both the regular rhyme scheme and the steady four-stressed line. The family mourners, on the other hand, experience the antithesis of distance: the intense grief and heartbreak into which they have been abruptly initiated. That abruptness is further heightened by the poet's running of the prose introduction into the poem's opening lines:

> *She has died suddenly, aged twenty-nine years, in Dublin. Some of her family travel from the country to bring her body home. Having driven all morning through a storm*
>
> They dither softly at her bedroom door
> In soaking overcoats, and words forsake
> Even their comforters. The bass of prayer
> Haunts the chilly landing while they take
> Their places in a murmur of heartbreak.
>
> (22)

The landing has not yet assumed significance among Kinsella's domestic symbols—it will make its first appearance as "a landing place" in the conclusion to the volume's title poem—but already here it serves as the frontier into heartbreak that Maura's family must cross. The mourning scene reads once again like a scene from *Dubliners*, for Kinsella has an acute Joycean eye for detail: for the mourners' "dithering," their soaked overcoats, for Maura's cracked laugh, for the photograph with "Her arm tucked tiredly into mine," and in death her hair spread out on the pillow. Yet her death is seen in distinctively Kinsellan terms:

> Her body's tact
> Swapped child for woman, woman for a ghost,
> Until its buried sleep lay uppermost;
>
> And Maura, come to terms at last with pain,
> Rests in her ruptured mind, her temples tight,

> Patiently weightless as her time burns down.
> Soon her few glories will be shut from sight:
> Her slightness, the fine metal of her hair spread out,
>
> Her cracked, sweet laugh.
>
> (22–23)

For Maura has "come to terms at last with pain," known suffering and gained understanding; she takes her place alongside the many Kinsella female figures whose experience serves to enlighten the less knowledgeable poet. Even the detail of the woman's hair spread out upon the pillow will be repeated in subsequent poems to acquire a sinister seductiveness and symbolic status. Yet no such sinister quality is meant here and the sincerity of the poet's feelings are never doubted: the poem's title from Webster's *Duchess of Malfi* (4.2.266), "Cover her face; mine eyes dazzle; she died young," reflects the poet's feelings, despite its literary source and his further reference to Ophelia. More distinctively Kinsellan imagery is that of appetite, in which Maura "drank the furnace of the Lamb, / Draining one image of its faint *I am*," and closed "her dream in hunger." As the first and later images of "the fruit of justice" and the need to "bite its ashen bread" suggest, the images' origin is biblical. The transcendent quality reflected in Kinsella's image of "the crystal soul" is achieved by accepting suffering in the soul's appetite to endure heartbreak. The consolation the poet offers Maura's mourning relatives depends more upon his evolving faith in the necessary experience of the world's dialectic than upon any religious faith in a divine will:

> Mother, brother, when our questions cease
> Such peace may come, consenting to the good,
> Chaste, biddable, out of all likelihood.
>
> (24)

The second section, "Moralities," which first appeared in 1960, is here revised, with some poems such as "A Toast" and "The Nest" being altered quite radically;[9] others, such as "Designs after Dürer,"[10] which encouraged the analogy with a medieval morality, are not reproduced. The poems are short, epigrammatic, reminiscent in part

9. In *Moralities* (Dublin: Dolmen Press, 1960) "A Toast" was titled "The Overrun," and "The West" was titled "Under Scorpio." Both were radically revised in *D* (1962) and neither poem was included in *Poems and Translations* (1961).

10. Miller, *Dolmen XXV*, 32.

of middle Yeats, and not especially successful. The arrangement under headings of "Faith," "Love," Death," and "Song," with "Interlude: Time's Mischief" separating the quartet into two halves, intrudes as programmatic; the overall achievement is uneven.

The section's most successful poems illustrate love, whether in the person of Pierce Ferriter riding through "Seventeenth-Century Landscape: Near Ballyferriter" or as "Pierce's bride" in tragic sisterhood with Deirdre of the Sorrows ("Sisters"). Pierce Ferriter, distinguished both as patriot and poet, was executed for rebellion against Cromwell and, in her grief, his wife, Sybil, threw herself from the castle walls onto the rocks below in the manner of a seventeenth-century Deirdre. Their grim sisterhood takes on tragic proportions just as Pierce's statement, "On shales of desolation ends my race" (30), has political as well as personal significance. Pierce's death is an acknowledged landmark in the death of the Gaelic order: he was a distinguished poet as well as a Kerry landowner and a political rebel; his "race" indeed ended in "desolation," as Cromwell's Irish campaign and policy showed. Kinsella's interest in the Ferriters was encouraged by a crucial holiday spent in the Dingle Peninsula in 1959 (*FD* 67–69), but Pierce's full significance comes clearest to Kinsella's readers only much later with the publication of *An Duanaire* (1981). Indeed, in the same year as *Downstream* Kinsella declared finding himself "conscious of eschewing Catholic subjects or Irish subjects as being limited in themselves" and pointed to "Seventeenth-Century Landscape: Near Ballyferriter" and "Sisters" as the only instances "where the references are completely and exclusively Irish and where the actual facts behind the references would certainly be unknown to a non-Irish person."[11] While the Ferriters owe their place in "Moralities" primarily to their status as Irish exemplars of tragic love, their appearance signals in part a more far-reaching change that Kinsella experienced in the early 1960s and in which the Irish poetic tradition, including the myth of Deirdre and the literary achievement of Pierce Ferriter, was to prove central.

Even more successful, however, is another love poem, "A Garden On the Point" (31), in which child and mother, within an everyday setting of garden, clothesline, and garage wall, gain symbolic status. Easter and spring point to a return to life, movement, and light, while mother and child, sources of love in the poem, serve to bring an

11. *The Poet Speaks*, ed. Orr, 107.

unruly world to order. The garden tended is as much the self in need of cultivation as is the "point" an extremity or danger, which, like Kinsella's later abysses, must be endured. As the poem ends, moreover, we are reminded that the season that brings "great ebb tides" also depends for its transforming, resurrecting capability upon the conjunction of such contraries as light and darkness, life and death. As such, the poem resembles "Another September" in the previous volume and, for all its brevity, captures convincingly the emergence of threatening, normally submarine forces: "And now great ebb tides lift to the light of day / The sea-bed's briny chambers of decay." The full descent into a land of the dead has not yet begun, but individual poems are beginning to point in the poet's future direction.

II

Downstream's third section contains the volume's most ambitious and substantial poems: "Old Harry," "A Country Walk," and the title poem. The three poems also illustrate Kinsella's determined effort to break free of the double shadow of Yeats and the English verse tradition. For while Yeats is, as we shall see, to some extent "answered" in "A Country Walk," the dominant new influence in both the other long poems comes neither from Anglo-Irish nor English literature but from *European* literature: Dante. The shift is perhaps natural given the poet's concerns in both poems—not only of a large, public, social nature, such as the dropping of the atomic bomb or the Holocaust but, more particularly, of the moral question of humanity's potentiality for evil. The actual historical events play almost no part in either poem. Rather, Kinsella's concern is almost exclusively internal, and even in "Downstream," where an external landscape and occasion are described in vivid detail, we are made constantly aware of the internal nature of the journey through that landscape and its essentially moral significance.

In his conversation with Peter Orr, Kinsella described the poet's need to achieve a certain distance—his own term was "levitation"—and in so doing commented upon "Old Harry":

> [M]y attempt at levitation there has been to make the subject of the poem not so much the dropping of the bomb, which as a human being I regard as a morally ignorant act: the subject of the poem is not this, but is simply the possibility of the monstrous choice in the human brain, something

> which must be accepted because we have continuing evidence of it and always have had.[12]

Kinsella makes plain that he views the atomic bombing not as a sudden aberration but as "evidence" of the inherent human capacity for evil. Such evidence is founded on "choice," is "continuing," and is long-standing. In another statement in the same year (1962), he admitted to less levitation in respect to the poem and, while offering some accommodation to human imperfection, his view of "Bodily existence" as "fit punishment" is mordant in its irony:

> In "Old Harry" the theme is guilt and retribution; the context of the larger section, "The Twilight of Old Harry," is probably fairly clear. The luxury of a personal judgment has not been foregone, and it is unashamedly bitter; nevertheless, as suggested in the section entitled "The Ordeal," the vessel of decision is imperfect and, even in this case, a subject for pity. Bodily existence may constitute in itself a fit punishment for what is done with it.[13]

The two shorter poems, "Check" and "Tyrant Dying," are used to introduce the longer "Old Harry" by showing, in the first, a stage in human evolution as "A naked foot steps out onto bare baked mud" (39). Given Kinsella's early treatment of the natural world as representative of an instinctive loving state, it is appropriate that that world is described in idyllic, pastoral terms and that its response to the emergence of man is "a limitless neutrality." "Tyrant Dying" (40), the second poem, shows how misplaced that neutrality has been in the vivid description of the tyrant, whose "Fat hands" are like "talons" no longer capable of holding "The bone- and sinew-shattering pen" that has sent the tyrant's victims to torture and death. Time, on the other hand, is not only victorious but merciful, while angels descend to bring peace in a death that "the schoolbooks" will call "holy." While the transforming power of love is emphasized, even in the case of the tyrant, what awaits him is what awaits us all: the "Nothingness . . . dark as a propped axe," in which even previously blind, tyrannical eyes, as they "turn inward," will be rudely illuminated.

12. Ibid. John Montague has written of the problems of writing successful poems about the atom bomb and has criticized Kinsella for dignifying " 'Old Harry' with a moral complexity alien to his [Truman's] character." He also remarked that "to compare the hapless inhabitants of Hiroshima and Nagasaki to 'the notorious cities of the plain' is a frightening inference." See "The War Years in Ulster," in *The Figure in the Cave*, ed. Quinn, 34–35.

13. Kinsella, *Poetry Book Society Bulletin* 34 (September 1962).

When Kinsella published "Old Harry" in *Studies* (Summer 1961), he provided this skeleton key in the form of a prefatory note: "A *moral tale of guilt and its retribution*. The Ordeal—*Death states the theme. He indicates the region of sin, in which the human flesh and spirit are required to undergo the ordeal of existence*. The Twilight of Old Harry. —*The example is presented: an aged man; his choice; his guilt, his victims; his half-awakening; his punishment*."[14] The scheme's divisions correspond to the poem's several sections.

Kinsella had already noted the devil's work in "A Pillar of the Community" (29); "Old Harry" refers both to the devil's nickname and to Harry Truman, the U.S. president whose decision it was in 1945 to drop the atomic bomb on Japan. In the opening section, "The Ordeal," Kinsella offers the image of a "sour ordeal" to describe the role of appetite and suffering in the self's necessary evolution toward fulfillment and wholeness. Appropriately enough, his "grim instructor" is Death itself, who points to the role played by the antithetical figure of "Master Love." We have seen the conjunction of love and death in previous Kinsella poems. Love's title, however, is nicely ironic: like the master of a vessel, Love initiates and establishes man's course, moving "in the criminal darkness / Before our dust was chosen or choice began." For it is desire or appetite that is at the heart of love and the main mover behind the human journey. Yet such a journey involves enduring that "sour ordeal" by way of which "*the innocent spirit*" is married to a "flesh [that] proceeds to its harmonious end," while "*the guilty*" are destined to temporal existence, the "fit punishment" to which Kinsella referred in his prose statement: "The spirit that invites / The criminal darkness to the human womb / Repays with flesh and blood." It is the latter path—into "the region of sin"—that is described in "The Twilight of Old Harry."

The poem begins and ends with Old Harry's journey through a wood, while the middle sections consist of recollections of the decision to drop the bomb and the subsequent destruction. The natural world responds instinctively with terror—"Pink eyelids dipped in terror; softly, possessed, / Voles flew like shuttles through the brush"—while this agent of evil and destruction is reduced in vigor ("A crumpled lion") and to moral, if not literal, blindness ("His glasses flared suddenly, two sightless coins"). Yet the poem proceeds to his recollection of military and political advisers assembled like bacteria ready to

14. *Studies* 50 (Summer 1961): 186.

invade the body ("All the war organisms of a continent!"). His choice, as Kinsella indicates with biting irony, is to impose "reason," to seek "The greater terror for the lesser number," with "Jaw jutting with power for good." While Kinsella concedes Truman's struggle "for righteousness," he permits little irony in describing the effects of the nuclear explosion:

> Then the notorious cities of the plain,
> Groves of the temporal, lost their flesh and blood,
> Tiles, leaves, wild cries, stripped away by gales of light.
>
> Lascivious streets before they shrivelled up
> Heightened their rouge and welcomed baths of pure flame;
> In broad daylight delicate creatures of love
>
> Swayed in a rose illumination of thighs,
> Their breasts melted shyly and bared the white bone;
> At that sight men blushed fiercely and became shades.
>
> (43)

The poet acknowledges that Hiroshima and Nagasaki are "notorious cities," "cities of wickedness," but their utter devastation in turn undercuts Old Harry's righteousness:

> Where once the cities of wickedness had stood
>
> An eye socket with nerves and ducts smouldering,
> A mouth with torn uvula and with no tongue,
> Moistened like two wells the plain's enamelled face.
>
> (43)

Moreover, the reduction to a Swiftian Yahoo existence is vividly caught in section 4, where "Odours of darkness," "blind terror," and "flesh-severing embraces" highlight the conjunction of love and hurt, heart and pain. The vision is no more fearful than that of Old Harry whistling his way home, all recollections done. The concluding "Vale," likewise, unsettles: it may be, through God's goodness, that all things come to dust, that death ends all, but, addressing the "Rightly terrified sentinels of the world," the poet concludes: "In certain cases death is a criticism." That it will be in Old Harry's case we are not left to doubt.

"A Country Walk" is a more readily accessible poem: following the persona's walk through a landscape, the narrative is straightforward, relies upon traditional imagery, and provides a more effective form for

Kinsella's social criticism. While the scope may be less universal than the atomic warfare of "Old Harry," the poet's concern remains the human capacity for evil, for greed, enmity, and war. The setting now is rural (in fact, Enniscorthy, Co. Wexford). In the course of his walk, the persona, like Yeats atop his tower, calls up images and memories of Ireland's history implicit in the landscape. At the same time the reader is made aware from the outset of the nature of the narrative, which reflects an internal as well as an external reality. In Kinsella's own description, the poem "begins in petty agitation and ends in creative calm. The instrument of inner change is the gradual intrusion of the outer world; the final focal moment, where road and river intersect, is one of total awareness of the self in its physical and metaphysical surroundings."[15]

The poem begins in dissatisfaction—the walker is "Sick of the piercing company of women"—a dissatisfaction eased only as the walker proceeds through the "hushed stations" of the dead trees to find peace and renewal by way of the familiar Irish and traditional archetype, the holy well. The passage is worth quoting to illustrate the physical immediacy of Kinsella's writing here: it possesses a sensuousness that persuades the reader of the protagonist's conversion from angry dissatisfaction to joy, and that permits the abstract generalization with which the lines conclude:

> I clapped my gloves. Three cattle turned aside
> Their fragrant bodies from a corner gate
> And down the sucking chaos of a hedge
> Churned land to liquid in their dreamy passage.
> Briefly through the beaded grass a path
> Led to the holy stillness of a well
> And there in the smell of water, stone and leaf
> I knelt, baring my hand, and scooped and drank,
> Shivering, and inch by inch rejoiced:
> Ferocity became intensity.

The transformation is set in motion through the regenerative element of water, as the walker drinks from the holy well. The landscape contributes vitally as a spiritual force, made plain by the persistent religious imagery: just as the trees adopt "stations" (as in the Stations of the Cross), so too the grass is "beaded" (like a rosary) and leads to

15. Kinsella, *Poetry Book Society Bulletin* 34 (September 1962).

the holy well. On the other hand, the country town, outlined against the sky, offers little consolation, with "ruined aquaduct," "vast asylum," "Tall towers ochre where the gutters dripped; / A steeple; the long yielding of a railway turn / Through thorn and willow; a town endured its place. . . ." To the very act of enduring, however, Kinsella attributes considerable moral and epistemological importance: to endure is a necessary feature of man's spiritual growth toward fulfillment and understanding. That process proves central in subsequent volumes, beginning with *Nightwalker.* Moreover, because the place is also "Mated . . . with time," the walker becomes conscious, as he approaches "a speckled ford," of the historical events associated with the place, from the time of Cuchulain and the early Irish sagas, through the times of the Norman invasion and of Cromwell, down to the Easter Rising of 1916 and the Civil War of 1922–1923.

Despite his dismissal of the town as "an omphalos of scraps," the persona has been brought to an ancient matrix, to origins indeed. In tracing such a progress to this primordial source Kinsella draws upon traditional, archetypal imagery. The very walk itself with the persona's progress through a landscape is a recognizable metaphor for the self's journey toward enlightenment and, while Kinsella would have known of Auden's use of this traditional structural image—indeed, one Irish critic has described the poem as "a completely Irish poem in the English Blank Verse 'rural meditation' tradition"[16]—he was also familiar with its early Irish equivalent, the *immram* (voyage poem), and Joyce's Stephen and Bloom on their *peregrinatio* through the streets of Dublin. This is true too of his use of the ford: like frontiers, borders of time or space, or, most obviously, crossroads, a ford represents the route by which passage is achieved, a crucial meeting place of opposites, a strategic site on which battles are often fought. Again, such meanings have primordial origins and timeless relevance:[17] the Irish tradition supplies numerous examples of such archetypes, as Kinsella makes plain here. Indeed, "the tales" to which he refers he proceeded

16. Seán Lucy, "What Is Anglo-Irish Poetry?," in *Irish Poets in English*, ed. Seán Lucy (Cork: Mercier Press, 1973), 24.

17. Jung associates Hecate, a later Kinsella figure, with crossroads; see *Symbols of Transformation*, 370–71. For the significance of boundaries and of points where opposites coincide, see Alwyn Rees and Brinley Rees, *Celtic Heritage: Ancient Tradition in Ireland and Wales* (London: Thames and Hudson, 1961), 94, 346–47. Kinsella's own note to the *Táin*, 263, refers to Rees and Rees, *Celtic Heritage*, 94, in elucidating the symbolic character of the ford.

to translate in his influential version of the *Táin* (1969). The ford, then, like Heaney's bog, is a memory bank, but its memories are all tragic, of combat, defeat, and death, and indicate not so much progress as fearful repetition, of a cyclic pattern recurring down to the present:

> Those murmuring shallows made a trampling place
> Apt for death-combat, as the tales agree:
> There, the day that Christ hung dying, twin
> Brothers armed in hate on either side;
> The day darkened but they moved to meet
> With crossed swords under a dread eclipse
> And mingled their bowels at the saga's end.
> There the first Normans massacred my fathers,
> Then stroked their armoured horses' necks, disposed
> In ceremony, sable on green sward.
>
> (46)

Like many an ancient tragedy, the conflict involves individual families as well as whole societies. The ancient combat of Cuchulain and Ferdia (*Táin* 168ff.) on the day of Christ's Crucifixion set brother against brother: such division suggests not just tragic fratricidal enmity and distortion of normal personal relationships, but division within the self. That the "Normans massacred my fathers" suggests an ongoing connection between past and present. Moreover, Kinsella treats the Norman invasion with deliberate irony, pointing to the invaders' "ceremony" and using terms suggestive of heraldry or courtly tradition ("sable on green sward"). But the poet's irony is evenly distributed, toward Cromwell ("knot-necked Cromwell and his fervent sword / Despatched a convent shrieking to their Lover"), but also toward the "rebel host" who "piked in groups of three / Cromwell's puritan brood, their harmless neighbours." Brother against brother, neighbor against neighbor: such is the evil to which men can be driven by enmity and bigotry. And while Kinsella's sympathies lie with the suffering Irish, his description of "the martyred countryside" and the Irish kernes ("Root eaters, strange as badgers") is both properly compassionate and ironic at the same time, with the two elements counterbalancing one another. More recent events in this century, when "Brother met brother in a modern light," are more sharply criticized: freedom has been gained at a fearful cost, the exchange of "A trenchcoat playground for a gombeen jungle." He will offer a similar indictment, this time of Ireland of the sixties, in "Nightwalker."

Here the debasement of political principle is savagely caught in what also constitutes Kinsella's revisionist reply to Yeats and the older poet's elevation of the events of the Easter Rising:

> Around the corner, in a open square,
> I came upon the sombre monuments
> That bear their names: MacDonagh & McBride [*sic*],
> Merchants; Connolly's Commercial Arms . . .
>
> (48)

The Ireland of the Free State and the Republic has changed utterly, giving birth not to some terrible beauty but to Paudeen's greasy till, in which Catholic conservative attitudes and policies make a mockery of the rebels' sacrifice. Yet the poem, which began in dissatisfaction, ends not in bitterness but with the positive emergence of the Evening Star, Hesperus, associated with Venus, acknowledged by way of the fragmentary quotation from Virgil's Tenth Eclogue ("*Venit Hesperus*") and culminating in the release of expression: "Heart and tongue were loosed." What enables the persona to achieve such transformation is one more initiation or baptism of water at another ford as he stands on a bridge spanning the river and is made aware of temporal flux. For while that flux reflects a "shallow, shifting world," it is also the source of renewal. Ireland's debased commercialism, of which the poet was so critical earlier, is replaced, through the fusion of light and dark, by "sweet trade," a "commerce" (transaction, intercourse, exchange) that makes possible love between people and unity within the self. A similar dialectical synthesis is present in the conjunction of Hesperus's crystalline transcendence and the river's flood.

The same structural imagery of a journey and the transforming character of water are present in the third long poem in this section, the title poem, "Downstream" (50–56). According to Kinsella, "The journey in 'Downstream' is more openly 'meaningful' than that of 'A Country Walk,' but a similar process of increasing awareness is involved. During the poem, events so arrange themselves as to impose on the traveller an emotional acceptance of the reality of death, and the beginning of a possible understanding."[18] The narrative involves two people rowing in a skiff one evening toward Durrow; their journey's progression is accompanied, after the manner of Conrad, by their increasing penetration of some heart of darkness. Again, after

18. Kinsella, *Poetry Book Society Bulletin* 34 (September 1962).

Conrad, that darkness is recognized ultimately as something within, as the fearful potentiality for evil. Rather than Conrad, however, it is Pound or Dante[19]—Kinsella is deliberately vague—whose cantos are zipped into the narrator's jacket, although the terza rima maintained throughout further substantiates the analogy with Dante.

Perhaps because Kinsella's vision is still founded more upon literature than experience, the poem opens with curiously literary and decorative imagery—"The West a fiery complex, the East a pearl"—despite Kinsella's more threatening appetitive "hungry stream." Moreover, such artifice persists with descriptions like "the mirrored heavens' liquid casque" and the rowers' "tinkling blades." The Yeatsian swan crashing downstream does nothing to diminish the "literariness" of the situation in which the two personae talk of poetry:

> Entranced by the river's mirror-echoings,
> We swam in tranquil twilight, talking then
> Of poetry; I chose the silken kings,
>
> Luminous with crisis, epochal men
> Waging among the primal clarities
> Productive war. Spurred by the steely pen
>
> To cleansing or didactic rages, these
> Fed the stream in turn and deeper still
> Drove its course; then, fading by degrees,
>
> They shed their natures on the growing chill.
> I named them and the transitory eve
> Returned their names with force and warmth until,
>
> The gathering shades beginning to deceive,
> Night stole the princely scene. I closed the page
> And wiped the dewy cover on my sleeve.
>
> (51)

Such artifice is soon replaced by a deliberately harsh tone and equally harsh imagery: "Stabbing the stream, we grooved / Bloodvelvet furrows in its pearly face." Yet this alternation of descriptive manner

19. Kinsella admitted being influenced by Pound; see *Viewpoints*, ed. Haffenden, 103–4, 106; and Deane, "A Conversation," 86. Kinsella also favorably reviewed *Section: Rock Drill 85–95 de los cantares*; see "The Hundred Cantos of Ezra Pound," *Irish Press*, 26 October 1957, p. 4. Elsewhere he praised Dante for writing the kind of poem he most admired; see *The Poet Speaks*, ed. Orr, 108.

parallels a similar dichotomy experienced within as the narrator stares at the night sky:

> *Urmensch* and brute, in glassy unconcern,
> Where specks of alien light icily hung
> Sprinkled in countless silence—there to learn
>
> How the remote chaotic, far outflung
> In glittering waste, may shiver and become
> A mesh of order, every jewel strung!
>
> Mind shifted in its seed; . . .
>
> (52–53)

Moreover, while the narrator is made conscious of a supreme order in sorry antithesis to the chaos below, he is reminded also, through the quintessentially Joycean peal of thunder, of the Promethean nature of his transcendental dream: "honouring the birth of soul again, / The dim horizon uttered a word of thunder, / A soft flash of far Promethean pain." The voyagers' direction becomes increasingly dark and Stygian; it also proves, significantly, to be a *chosen* descent: "The waters of our choice / Gathered, plunging deeper into Styx."

The infernal character of this spiritual journey is intensified as, with "wary face," the two personae are confronted with increasing difficulty and threat: "Thick slopes," "matted arch," "slant pike," "black cage," "Furred nightbrutes," "rat-trails." But the initiation into the heart of darkness comes by way of, first, the tale of a death on the river and, second, by the extension of that death to the horrors of World War II. By this stage the two travelers have become "co-shadows," brothers indeed, like those in deadly combat in "A Country Walk," or the two halves of the same self. Appropriately enough, the narrator experiences "the cold of hell," not out of awareness of death but of death "in trouble." Once again the potential for evil is made clear, now in scenes worthy of Dante or Hieronymus Bosch,[20] as the narrator parallels Ireland's dark history ("—Ourselves through seven hundred years accurst—") with surely a calculated parodic echo of Sinn Fein ("Ourselves") and the fearful culmination of modern European history in the gas chambers of Nazi Germany:

20. Cf. Bosch, "The Hay Wain," a triptych of man as a wanderer passing through the wicked world; see Charles de Tolnay, *Hieronymus Bosch* (N.p.: Reynal, 1966), 116–33. Kinsella made the same conjunction of Bosch and Nazi Germany in "The Divided Mind," in *Irish Poets in English*, ed. Lucy, 214–15.

the soil of other lands

Drank lives that summer with a body thirst
While nerveless by the European pit
—Ourselves through seven hundred years accurst—

We gazed on barren earth obscurely lit
By tall chimneys flickering in their pall,
The haunt of swinish man—each day a spit

That, turning, sweated war, each night a fall
Back to the evil dream where rodents ply,
Man-rumped, sow-headed, busy with whip and maul

Among nude herds of the damned. It seemed that I,
Coming to conscience on that lip of dread,
Still dreamed, impervious to calamity,

Imagining a formal drift of the dead
Stretched calm as effigies on velvet dust,
Scattered on starlit slopes with arms outspread

And eyes of silver . . . when that story thrust
Pungent horror and actual mess
Into my very face, and taste I must!

(54)

The journey has been an internal one, of enlightenment, in which external and internal marry with increasing ease: "The river bed // Called to our flesh from under the watery skin / And, breathless, our shell trembling across the abyss, / We shipped our oars in dread. Now, deeper in, . . ." The river's skin corresponds in literal and figurative sense with the humans' flesh; their shell of a skiff is both their womb and tomb. The medieval monastic site of "gentle Durrow" may offer comfort from "the ache of time," but participation in, rather than retreat from, the world is sought. Kinsella's progress is indeed to depend upon proceeding more deeply inward; tissue, embryo, and digestion will replace the more external "skin" while the shell image will develop naturally into the "egg of being" in *Notes from the Land of the Dead*.

What has died in the course of this journey is the narrator's old and ignorant self and, rather than seek peace through abnegation of self and will, the protagonist reaffirms the need for individual will, choice, and moral responsibility. Appropriately enough, it is with the swan—"A soul of white with darkness for a nest"—that the protagonist identifies rather than with Durrow's "teacher and saint" in their "acre of abstract love," for the two rowers themselves are similarly engaged in "Searching the darkness for a landing place." This last trope, as critics have rightly suggested, proves increasingly central to Kinsella's work.[21]

The version in *Downstream* quoted so far is not, however, Kinsella's preferred final version: the poem was drastically revised when published in the *Massachusetts Review* (Winter 1964); it underwent further minor revision before publication in its final form as the closing poem in *Nightwalker* (1968). Once more Kinsella's practice must be examined, and once more it must be acknowledged that his editing transforms an interesting and significant poem into a statement of major importance in the development of his art. The poem's essential meaning does not vary: it remains throughout a narrative of a journey into the self, with enlightenment about one's capacity for evil and the world's dialectical nature. Its overall technique also remains an *arrangement* of experiences, much as Kinsella earlier described a poem like "Ulysses" *(Another September)*: "events so arrange themselves as to impose on the traveller an emotional acceptance of the reality of death, and the beginning of a possible understanding."[22]

In the two years separating the *Downstream* from the *Massachusetts Review* version, however, the poem underwent major revision, with its length cut in half from 163 lines to 83, the length on which Kinsella finally settled.[23] While the 1964 and 1968 versions vary in minor wording, resulting in increased sharpness of tone and phrasing, the major differences exist between the 1962 and 1964 versions. Not only is the poem reduced by half but the elaborate device of artifice, whether of language or attitude, that takes up the first 42 lines, and the subsequent dichotomies of illuminated night sky and earthly darkness, of order and chaos, man as "*Urmensch* and brute," are all

21. Edna Longley, "Searching the Darkness: Richard Murphy, Thomas Kinsella, John Montague, and James Simmons," in *Two Decades of Irish Writing*, ed. Dunn, 118–53. Robert F. Garratt argues that from *NLD* onward it is the *searching*, rather than the *finding*, that is emphasized; see "Fragilities and Structures: Poetic Strategy in Thomas Kinsella's 'Nightwalker' and 'Phoenix Park,' " *Irish University Review* 13 (Spring 1983): 89, and his *Modern Irish Poetry: Tradition and Continuity from Yeats to Heaney* (Berkeley and Los Angeles: University of California Press, 1986), 184.

22. Kinsella, *Poetry Book Society Bulletin* 34 (September 1962).

23. Skelton rightly noted "the almost decadent romanticism of the imagery" and the "adjectival richness" of the 1962 version replaced by the "more rigorous and disciplined structure" of 1964; see "The Poetry of Thomas Kinsella," 101–4.

dispensed with. Instead, the poem begins in medias res, prefaced by four italicized lines serving as commentary upon and summary of the process to be explored:

> *Drifting to meet us on the darkening stage*
> *A pattern shivered; whorling in its place*
> *Another held us in a living cage*
> *Then broke to its reordered phase of grace.*
> (1964, 323; N 83)

The reader is placed immediately on a journey downriver, no longer identified as Durrow but given universal relevance; moreover, comparison of these opening lines in the 1964 and 1968 versions will indicate the nature and validity of Kinsella's editing:

> Again in the mirrored night—a liquid mask—
> We sank our oars, bowing both in team;
> The ripples scattered, dying, to their task
>
> Under ghost alders stooped above the seam
> Of calm and current, mowing like the blind.
> We gave our frail craft to the hungry stream.
> (1964)

> Again in the mirrored dusk the paddles sank.
> We thrust forward, swaying both as one.
> The ripples scattered to the ghostly bank
>
> Where willows, with their shadows half undone,
> Hung to the water, mowing like the blind.
> The current seized our skiff. We let it run. . . .
> (1968)

The differences, while not extensive, are nevertheless significant in their elimination of weak expression. Night gives way to dusk since night will eventually fall to signify increasing darkness of self; the awkward metaphor for the night sky's reflection in the river ("a liquid mask") is replaced by the single-line first sentence, with the finality of the period capturing the sinking motion of the paddles. Greater physical immediacy is gained by the new verb "thrust," while the team action of the 1964 rowers is replaced by the sense of oneness in 1968. As we have seen in the 1962 version, Kinsella sought to relate the two oarsmen as coshadows. Willows replace alders to improve the alliteration upon the "w" sound, while the appetite of "the hungry stream" is enacted rather than simply asserted—"The current seized our skiff"—thereby increasing the sense of drama and impending threat. By drastically reducing the poem's length in the 1964 version Kinsella has sharpened the reader's focus upon the tale of the dead man, the barbarism of World War II, and the protagonist's experience of darkness and need for endurance. The earlier antitheses are dispensed with—of monastic retreat and active participation, of saints and scholars living according to divine will set off against the individual will and moral choice of the rowers. The final, leaner version of 1968 proves the most effective because it is also the most convincing and satisfying; Kinsella's technical advance thus preludes the major work beginning with *Nightwalker*.

III

The poems in *Downstream*'s final section lack the substance and scope of the three long poems, but the direction of Kinsella's progression toward understanding is maintained. The vision is no less dark but the bitterness of tone gives way to a greater pity and compassion. In the bleak island setting of "Brothers" (61), where a man and his dog walk "Over high ridges of rock, through tempest of salt and sun / And pounding wind," the man comes to recognize his "brotherhood" with the dog in their confrontation with the antagonistic forces of nature, and, with characteristic Kinsella insight, sees through the animal's body as through glass:

> A model of sinews, fragile tissue and channelled blood,
> Of living translucencies crimson in the driving gale,
> To horrify and instruct. In the spasm of Sentience
> Beast and man are made one.
>
> (61)

Other poems, tracking the evolutionary process toward understanding, take place on the borders of change, like "Chrysalides" (59), which describes adolescents on the verge of the transition into adulthood. Experiencing "A tolerance we shall never know again," the adolescents on their bicycle tour are described in appropriately tolerant terms, whether descending from late sleep into country kitchens "Like calves poking our faces in with enormous hunger," or left a late-night snack: "When by a window ablaze softly with the virgin moon / Dry scones and jugs of milk awaited us in the dark." In such virginity they remain insensitive even to the dark itself—that crucial Kinsella state of threat, uncertainty, and testing—or to the "lasting horror" of the cannibalistic mating practice of ants. Love and death indeed marry, but that marriage is known only beyond that frontier the young boys have yet to cross. Time, if only temporarily, is suspended.

"Mirror in February," the volume's concluding poem and the most significant of this final section, operates on similar frontiers, as a man in his thirties looks in the mirror at himself when shaving one February morning. While a similar confrontation with one's face is experienced in *Ulysses* by Stephen Daedalus in the famous opening scene at Sandycove with Buck Milligan and his shaving mirror, the situation is distinctly Kinsellan: at dawn, as night is replaced by day; in February as the natural world moves toward spring and renewal; in the enclosed world of a bedroom, normally the place for rest and refuge, where the man, confronting himself in the mirror, undergoes a most unsettling experience. Indeed, Kinsella's male personae often subject themselves to such self-scrutiny before mirrors: reflected image and imagined self conflict and the viewer is forced to self-revaluation. Mirrors, moreover, have been traditionally associated with luck and with one's shadow self. It is hardly coincidental, then, that the Irish for "mirror" *(scáthán)* and for "shadow" *(scáth)* are commonly derived.[24] In "Mirror in February" the man approaches another Kinsella frontier as he examines his face in the mirror, and finds not just his "dark exhausted eye, / A dry downturning mouth," but his soul:

> Now plainly in the mirror of my soul
> I read that I have looked my last on youth
> And little more; for they are not made whole
> That reach the age of Christ.
>
> (63)

The man learns, however, not only "that it is time to learn" but about time itself and in particular the humanity of his own mortality. Exterior and interior landscapes once more coincide, when he appreciates that the trees outside have benefited from pruning—a rather heavyhanded analogy but one epitomizing the discipline and endur-

24. P. W. Joyce noted that the Old Irish for "mirror" is derived from "*scáth-derc,*" "shadow-seeing" or "shadow-seer"; see A *Smaller Social History of Ancient Ireland*, 2d ed. (London: Longman, Green/Dublin: M. H. Gill, 1908), 381–82. Kinsella refers to Joyce in *Her Vertical Smile* (1985) and uses various illustrations from the *Social History* in both *SPsyche* (1985) and *Out of Ireland* (1987).

ance of suffering to which Kinsella will increasingly encourage his personae. Yet such endurance does not come easily: the flesh quails, he feels distaste, and whatever grace he musters is gained with difficulty. That we need to cross such a frontier Kinsella has shown us already; what is more evident here than in previous work is the poet's feeling for and tolerance of human inadequacy, important dispositions to set against his sometimes severe and bitter condemnation:[25]

> Below my window the awakening trees,
> Hacked clean for better bearing, stand defaced
> Suffering their brute necessities,
> And how should the flesh not quail that span for span
> Is mutilated more? In slow distaste
> I fold my towel with what grace I can,
> Not young and not renewable, but man.[26]
>
> (63)

Kinsella, conceding that his early poetry is not only tragic but nihilistic in vision, added that such nihilism was qualified significantly by the "artistic response" that makes tragedy "more acceptable." He avers that "[t]he artistic impulse justifies reality and man's part in it."[27] The thesis goes beyond the function of the earlier verse, which was "to make real, in whatever terms, the passing of time, the frightening exposure of all relationships and feeling to erosion."[28] Rather than seeking to preserve experiences in the face of ravaging time, the poet now seeks understanding and acceptance. It is a search to which Kinsella's subsequent volumes bear impressive and eloquent witness.

25. Skelton warned against reading Kinsella as a humanist and compared him with Graham Greene; see "The Poetry of Thomas Kinsella," 108. Cf. Boland, "Downstream," 21.

26. John C. Kelly commented upon the rhyme scheme reinforcing the mirror image: the odd rhyme in the first two stanzas is the last line (abacbc*d*), resolved in the final stanza (abacbc*c*) by the reassuring concluding couplet ("can/man"); see *Studies* 51 (Winter 1962): 550. However, Kelly overlooked the further complication of the scheme in which imperfect rhymes link stanzas ("mouth/growth/youth" and "Christ/defaced/distaste"), and in which the preceding stanza's final line rhymes with ll. 2 and 5 of the subsequent stanza. Such linking goes beyond mere sound: the *mouth* proves indeed the source of *growth* but, in its avidity here, indicates the blight on *youth*; the protagonist, while *defaced* like *Christ* and trees, "awakens" to a "grace" founded not on Christian faith but on "*distaste*" and an essentially limited humanism.

27. *Viewpoints*, ed. Haffenden, 107.

28. Kinsella, *Poetry Book Society Bulletin* 17 (March 1958); cf. *The Poet Speaks*, ed. Orr, 106.

three

Balance in the Violent Zone

W. J. McCormack, in a striking phrase, described *Nightwalker* as "that Red-Sea-dividing collection."[1] While one might take exception to such hyperbole, the volume's significance is nevertheless clear: it evidences a poet gaining his majority. Possessed now of what might be called a worldview, together with the technical expertise to express that view, Kinsella begins to work within a framework of myth and symbol that convincingly carries the weight of his convictions. Certainly, in the period between *Downstream* and *Nightwalker*, Kinsella's poetry underwent important sea changes. The long poems ("Nightwalker" and "Phoenix Park") in the latter volume are clearly more substantial than the three long poems ("Old Harry," "A Country Walk," and the title poem) in *Downstream*, and are more accomplished and assured in their vision. "Nightwalker" indicates also a major technical development: the formal, sometimes mannered work of the first volumes, written with some awareness of the double shadows of Yeats and English verse, gives way to less formal, less ordered, more fragmented, even dislocated narratives. Kinsella has confessed

1. McCormack, "Politics or Community: Crux of Thomas Kinsella's Aesthetic Development," *Tracks* 7 (1989): 63.

that the "early strict forms were borrowed and imposed: a form of apprenticeship and something that had to go."[2] The new direction is downward and inward, into the unconscious world of dark, primordial forces working within a timeless and universal process. *Nightwalker* indeed signifies an important stage in Kinsella's evolution: his literary apprenticeship has been served, and the subsequent poems are more readily distinguishable from those of the first volumes. Kinsella may have benefited from the "more experimental poetic climate" of the United States, as John Montague has suggested:[3] he had long been aware of Pound's *Cantos* and now regarded William Carlos Williams, as he had previously regarded Auden, as an enabling voice, one who could provide him with "leverage out of a rather clamped condition."[4] Moreover, his commitment in the early 1970s to the sequential form was reinforced in some measure by the example of Robert Lowell.[5] In all such instances Kinsella recognized what greater liberation of form could achieve. At the same time, other, intrinsically Irish, influences proved more essential to Kinsella's evolving poetic.

While major changes were in the making, McCormack's biblical image needs careful qualification: for all Kinsella's emergence as a major poet, his work remains ultimately of a piece, possessed of an impressive unity of purpose. No less than Yeats, Kinsella sought to "hammer his thoughts into unity," although never to the extent of creating a formal system. By this stage in his career he began to rely upon a more coherent and discernible worldview, and to employ recurrent myths and symbols, but neither Yeats nor the English poetic tradition proved helpful to him in these tasks. Rather, help came in part from quintessentially Irish sources—from both Joyce and the Gaelic tradition, from Ó Rathaille back to the earliest writings, to Amergin and the *Book of Invasions*—and from his reading of the psychoanalyst Carl Gustav Jung. These exemplars in their different

2. O'Driscoll, "Interview," 63.

3. Montague, in *Contemporary Writers*, ed. Vinson, 835. Edna Longley, however, has been critical of transatlantic alliances of the kind promoted by Kinsella, Montague, and Heaney; see her *Poetry in the Wars* (Newcastle upon Tyne: Bloodaxe, 1986), 168.

4. Quoted in Dillon Johnston, *Irish Poetry after Joyce*, 253. Cf. "Hiberno-American cross-fertilisation" (Haffenden's terms), in *Viewpoints*, ed. Haffenden, 105–6. In the mid-fifties Kinsella reviewed Wallace Stevens's *Collected Poems*, Marianne Moore's *Predilections*, and Richard Wilbur's *Poems, 1943–1956* (see *Irish Press*, 23 June 1956, 16 February 1957, and 14 December 1957); and praised modern American poetry, in "New Found Land," 184–86.

5. Johnston, *Irish Poetry after Joyce*, 104.

ways contributed more vitally to the forging of Kinsella's own language than either Yeats or the English poets. They showed him the way back into his past, both his national and his family, private inheritance, and provided at one and the same time a continuity and a way forward. Seamus Heaney, whose own path has both coincided with and diverged from that of Kinsella, has commented upon the latter's development and "trust in the continuing efficacy" of the Irish literary tradition:

> He . . . has been concerned to widen the lens, to make Irish poetry in English get out from under the twilight shades of the specifically English tradition. In his own work he has long since—and deliberately—given up considerations of "the reader's comfort." He has strenuously punished the lyricist in himself who carried off such stylish performances in the early books. As the influence of Pound and indeed of Ó Rathaille has taken hold, he has gradually evicted traces of Audenesque, iambic—strictly English—melody, in order to find a denser, more laconic, more indigenous way with the poetic line. When I say "indigenous" I do not mean the alternative charm of some kind of "Irish note" but rather something genetic at the roots of Kinsella's own Dublin speech. In fact, the rhythms of Joyce's prose are finally more relevant to his endeavour than the metrics and assonances of the native tradition.[6]

Indeed, Kinsella has resisted (apart from the rarest of instances) the temptation to reproduce Gaelic metrical and assonantal intricacies, leaving such to his predecessor, Austin Clarke. The Irish tradition, like any other in its most insular mode, can also cramp the contemporary poet. What really distinguishes Kinsella's work from *Nightwalker* on is the extent to which he becomes his own man, capable of raiding exemplars of various kinds—Dante, Joyce, Jung, the *Book of Invasions*—and, while reconnecting with the native Irish material, in all such instances using them to speak not just *to* him but *for* him, and, by extension, for all humanity.

I

Coinciding with these developments Kinsella expresses a different attitude toward the writing of poetry itself. Poems like "The Laundress" and "Dick King" are, in Kinsella's terms, "set pieces,"

6. Heaney, *The Government of the Tongue*, 32.

written under the delusion that poetry is a passive affair. He had previously believed that the poet's prime consideration was to stay alert; now he sees that he can "push for poetry" and it will come,[7] that imagination also involves will. Certainly will had previously proved crucial; in "Baggot Street Deserta," for example, "the will to work is laid aside" but, ironically, the poem still gets written after this relapse. Kinsella's figures constantly will themselves on to acts of heroic defiance and endurance. Now, however, the "push for poetry" parallels Kinsella's intensified investigations of the self, particularly of its darker recesses, of the unconscious and the historical or racial self or collective unconscious. More than being a mere observer, the poet now becomes an active participant in a process of self-discovery in which will and imagination serve the exploring, probing consciousness drawn down into contact with the very processes of life and creation. Hence, writing of the next volume, *Notes from the Land of the Dead,* Seamus Deane has argued that "[i]n the end there is no difference between the will and the imagination. The will is the imagination in extremis."[8] The beginnings of that extremity appear in *Nightwalker.* In the process of investigating his own self and his origins Kinsella recognized older, primordial forces at work, so that the poetry of this period increases in complexity and scope. At a time when his use of distinctively Irish material intensifies, Kinsella's vision gains correspondingly in universality.

In the same month in which *Downstream* was published (September 1962), Kinsella pinpointed for Peter Orr his distinctive themes, love, time, death, and the artistic act:

> My earliest poems were about the artistic act and I still do them, but they are becoming slightly more elaborate and in a peculiar way the idea of artistic creation and the idea of the passing of time are becoming fused together. I have not yet written a poem in which this process is embodied. I have a distinct feeling, for instance, that one of the main impulses to poetry or, for that matter, to any act, is an attempt more or less to stem the passing of time; it's the process of arresting the erosion of feelings and relationships and objects which is being fought by the artist, not particularly because one relationship or one object has all his love at the moment, but simply that he is there to combat the erosion. . . . The function of

7. Project Arts Theatre poetry reading, Dublin, 26 March 1982.

8. Deane, "The Appetites of Gravity: Contemporary Irish Poetry," *Sewanee Review* 84 (Winter 1976): 201–2.

> the poet has something to do . . . with this business of stemming the flow of time.[9]

Like other poets before him, he recognizes the conservative nature of his art and uses essentially conservative terms—"stemming," "arresting," "combating" the eroding force of time. In the face of temporal flux, the poet preserves the instant; Philip Larkin's characteristically deflationary image was of "pickling."[10] Such stasis parallels Kinsella's conception of the poet as an observer rather than as a participant, whereas a poem's "embodiment" of process—a central feature of the later work—requires more active and dynamic form.

By the time of another interview a decade later, both conception of poetry and choice of form had clearly undergone a major change; now Kinsella told John Haffenden that the function of poetry was the achievement of understanding, "the eliciting of order" out of the chaos of experience. At the same time, he noted that "[i]mages and symbols are a way of embodying the kinetic in the static."[11] As we shall see when we turn to his later poetry, from *Notes from the Land of the Dead* onward, Kinsella pursues other strategies by which to embody the kinetic, particularly through repetition and montage. In 1962 one strategy involved pace: "I am striving continually for greater clarity and directness and regular pace—fitting the pace to the poem and making it an immediately comprehensible whole as far as possible."[12] The point would not be lost on William Carlos Williams, although Kinsella's continuing commitment to "regular pace" suggests that English rather than American poetic practice is still what he has in mind. Yet such regularity proved inadequate when the poet confronted the more dynamic kinesis he sought to express: the way was being prepared for Kinsella's free-form poetry, in which paragraph replaces stanza; where poems remain open-ended, with in some cases punctuation withheld entirely; and where pace is effected by spacing to reflect changes of direction or meaning. Rather than *describing*,

9. *The Poet Speaks*, ed. Orr, 105–6.

10. "I want to express the experience in a poem so that it remains preserved, unchanging; and then I hope that other people will come upon the experience, pickled as it were in verse, and it will mean something to them"; see Unsigned, "Speaking of Writing—XIII: Philip Larkin," *(London) Times*, 20 February 1964, p. 13. Cf. "verbal pickling," in Philip Larkin, "Writing Poems," *Required Writing: Miscellaneous Pieces, 1955–1982* (London: Faber and Faber, 1983), 83.

11. *Viewpoints*, ed. Haffenden, 113.

12. *The Poet Speaks*, ed. Orr, 108.

Kinsella's later poetry *embodies* experiences, offering a more dramatic and immediate version than description permits. These shifts—from description to embodiment, from stasis to kinesis, from the preservation of to the understanding of experience—represent the poet's commitment, from at least *Nightwalker,* to a theory of process and of knowledge as "becoming." At least one critic has seen Kinsella's poetry as developing from portraiture to confessionalism.[13] However, the Irish poet's experience of contemporary American poetry, improved at firsthand from his life and work in the United States after 1965, is only one of several factors contributing to his development, and confessional poetry, of the kind associated with Sylvia Plath, Anne Sexton, and John Berryman, proves an inadequate description for Kinsella's poetry of the 1970s. Neither American confessionalism nor that other controversial poetic invention of the decade, the black mythic world that the British poet Ted Hughes portrayed in *Crow* (1970), contributed significantly to Kinsella's poetic development. His major exemplars, as we shall see, are to be found closer to home.

Kinsella returns to "the function of poetry" in the third section of *Nightwalker,*[14] and while he remains preoccupied with the instant and the passing of time, his treatment of poetry's function is anything but static. It is not merely that the poet is constantly conscious of the world's appetite and capacity for chaos and disorder, but that he participates in rather than observes that appetitive process. Indeed, the grub's direction in "Leaf-Eater" (52) is back upon itself, to eat the very leaf on which it presently crawls. It is a process that the poem's single sentence, syntax, and enjambments capture exactly and with a characteristically ironic tone. It may be, likewise, that the instant in " 'To Autumn' " (49) is held in some transcendent timelessness, but the world's dominant character remains one of process. Insects are engaged in "bedlam"; the poet Keats, who provides both title and fragmentary lines from his famous ode, is through the season made conscious of the conjunction of life and death, himself "a phantasm of flesh" and a fusion of stasis and flux ("still writing"). The adverb "still" is used ambiguously, as in Keats's ode ("Thou still unravish'd bride of quietness"); similarly, light appears on the brink of giving way to darkness, with the "gleam" held only "a frail instant." What makes such illumination possible is the awareness—shared by both the ro-

13. Redshaw, "The Wormwood Revisions," 113.
14. Kinsella, *Poetry Book Society Bulletin* 55 (December 1967).

mantic poet and by Kinsella—of the dynamic process of "disintegrating materials" which, by that very disintegration, brings integration into being.

The poem is paired with another involving a second poet, this time from the Irish tradition. "The Poet Egan O'Rahilly, Homesick in Old Age" depends to no small extent upon Aogán Ó Rathaille's original poem in Irish, "Is Fada Liom Oíche Fhírfhliuch" ("The Drenching Night Drags On"), an interesting example, as is " 'To Autumn,' " of what has come to be termed "intertextuality."[15] As in the latter poem, Kinsella, through the adverb "still," associates writing both with suspension of time and with persistence: "the lists of praises / I make for you still in the cooling den of my craft." As the late poem "At the Western Ocean's Edge" (*FCC* 26) indicates, Ó Rathaille increasingly assumes a major role in Kinsella's canon. The eighteenth-century poem, which is his source here and which Seán Ó Tuama has described as "one of the most memorable poems in all Irish literature,"[16] places the dispossessed Ó Rathaille in the midst of process and disintegration. Kinsella's own poem, like its Irish source, begins with a portrait of suffering humanity, here struggling to stand upright but achieving at best "decrepit progress" and focusing in good Kinsella fashion upon appetite and digestion:

> He climbed to his feet in the cold light, and began
> The decrepit progress again, blown along the cliff road,
> Bent with curses above the shrew his stomach.
>
> (48)

Kinsella takes over the persona of Ó Rathaille, much as he had done previously with the persona of Clarence Mangan in *Another September*, to dramatize not only the world's appetite and the parallel

15. Kinsella's translation of Ó Rathaille's poem is included in *Duanaire*, 141, and *TNOBIV*, 196–97. Comparing Kinsella's own poem, "The Poet Egan O'Rahilly, Homesick in Old Age," with the *Duanaire* version, Heaney notes "the difference between his freedom as a creative poet and his obedience as a translator"; see *The Government of the Tongue*, 35. An earlier version of Kinsella's own poem, in which the narrative is given in the present tense together with other minor variants, appeared in *Dublin Magazine* 5 (Summer 1966): 23. For "intertextuality," see Jonathan Culler, *The Pursuit of Signs: Semiotics, Literature, Deconstruction* (London: Routledge and Kegan Paul, 1981), ch. 5.

16. Seán Ó Tuama, "Gaelic Culture in Crisis: The Literary Response, 1600–1850," in *Irish Studies: A General Introduction*, eds. Thomas Bartlett, Chris Curtin, Riana O'Dwyer, and Gearóid Ó Tuathaigh (Dublin: Gill and Macmillan/Totowa, N.J.: Barnes and Noble, 1988), 36.

with Ó Rathaille's own suffering stomach but also the eighteenth-century poet's endurance in the face of fearful odds: the natural forces (cold, dark, wind, waves) and the past (the flight of the Wild Geese, those Irish aristocrats who fled to Europe after the 1691 Treaty of Limerick and the introduction in 1695 of the Penal Laws against Catholics). Both nature and history, external and internal, combine to bring the wandering poet to the same extremity that drove the "Princes overseas." Yet Ó Rathaille endures and provides nourishment for the "starving children," the Irish people abandoned by their princes in the face of the more powerful alien English appetite. The poem thus relates natural, historical, and political worlds, and sees the artist functioning among these interacting forces. Indeed, Kinsella goes beyond his Irish source and, rather than raging bitterly with Ó Rathaille against the natural elements and Irish dispossession, stresses heroic suffering and the poet's craft in confronting his persistent and victorious antagonists, who multiply like runaway cells and, "recruiting the sea," gain domination over the natural as well as the political world:

> He pressed red eyelids: aliens crawled
> Breaking princely houses in their jaws;
> Their metal faces reared up, chewing at light.
>
> "Princes overseas, who slipped away
> In your extremity, no matter where I travel
> I find your great houses like stopped hearts.
>
> Likewise your starving children—though I nourish
> Their spirit, and my own, on the lists of praises
> I make for you still in the cooling den of my craft.
>
> Our enemies multiply. They have recruited the sea:
> Last night, the West's rhythmless waves destroyed my sleep;
> This morning, winkle and dogfish persisting in the stomach . . ."
>
> (48)

Other poems in this third section of *Nightwalker* pursue a similar progress: in both "Before Sleep" and "Magnanimity," for example, part of the poet's discipline is to confront chaos and to endure the world's appetite. Hence, the poet-persona in the former poem assumes his responsibility: "Yes: in the morning I will put on the cataract, / Give it veins, clutching hands, the short shriek of thought" (45). In the latter poem, Kinsella places Austin Clarke at Coole Park, which, despite the house's destruction, is resonant still in its associations with Yeats. But whatever magnanimity Clarke might summon to forget Yeats's enmity,[17] Kinsella calls for similar magnanimity in the face of time's destructiveness—whether that destructiveness show itself in Clarke's own losing battle against property development (epitomized by that distinctively Yeatsian noun, "commonness") or of the world's appetite (captured by verbs distinctively Kinsella's): "Helpless commonness encroaches, chews the soil, / Squats ignobly. Within, consciousness intensifies" (46). The Yeats inheritance, no longer threatening, is absorbed and modified by such quintessentially Kinsellan verbs ("chews," "Squats"). Survival within such a destructive environment requires more than alertness or observation; enlightenment will only come through persevering and unshrinking self-examination, provided that magnanimity is not overtaken by bitterness and enmity.

It is a measure of the distance Kinsella has traveled beyond his early exemplars Yeats and Auden that in "Death in Ilium" (50), written as part of the celebration of the centenary year of Yeats's birth, 1965, he can afford to employ imagery characteristic of both poets. For the analogy with the death of Hector in Ilium is a clear acknowledgment not just of Yeats's heroic stature and myth but of his distinctive use of Troy as a symbol for Dublin. The language, rhythm, and imagery, however, are more reminiscent of Auden, for example, in Kinsella's use of general abstract nouns (Attention, power, Truth), a three-stressed line (as in Auden's "September 1, 1939"), and imagery of the body reminiscent of Auden's urban imagery. But it is the more essentially Kinsellan "shadow-eaters" possessed, like creatures out of Dante's Hell, of "tough nose / And pale fang" and driven by ravenous but foiled appetite through whom the dead poet "grows whole and remote."

"Soft Toy," however, best expresses Kinsella's new conception of the artistic act, as the persona of the limp toy assumes the discipline of the creative self confronting darkness and terror. The relationship between toy and child begins in passivity—"I am soiled with the

17. Kinsella quotes Austin Clarke's lines, "So, I forgot / His enmity," from "The Abbey Theatre Fire," in *Flight to Africa* (1963), in *Poems 1955–1966*, ed. Liam Miller (Dublin: Dolmen Press, 1974), 249. An earlier version of Kinsella's poem appeared in *A Tribute to Austin Clarke on His Seventieth Birthday, 9 May 1966*, eds. John Montague and Liam Miller (Dublin: Dolmen Press, 1966), 7–8. The opening six lines were much revised in N.

repetition of your loves and hatreds," "I lie limp with use and re-use, listening"—but with the acknowledgment that "I understand," the toy's progress begins to be formulated:

> Knowledge
> Into resignation: the process drives deeper,
> Grows clearer, eradicating chance growths of desire
> —And colder: all possibilities of desire.
>
> (51)

By the final stanza, however, that progress is made concrete as the toy takes shape as the child's shadow or other self, crushed and discarded in the child's "need / To grow," confronting the dark and acquiring the necessary instruments: "eyes that cannot close," "a blunt probe," and "a cold pitted grey face" like that of so many of Kinsella's moons. Indeed, one might compare the toy's new face with the lunar landscape at the conclusion to "Nightwalker." Knowledge has proceeded through resignation to clarity and coldness. The toy's "button-brown hard eyes" confront the world's destructive nature with the same heroic ability to endure as the "red eyelids" of Ó Rathaille or the "ancient glittering eyes" of Yeats's Chinamen in "Lapis Lazuli." Instead of Yeatsian tragic joy and ecstasy, however, Kinsella offers only further endurance, as in the previous poems, although the ultimate goal, assuming it may be achieved, will be wholeness and enlightenment. The relationship between child and toy is tyrannical: the toy is crushed, thrown aside, subjected to the child's whim. Yet it is the soft toy that faces the dark "with eyes that cannot close," eyes that constitute "the cold, outermost points" of the child's will. (The imagery—of dark, will, "cold outermost points"—recalls the concluding lines of "Baggot Street Deserta," where it is allied similarly to the imagination and the poetic process.) Although the child experiences "dull terror" only unconsciously, while asleep, and is both agent and recipient ("as you thrust, are thrust"), the result nevertheless is his "opening brain" as "all possibilities of desire" are experienced:

> My button-brown hard eyes fix on your need
> To grow, as you crush me with tears and throw me aside.
> Most they reflect, but something absorb—brightening
> In response, with energy, to the energy of your changes.
> Clutched tightly through the night, held before you,
> Ragged and quietly crumpled, as you thrust, are thrust,

In dull terror into your opening brain,
  I face the dark with eyes that cannot close
—The cold, outermost points of your will, as you sleep.
  Between your tyrannous pressure and the black
Resistance of the void my blankness hardens
  To a dull probe, a cold pitted grey face.

(51)

II

Commenting upon the volume for the Poetry Book Society in December 1967, Kinsella referred to its "subject in general" as "a developing view of life as ordeal."[18] From the outset of his career he has been preoccupied with loss, death, time, and mortality, and increasingly he has extended his concern to include public, social, and political subjects. His predominant tone has been bleak, even at times depressive; he has been alert to threat and destruction, and, with the exploration of more public matter, that tone has deepened and darkened as he has confronted the barbarism of this century and humanity's unfailing capacity for evil. However, what marks off the poems in *Nightwalker*, among other things, is the formulation of a worldview that collects previous themes and preoccupations and shapes them into a more comprehensive scheme. Central to this scheme is the archetypal "ordeal" in which the individual self suffers and learns to endure. It may be that his faith in purgatorial suffering derives from Kinsella's Catholic upbringing, but such faith is inherent in numerous myths, traditions, and value systems of which he is well aware: classical Greek tragedy, for example, where understanding is gained through suffering; or the Great Goddess mysteries, in which, Erich Neumann writes, the Goddess "grants life only through death, and development toward new birth only through suffering—that as Lady of the Beasts and Men she confers no birth and no life without pain";[19] or the Irish tradition itself, where the Book of Ballymote describes twelve different kinds of ordeal as a means of "determining truth or falsehood, guilt or innocence."[20] Kinsella's sources are less

18. Kinsella, *Poetry Book Society Bulletin* 55 (December 1967). The volume was the winter "recommendation."

19. Erich Neumann, *The Great Mother: An Analysis of the Archetype*, Bollingen Series, vol. 47, trans. Ralph Manheim (1955; Princeton, N.J.: Princeton University Press, 1970), 279.

20. Joyce, *Smaller Social History of Ancient Ireland*, 128–30.

important than the value he saw in such a scheme. He himself declared in 1979–1980 that he admired the "system" by which one persisted, despite failure, describing it as "a marvellous and fruitful system, never repeating itself."[21] Intrinsically dynamic and transformative, process resists mere repetition, is infinitely variable, and is always becoming.

The "countermoves" to seemingly bleak, purgatorial process are the positives of love and the artistic act:

> The ordeal is around us and in us—the ordeal of mankind and the ordeal of each man. Its qualities do not change: the same high hopes, the same disappointments, the same hideous discrepancy between what one might and what one can and does. In the private context, as the ordeal bears down on us one by one, the weight may be lightened by the experience or the ideal of love.[22]

The process may be dialectical, but progress toward enlightenment and the shaping of chaos into order, becoming into being, are nevertheless held out as possible. The same shaping, for example, is evident in Kinsella's organization of the volume, the significance of which we have already seen. That significance takes the form not simply of the interweaving of themes, but of leading the reader through various experiences or of progressing through a landscape in order to gain order, enlightenment, and fulfillment. The condition for such an ordered whole self Kinsella calls "understanding," the construction of meaning in the midst of meaninglessness.

"Structure" thus becomes a key Kinsella term, but the interweaving or "arranging" of experiences provides at the same time an important warning signal. Whatever structure the poet experiences will not be imposed externally but will instead be revealed, discovered by assembling disparate images and events and allowing a structure of meaning to evolve. We have seen the process at work, if only embryonically, in the earliest poems. That technique now undergoes considerable and valuable refinement. In *Nightwalker* the technique begins to come into its own; by the time of the subsequent volume, *Notes from the Land of the Dead*, its evolution, if not final, is achieved. Hence, in 1967 the poet described *Nightwalker* in the following terms:

21. *Viewpoints*, ed. Haffenden, 102.
22. Kinsella, "The Divided Mind," 215.

> The first two sections of the book begin with certain private experiences under the ordeal, and follow with countermoves—love, the artistic act—which mitigate the ordeal and make it fruitful, and even promise a bare possibility of order. The poems in the third section are about a few poets, and the function of poetry. In the last section the feeling reaches out to the Irish historical landscape and the "new" Ireland, and inward to the imaginative hunger that (I believe) gives to existence whatever significance it may have. These poems are trying (as the whole book is) to find a balance in the violent zone, between the outer and the inner storms, where human life takes place.[23]

The experience of the ordeal, then, goes beyond mere education in resignation or endurance; it can be made "fruitful," particularly through love and the creative act. Indeed, in the 1979–1980 interview with John Haffenden the poet stressed the positive aspects of his system: "love, continuity and amplification." While agreeing with Haffenden that he might previously have stressed the system's negative aspect of mutilation, he remained "content to rest in the potentiality, the possibility of an order inherent in experience—however dark."[24] Order or balance, then, is to be striven for, whether in the self's experience of the world or within the self itself, and, no matter how dark those experiences, such order or balance remains a "potentiality" to be sought.

However, the volume begins on a less obviously positive note with experiences of mortality and death, evidence of the world's destructive appetite. The young girl in a hospital bed in "Our Mother" "sleeps on her new knowledge" gained through pain, and in her dream confronts a Gorgon face; this classical image suitably indicates its mythic, archetypal, primordial origin. "In Greece," Neumann tells us, "the Gorgon as Artemis-Hecate is also mistress of the night-road, of fate, and of the world of the dead." Her symbol is the key and she is "mistress of birth and conception."[25] More, the confrontation with the Gorgon, like the relationship between child and soft toy, suggests a shadowy self or unconscious and leads to the girl's participation in or digestion of the appetite the Gorgon face represents:

> She dreams a red Gorgon-mask
> Warped in the steel kidney dish,

23. Kinsella, *Poetry Book Society Bulletin* 55 (December 1967).
24. *Viewpoints*, ed. Haffenden, 103.
25. Neumann, *The Great Mother*, 170.

The tender offals of her core
Worming around the raw stare.

Her mother watches, struck dumb.
Tears of recognition run
For the stranger, daughter, self, on whom
In fascination her eyes feed,

As mine on her . . .

(11)

The initiation into pain and life's appetite is undergone by the young girl, but the experience is shared, like some religious wounding or mystery, by the poem's three female figures. Indeed, they parallel the archetypal triple-faced Great Mother ruling over the moon's waxing and waning and over life's process. Each is at a different stage in that process, whether child, mother, or old woman. The male poet-narrator is thus set off against them, participating in the same life–death cycle but lacking their intimate, shared wisdom, and is rendered motionless, caught under their Medusa-like stare: "Living, dying, I meet their stare / Everywhere, and cannot move."

Both appetite and the marriage of opposites are prominent in subsequent poems, the most effective of which is "Ballydavid Pier" (14–15). There the poet recollects seeing, amid the scum and detritus of shells, bones, and claws, "a bag of flesh, / Foetus of goat or sheep." The luminous quality of the tide parallels the self's illumination, a vision into the real nature of things akin to Keats's experience at Teignmouth ("I saw / Too far into the sea; where every maw / The greater on the less feeds evermore:— / But I saw too distinct into the core / Of an eternal fierce destruction . . .").[26] Indeed, the experience may owe something to another literary source: that of "A bloated carcass of a dog [which] lay lolled on bladderwrack" in Joyce's *Ulysses* (411). But there is nothing literary about Kinsella's poem, which unites gross physical immediacy and abstract meditation; the "allegory" he sees enacted is straightforward in its Darwinian evolution of worlds,[27] a "structure" that gives shape and meaning to the experience:

26. "Dear Reynolds, as last night I lay in bed," in *The Poems of John Keats*, ed. Jack Stillinger (Cambridge: Harvard University Press, 1978), 244.

27. Johnston suggests parallels here with Pierre Teilhard de Chardin's "evolutionary teleology"; see *Irish Poetry after Joyce*, 105.

Allegory forms of itself:
The line of life creeps upward
Replacing one world with another,
The welter of its advance
Sinks down into clarity,
Slowly the more foul
Monsters of loss digest.

(14)

As the poem proceeds, however, that "structure" is extended from the drowned foetus in the sea to the unborn child in the womb and then to the self in the process of discovery and wholeness:

The ghost tissue hangs unresisting
In allegorical waters,
Lost in self-search
—A swollen blind brow
Humbly crumpled over
Budding limbs, unshaken
By the spasms of birth or death.

(15)

The tissue image, to which Kinsella turns increasingly in this and subsequent volumes, points to the biological and anatomical worlds upon which he so frequently draws. Such imagery naturally complements the poet's attention to process and evolution.[28] The tidal ebb and flow described in the poem's conclusion remind the reader of the endless change in "The line of life" Kinsella has traced, and in the glimpse of the foetus glistening "like quicksilver" one sees both its transience and its significance. "The misbirth" rises to the sea's surface in the manner of the poet's experience of his own unconscious, and it glistens mercurially, an appropriate image of a future favorite Kinsella figure: Mercury-Hermes, messenger of the gods and bringer of news from the underworld.

Another such messenger surfaces in "Traveller," where the poet undertakes a night journey to reach his wife, who is struggling for survival in a hospital room some eighty miles away. It is late at night ("An hour to midnight"), and the surrounding darkness increases the poet-husband's worries, including his guilt at leaving behind their children "In their strange bed." All the poem's details give concrete

28. Cf. "Tissue forms about purpose" (*N* 16), "Delicate distinct tissue begins to form" (*N* 82; *NLD* 2); cf. *One* 28.

substance to the persona's overwhelming sense of threat and appetite. The reader is led from the children's innocent "apple-tasted night" (a curious Dylan Thomas inheritance and an epithet employed previously in an early poem, "Second Song" (*Poems* 11)) to the father's catching sight on the road before him of that distinctively Kinsellan predatory creature, an owl eating. Once more the direction is inward, toward self-examination, as the self pursues its corresponding night-time journey:

> The brain, woken to itself and restless,
> Senses their black mouths muttering in the darkness:
> Phrases, echoes of feeling, from other journeys
> To bait and confuse the predatory will
> And draw it aside, muttering in absent response,
> Down stale paths in the dark to a stale lair,
> In brainless trance, where it can treadle and chew
> Old pangs blunter and smoother, old self-mutilations.
> (21)

The journeying self is thus made aware of tempting voices leading toward sterility, "Down stale paths in the dark to a stale lair," the "brainless trance" lacking illumination, the appetite leading simply to "old self-mutilations." Kinsella's evolving myth of ordeal might conceivably lead to negative bleakness, sterile suffering, inward-looking gloom. Instead, the poet's vision of the owl draws his attention back to the positive value of confronting darkness and submitting to threat, for the bird represents another divine figure, the goddess Hecate, whose symbol is the owl.[29] Owl, Hecate, and poet's wife come together to symbolize the muse, the White Goddess, the triple-faced Great Mother, a significance substantiated further, as in "Our Mother" and other *Nightwalker* poems, and pursued in *Notes from the Land of the Dead*. While Hecate offers the dark face of the triple goddess, she represents also the poet's need to experience her underworld. Descent into that dark hell entails neither masochism nor Jansenism: the unconscious must be explored if the self is to be made whole, just as the threat to the poet's wife must be confronted and endured. The objectives are survival and understanding.

29. Robert Graves notes that owls are "messengers of the Death-goddess Hecate, or Athene, or Persephone: from whom, as the supreme source of prophecy, they derive their reputation for wisdom"; see *The White Goddess: A Historical Grammar of Poetic Myth* (New York: Vintage, 1948), 222.

"Wormwood," *Nightwalker*'s second section, has as its epigraph Apocalypse, 8:10–11:

> *and a great star fell from heaven, burning as it were a torch; and it fell on the third part of the rivers and upon the fountains of waters; and the name of the star is called Wormwood; and the third part of the waters became wormwood; and many men died of the waters, because they were made bitter.* (27)

Kinsella pinned his hopes, he said, commenting upon the volume, "on the reader's giving due weight . . . to the third part of the waters, in 'Wormwood,' and not all, becoming bitter."[30] More recently, he used "Wormwood" to disprove the persistent charge against him of pessimism, arguing, simply, that "it remains a positive response."[31] For, it must be emphasized, death of the waters is not inevitable; indeed, Kinsella makes explicit that it is also not desirable. Understanding is not attained through bitterness, and those who criticize him for expressing a despairing bleakness and a depressive blackness have failed to distinguish the positive elements in his vision. The point is made even more explicitly in the prose statement prefacing "Wormwood" and addressed to his "Beloved" as "A little of what we have found . . .":

> It is certain that maturity and peace are to be sought through ordeal after ordeal, and it seems that the search continues until we fail. We reach out after each new beginning, penetrating our context to know ourselves, and our knowledge increases until we recognise again (more profoundly each time) our pain, indignity and triviality. This bitter cup is offered, heaped with curses, and we must drink or die. And even though we drink we may also die, if every drop of bitterness—that rots the flesh—is not transmuted. (Certainly the individual plight is hideous, each torturing each, but we are guilty, seeing this, to believe that our common plight is only hideous. Believing so, we make it so: pigs in a slaughter-yard that turn and savage each other in a common desperation and disorder.) Death, either way, is guilt and failure. But if we drink the bitterness and can transmute it and continue, we resume in candour and doubt the only individual joy—the restored necessity to learn. Sensing a wider scope, a more penetrating harmony, we begin again in a higher innocence to grow toward the next ordeal.
>
> Love also, it seems, will continue until we fail: in the sensing of a

30. Kinsella, *Poetry Book Society Bulletin* 55 (December 1967).
31. O'Driscoll, "Interview," 64.

> wider scope, in the growth toward it, in the swallowing and absorption of bitterness, in the resumed innocence. . . . (28)

The poet's wife has served from the beginning not just as a source of love and inspiration but of wisdom and illumination. To borrow her equivalent in the Irish tradition, she is the muse-skywoman-*aisling* figure. Yet Kinsella's sources are now multiple and various: not just the Irish *aislingi* but the biblical wormwood and apocalypse; the Dantean–Yeatsian "bitter cup" that must be drained; the progress from innocence through experience to some "higher innocence," a dialectic traced earlier by William Blake; and, not the least, Jonathan Swift with imagery of "pigs in a slaughter-yard." The shaping of these various exemplars into a coherent scheme gives added force and direction to Kinsella's poetry.

From the adjectival baroque of the original "Downstream" Kinsella has progressed to Lear-like nakedness, and what is offered is an unaccommodated vision. "Open this," the reader is told in the second section's opening untitled poem, "and you will see / A waste, a nearly naked tree / That will not rest till it is bare." The poem in *Wormwood* (1966) was originally titled "On a Gift in the Shape of a Heart," so that the instruction "Open this" was intended to reveal explicitly a waste of the heart. The life–death process in which man and tree participate drives on both, as the poet makes clear in his riddling question, reminiscent of those posed by Lear's Fool: "What cannot rest till it is bare, / Though branches crack and fibres tear?" The poems in "Wormwood" all focus on love, but it is a love under threat, a love whose underface or shadow is sinister and savage but which alone can transmute bitterness. The dream therefore in the title poem (30) is a recurrent one—of an axe sinking into "A black tree with a double trunk—two trees / Grown into one." The analogy with the poet and his wife is clear, and is paralleled in Yeats;[32] but, more characteristically Kinsellan is their grafting union as "A slowly twisted scar." It is a nightmare that must be endured—"I will dream it again" —but that, through the persistence of love, becomes what in "Phoenix Park" he calls "the one positive dream" (74, 77–79). In "Remem-

32. In "Baile and Aillinn" the lovers' eternal union is likened to "two sweet blossoming apple-boughs / That have one shadow on the ground" (ll. 153–54). The earlier "The Two Trees" offers a less desirable expression of the same image. Kinsella uses the image again: "A tree with a twisted trunk; / two trees grown into one. / A heart-carving grown thick, / the cuts so deep"; see *SPsyche*, Poem VIII, *BF* 27.

bering Old Wars" (34) he offers a calculatedly unromantic view of love —"What clamped us together? When each night fell we lay down / In the smell of decay and slept, our bodies leaking"—and, equally characteristically, has the couple labor to become "upright" in a fearful renewable cycle: "We would renew each other with a savage smile." Yet the section ends by recognizing that love alone remains; all the other "props" are gone, leaving "Love the limiter" (35). Like Blake, Kinsella appreciates the need for boundaries if order is to be shaped and the void of "nothing" counterbalanced. But the boundaries must derive from love, even if the lovers' arms are "iron."

Among the most effective and moving of the "Wormwood" poems is "The Secret Garden," commissioned originally for a commemorative volume celebrating the four hundredth anniversary of Shakespeare's birth.[33] Its original, not wholly accurate, epigraph from *Othello*, "Our bodies are our gardens, our wills our gardeners" (1.3.324), indicates less Kinsella's source, since his imagery was already well established, than the poet's emphasis upon will and the Voltairean need to "cultivate one's garden." The speaker's love is focused here not upon the wife figure but upon a child, a son whose innocence the father both cherishes and gains strength from. For the son has "pearl flesh," an image directing the reader to the archetypal "pearl" symbolizing the "divine child" of which the Christ child is only one example.[34] Precious, protected like an embryo in the shell's womb, the son symbolizes "the germ of wholeness"[35] yet to be born into the world of suffering. The action of Kinsella's poem, then, involves on one level a parent's loving concern for his child in the midst of temporal threat and decay. Beyond that, however, is the level of symbol on which the action transcends personal familial relationships and comments upon the self's transformation on its journey to wholeness and individuation.

What is impressive about "The Secret Garden" is the ease with which Kinsella has acquired depth and complexity of meaning, in

33. A first version appeared in *Fifteen Poems for William Shakespeare*, ed. Eric W. White (Stratford-upon Avon: Shakespeare Trust, 1964), 11, and was revised for *Wormwood* (1966). The final *N* version is considerably revised, improved by greater precision and tauter syntax.

34. Carl Jung, *Psyche and Symbol: A Selection from the Writings of C. G. Jung*, ed. Violet S. de Laszlo (New York: Doubleday, 1958), 122–23.

35. Jung, *Symbols of Transformation*, 329–30.

which allegory has now attained the richness of myth, gained by effective but simple technique. Image becomes symbol, in the form of garden, bramble, child, pearl, kernel, sun, dew, and gardener, and —above all—Kinsella's distinctive "sour encounter." End-stopped and single-sentence lines, of which there are many examples in this twenty-one-line lyric, capture appropriately a sense of impedance, of ways blocked whether by threat or fear. Whatever growth occurs in the garden is toward increasing difficulty, toward a stasis in sharp contrast to the child's rapid movements, but which the parent-speaker, for all his efforts at cultivation, seems affected by. The ultimate stasis is loss of will and the self's spiritual death, a withering that is also the self's progress: the Shakespearean punning upon "wither" / "whither" reinforces the paradox of progress embracing decline. Proceeding ("whither") depends fundamentally upon one's capacity to suffer negation ("wither") and to endure:

> The place is growing difficult. Flails of bramble
> Crawl into the lawn; on every hand
> Glittering, toughened branches drink their dew.
> Tiny worlds, drop by drop, tremble
> On thorns and leaves; they will melt away.
> The silence whispers around us:
> Wither, wither, visible, invisible.
>
> (32)

The situation Kinsella describes is reminiscent of some of Blake's *Songs of Innocence and Experience:* parent and child come together, reenacting the Fall from grace but also making possible a new "fall" into consciousness. The child must be set free from the protective womb of the secret garden to experience the world's real nature, to suffer pain and threat, to recognize his own mortality, to inherit "The first taint" from his father's touch, while gaining spiritual growth in the process:

> A child stands an instant at my knee.
> His mouth smells of energy, light as light.
> I touch my hand to his pearl flesh, taking strength.
> He stands still, absorbing in return
> The first taint. Immaculate, the waiting
> Kernel of his brain.
> How set him free, a son, toward the sour encounter?
>
> (32)

Although the son runs off "glittering into the sun" and the parent's efforts at cultivation seem undermined by his awareness of the superior forces of mortality and temporal flux, we should not underestimate the expression of will with which the poem concludes. For only through will's confrontation with those forces is the self able to progress to wholeness, as both the *Othello* epigraph and Kinsella's work generally illustrate:

> I cultivate my garden for the dew:
> A rasping boredom funnels into death!
> The sun climbs, a creature of one day,
> And the dew dries to dust.
> My hand strays out and picks off one sick leaf.
> (32)

The other impressive work in this section of *Nightwalker* is the long poem "The Shoals Returning," an elegy for the Dingle fisherman Gerry Flaherty, whose *sean nós* ("old style") singing moved and inspired both Kinsella and Ó Riada during their holiday in West Kerry in 1959. The "sour encounter" with the world's destructive appetite here takes the form of death by drowning, an all-too-familiar fate in the fishing communities of the West of Ireland. Moreover, the poem takes on a more distinctly Irish character, not merely through its setting but also through its very form. Where Yeats's "In Memory of Major Robert Gregory" draws upon the English elegy for form and techniques, Kinsella's poem falls more naturally within the Irish genre of the lament. The scope extends beyond the death of the individual, mourned though he may be, to acquire social, cultural, and political significance as that death is placed in the larger context. The "dramatic or story-telling voice," which Kinsella and Seán Ó Tuama identify (*An Duanaire* xxxv) as characteristic of much post-1600 poetry in Irish, is employed here as the narrator marks off the different phases of the action with the equivalent of stage directions or subheadings (*"He comes from the sea," "He sings," "He returns," "He disappears"*). On one level the lament focuses on the tragic death of a fisherman encouraged, ironically, by the reappearance of mackerel shoals off the west coast. A bare subsistence living for the past fifteen years, when the shoals were absent, has been temporarily relieved. Kinsella's distinctive perspective that incorporates threat and wounding corresponds naturally enough with the mundane scene:

The boats waited at Smerwyck,
Black-skinned, crook-backed,
On the grass by the drying boat-slip;
The rocky knife-sharp shore
Drained bare: crayfish stared:
Brutal torso of conger
Slid through a choked slit—
Naked savagery . . .

(40)

The act of fishing itself likewise acquires symbolic significance as depths are plumbed and fish hauled up:

Nets are shaken out
And swallowed into the sea,
The lines reach far down
And open everywhere
Among the haunted levels.
A million shadows here
Pursue their staring will
Along echoing cold paths.

(41)

Yet in this Gaeltacht community existing at one extremity of Ireland, it is the native Gaelic singing of Gerry Flaherty that impresses the narrator and articulates the insights gained from the fisherman's lifetime of hardship and suffering. Appropriately enough set within the province of Munster, traditionally conceived in Irish myth as the land of the dead, Flaherty serves as one more Kinsellan messenger of the gods, his voice emerging from the darkness of Kruger Kavanagh's Dunquin pub with all the distinctive resonance of an Irish Orpheus in the underworld. It is a voice akin to Kinsella's "instruments"—his later images of dissecting knife or surgical probe—but, more particularly, of the "snake out of the void" that moves in the poet's mouth at the conclusion of the *Nightwalker* volume:

A voice rises flickering
From palatal darkness, a thin yell
Straining erect, checked
In glottal silence. The song
Articulates and pierces. . . .

Men, sunk in shade, listen
On their benches, bodies tainted

With cold sea wind.
Their eyes respond; squat
Entities turn in cranial darkness
In the ravenous element
At the innermost turn of the shell.
(38–39)

In the later prose commentary to *Fifteen Dead* (1979), Kinsella describes the scene once more, defining the quality of Flaherty's voice as peculiarly fitted, in the Darwinian sense, to the vision it articulates, just as the equally appropriate muted appreciation of the audience of local fishermen completes the "act of communication":

> It was a special voice, adapted (like a reptile or an insect) to its function. Mere beauty of tone would have distracted, attracting attention for its own sake. And the singer's act of communication was thoroughly completed by his audience. They sat erect and listened, lifted their glasses and drank, and murmured phrases of appreciation. When the song ended there was a slight increase in the volume of general approbation but very little fuss. Something had been accomplished, and the entities which had combined to accomplish it separated and began to chat, in the smells of fish, rope, tobacco and porter. (*FD* 68)

Flaherty's is "the cry / That can prepare the spirit / To turn softly and be eaten / In the smell of brine and blood." As such, both his cry and the poet's lament are given a larger perspective in the poem's concluding paragraph, as Kinsella's narrative moves from the discovery of the dead man's upturned boat, complete with heavy mackerel catch, to a vision of "A withered man." With the same raised cheeks and jawbone as Flaherty's and illuminated by a similar lifetime of suffering and tragedy, the man serves to put the other's death in proper perspective. For the Dingle Peninsula is resonant with historical evidence of English repression: the poem refers to Smerwyck, for example, where the 1580 massacre of Catholics took place, and, by implication, to the tragic deaths of Pierce and Sybil Ferritur, about which Kinsella wrote in *Downstream*. English assaults upon the Irish language and culture ultimately failed in the past in the Dingle, although Flaherty and his *sean nós* singing remain in the present as isolated, rare, surviving examples. His death, then, has implications for the revival of traditional Irish music, to which Ó Riada was motivated by his 1959 holiday. But the withered man's identity has been prepared, if only obliquely, by an earlier reference to the Wave of

Tóime ("The Wave of Tóime snarls / With distance, shudders in its caves"). The reference, like Flaherty's *sean nós* singing, looks backward to an ancient Irish past: *Tonn Tóime* was one of the great waves of Ireland.[36] It is located, as Kinsella himself notes (*Duanaire* 139, 165), on the edge of Castlemaine Harbor where the poet Aogán Ó Rathaille lived in poverty after the Battle of the Boyne. We have already seen Ó Rathaille play a significant role in *Nightwalker* as spokesman for an abandoned people and for a threatened culture and language. A similar crucial significance is given him in the Kinsella–Ó Tuama edition, *An Duanaire*.

In "The Shoals Returning" Ó Rathaille assumes the same primordial enduring character of Yeats's heroic masks, and, like Yeats before him, Kinsella concentrates upon the face and in particular on the eyes. Both the parallel with Yeats and the concentration upon eyes we have already seen in "Soft Toy." The eyes have seen and suffered all, and possess the wisdom that comes from experience. Moreover, the eyes "Assess the crystalline plasm": the image may parallel Ó Rathaille's crystal imagery in his famous *aisling* "Gile na Gile" (*Duanaire* 150–53) or Yeats's "sweet crystalline cry" ("Paudeen"), just as the conjunction of withered man and coat provokes inevitable echoes of "Sailing to Byzantium." Certainly the crystal image in earlier poems (for example, "Cover Her Face") indicates transcendence. Here Kinsella's image suitably unites the clarity and rational structure of crystal with the more biological and organic "plasm." For "plasm" suggests a shaping process in which the imagination or creative self participates. Such meanings require also that union of contraries that is signified by the paradoxical "Formations of water," achieved, appropriately, "Under falls of air." (That same union is evident as the "reordered phase of grace," made possible in "Downstream" through the shivering of "pattern" (*D* 51, *N* 83), and known again in "Phoenix Park," as we shall see.) It is a vision of contraries of which the "withered man," Aogán Ó Rathaille, through poverty, hardship, and desolation, became aware. The lament for Flaherty thus concludes with a timeless vision embracing past and present, uniting *sean nós* singer, Ó Rathaille, and contemporary poet as all three participate in a process that culminates in understanding:

36. Supposed to be of "supernatural origin," the waves were believed to give "warning of the deadly danger, or foreboded the approaching death, of kings or chieftains, or bewailed a king's or great chief's death"; see Joyce, *Smaller Social History of Ancient Ireland*, 529.

A withered man, a coat
Across his shoulders, watches
From the cliff over the gorge
—A black outcrop thrust
Partly out of the soil
Into the salt wind.
The shale-grass shivers around him.
He turns a shrunken mask
Of cheekbone and jawbone
And pursed ancient mouth
On the sea surface.
A windswept glitter of light
Murmurs toward the land.
His eyes, out of tortoise lids,
Assess the crystalline plasm,
Formations of water
Under falls of air.

(42)

III

The volume's final section provides the most substantial and ambitious poems, "Nightwalker" and "Phoenix Park," which are linked by a short connecting poem, "Ritual of Departure." The section closes with "Downstream II," the final revised version of the previous volume's title poem, with Kinsella's reader, like the poem's protagonist, "Searching the darkness for a landing place" (*N* 86). In that respect, continuity between volumes is maintained, although it is the concluding four lines of "Phoenix Park" that serve as epigraph to the next volume, *Notes from the Land of the Dead,* and so provide the more literal link. Such explicit linking of the two volumes in a common search and sequence is thus blurred by the inclusion of "Downstream II," particularly since the poem's terza rima reflects Kinsella's earlier commitment to tight metrical forms in sharp contrast to the freer narrative of "Nightwalker." That said, the three long poems bring the volume to an impressive close.

"Nightwalker" pursues the protagonist's nocturnal journey through "the Irish historical landscape and the 'new' Ireland,"[37] more specifically through Dublin and its environs. The walker's direction is down-

37. Kinsella, *Poetry Book Society Bulletin* 55 (December 1967).

ward, into the self, but also into the corresponding darkness outside. Indeed, the spiritual decay, torpor, and death addressed in the poem are summed up in the term "Necropolis," while what emerges in this walk by an increasingly familiar nocturnal prowler is a savage indictment of Ireland's history during the poet's own lifetime, from independence in 1922 to the 1960s.

In "Downstream" and its revised version, Kinsella had accepted the challenge of the long poem. It was a form to which other poets were attracted at this time: as John Montague wrote in 1967–1968, he wished "to write a long poem or sequence . . . co-terminous with at least one whole aspect of one's experience."[38] Whereas Kinsella had sought from the outset to shape his volumes into a unity, his adoption of the sequence as a structure enabling such unity was still a few years away. Yet Montague may have unintentionally influenced *Nightwalker* through his own *Patriotic Suite* (1966). Montague's poem was written to disavow the Easter Rising of 1916 and the divisive nationalism generated by the Rising's fiftieth anniversary. He had found Ó Riada's score to George Morrison's film, *Mise Eire* ("I am Ireland") (1960), "overwhelming," so requiring "an antidote to the aisling of nationalism." When *Patriotic Suite* appeared, with John Derricke's Elizabethan woodcuts as illustrations, "Tom Kinsella in Carbondale was amused by the parody of Reidy's Band [Ceoltóirí Chualann] as savage woodkernes on the cover and provoked enough by the contents to produce *Nightwalker* as his much less playful response."[39] Montague, on another occasion, criticized Kinsella's poem for being "too heavy in movement and reference; he has discovered a new subject, but not, I feel, a new metric to energise it."[40] The point is well taken: as we shall see later volumes, the problems of the long poem are overcome through sequences of short lyrics. However, Edna

38. Montague, "Hugh MacDiarmid: The Seamless Garment and the Muse," in *The Figure in the Cave*, ed. Quinn, 154. Commenting upon the longer "epic" form sought by modern Irish poets "to apprehend the wholeness rather than the separate moments of a culture," Seamus Deane has seen poets producing "lyric sequences rather than structurally satisfying narratives." He includes N and *The Rough Field* as examples; see *Celtic Revivals*, 15.

39. John Montague, "Living for Ireland," in *16 on 16: Irish Writers on the Easter Rising, Letters from the New Island*, 7, ed. Dermot Bolger (Dublin: Raven Arts Press, 1988), 18.

40. Montague, "The Impact of International Modern Poetry on Irish Writing," in *Irish Poets in English*, ed. Lucy, 157.

Longley's criticism—"Form simultaneously becomes more meandering"[41]—is heavyhanded and misplaced, and indeed both criticisms of Kinsella's forms overlook what Seamus Deane later made explicit. While Deane concedes that the poems display "a certain cumbrousness" and "loss of elegance," the poet, rather than being seen to fail, "instead, . . . chooses to demonstrate the process by which he arrives at his moments of balance. The poem is not a structure; it is an action in which structures appear and disappear as part of a complex process in which the poet, as well as the reader, is involved. The earlier poetry, based on oppositions, gives way to a poetry in which a dialectical relationship was being sustained between modes and moments of order, modes and moments of dissolution."[42] Deane's exposition captures exactly both Kinsella's method and his purpose, as we shall see.

Kinsella's concern focuses primarily upon the spiritual failure of Irish society. The poem should be taken, he has said, "[n]ot as a political satire or as an exile's criticism but as a sad poem about violence."[43] While material matters are scrutinized and found wanting in the poem, Kinsella is particularly concerned with the moral vacuity that he views as the true source of Ireland's predicament, a vacuity that fails to find any balance in the violent zone explored. In referring to violence, therefore, Kinsella means more particularly the tension between order and disorder, light and darkness, structure and shambles; that is, his scope is larger than the merely political and ultimately embraces all existence. Likewise, while the poem's scope is public and social and the external setting is described with considerable immediacy, the drama is essentially internal, as the prefatory poem makes clear:

> Mindful of the
>   shambles of the day
> But mindful, under the
>   blood's drowsy humming,
> Of will that gropes for
>   structure—nonetheless
> Not unmindful of
>   the madness without,

41. Longley, "Searching the Darkness," 134.
42. Deane, *Celtic Revivals*, 142.
43. Kinsella, *Poetry Book Society Bulletin* 55 (December 1967).

The madness within (the
  book of reason slammed
Open, slammed shut)
  we presume to say:
            (N 56)

The protagonist is indeed "mindful," and his wandering around Dublin's streets parallels the explicitly dialectical pattern expressed here, whether the madness within and without or the slamming open and shut of the book of reason. The "shambles" suitably describes the chaos that must be ordered by the self in quest of "structure," a quest that involves intellect, blood, and will working together in wholeness of vision. That shambles is mental, spiritual, and social, and what is especially depressing is that in the protagonist's experience the forces of darkness, of irrationality, selfishness, and greed, appear to have gained the upper hand. The task is onerous in its scope and significance, and Kinsella concedes an element of presumption ("we presume to say") in the subsequent main body of the poem. The deflationary modesty, in fact, properly undercuts any charge of presumption: as Kinsella has commented elsewhere about his propensity to generalize, his generalizations are not arrived at easily but are all earned.[44] At the same time, he came in retrospect to view the poem differently. Speaking with John Haffenden in 1979–1980, he was no longer prepared to practice the role of social critic. No longer willing to judge a state of affairs moral or proper, he saw the artist as responsible for understanding rather than for moral or social improvement. "Nightwalker" was now dismissed as "that sort of full-throated outcry" that made him "a victim of that kind of rhetoric."[45] As we shall see later, this changed attitude toward poetry parallels the creation of a different kind of poetry, one employing a different kind of technique.

Here the poem opens with the Eliot-like pronouncement "I only know things seem and are not good," a parallel that illustrates how much Kinsella still depended upon Eliot (rather than Joyce) for his depiction of Dublin as a wasteland. Appearance, indeed, is shown up throughout the poem as hollow and deceiving; the nocturnal landscape is filled with shadowy figures—"Monsters of ivy squat in lunar glare"—and the very moon itself seems contaminated: "It hangs, like

44. Deane, "A Conversation," 88.
45. *Viewpoints*, ed. Haffenden, 107.

a fat skull, or the pearl knob / Of a pendulum at the outermost reach of its swing" or, even more ominously, as "A mask of grey dismay sagging open / In the depths of torture, moron voiceless moon. / That dark area, the mark of Cain" (57). Under such "lunar glare" the nightwalker recognizes the presence of spiritual death, whether in the form of the television watcher ("a shadow slumped in the corner") or of the suburban commuters waiting for their morning train, or of "Our banks and business and government" prepared to disregard principle in favor of profit and advancement. In savage parody of the compassionate appeal to the world's oppressed inscribed on New York's Statue of Liberty, Dublin's "Productive Investment" offers instead the wholly soulless "Lend me your wealth, your cunning and your drive, / Your arrogant refuse" (59). "Spirit-skeletons" are thus everywhere, whether exemplified by the two Germans who provoke recollections of Nazi barbarism, or by the photograph of "The Wedding Group," revealing a barbarism closer to home. The photograph —of Kevin O'Higgins, Rory O'Connor, and Eamon de Valera—was taken in happier times, at O'Higgins's wedding at which O'Connor served as best man. During the Civil War following the 1922 Anglo-Irish Treaty and the establishment of the Free State, O'Connor was among the seventy-seven Republicans executed, for his seizure of the Four Courts, on the order of Ernest Blythe and O'Higgins, then minister of justice, while de Valera (the Fox) continued to work against the treaty. In 1927 O'Higgins was himself assassinated in retaliation, while Blythe (the Weasel) became an Abbey Theatre director, responsible for the annual pantomime, and de Valera remained indifferent to "the horn of the Player King" (Yeats). Kinsella's "tragic tale," involving one of the more infamous events of the new nation,[46] vividly captures the abandonment of principle and the bitter and bloody internal conflict of the Free State's early years.

The present, however, offers no improvement. At Joyce's tower in Sandycove, past and present are superimposed in a dazzling montage. The copy of the *Irish Times* blowing in the gutter pictures "Our new young minister" complete "in hunting pinks," a picture that gives way to "a spectral stink of horse / And rider's sweat" and the protagonist's experience of a deathly world: "Note the silence. / Light never strays

46. See Harmon, *The Poetry of Thomas Kinsella*, 64. Noel Browne noted how in the 1950s "trigger words" like "seventy-seven" could provoke "white-hot hate" among Dáil members; see *Against the Tide* (Dublin: Gill and Macmillan, 1986), 228.

there. Nothing has a shadow there." And when he calls upon Joyce for help, to serve as a latter-day Virgil to guide Dante-Kinsella through Hell—"Watcher in the tower, be with me now"—the allusions to *Portrait of an Artist as a Young Man* and *Finnegans Wake*[47] place the new minister in a different perspective, not as "Father of Authors!" but as "The sonhusband" "mounting to glory / On his big white harse." Riding a different and political animal, the minister is motivated by expediency, ambition, and greed ("Marry the Boss's daughter" is a clear reference to Charles J. Haughey, then recently appointed minister in Sean Lemass's government and married to Lemass's daughter[48]). The hunting pack in the "New Ireland," which includes the Catholic hierarchy and the language revivalists, becomes "a pack of lickspittles." And amid disturbing recollections of a Christian Brothers' school, where history is distorted and literature is censored, the imagery of appetite is maintained with mordant irony, playing upon both biblical imagery and the Irish experience of "Soupers."[49] The protagonist is offered "Bread of certainty; scalding soup of memories, / From my drowsy famine—martyrs in a dish / Of scalding tears: food of dragon men / And my own dragon half" (66). The seamew answers its own cry, "*Eire, Eire . . . is there none / To hear? Is all lost?*" with the *rosc* (rhetorical poem or invocation) of Ireland's first poet, Amergin, finding comfort still in the earlier poet's assertion of the power of transformation:

> *Alas, I think I will dash myself*
> *At the stones, I will become a wind on the sea*
> *Or a wave of the sea again, or a sea sound.*
> *At the first light of the sun I stirred on my rock;*
> *I have seen the sun go down at the end of the world;*
> *Now I fly across the face of the moon.*
>
> (67)

47. Hugh Kenner noted the *Wake* references (*FW* 10:02, 10:11, 214:11–13, 627:1) in "Thomas Kinsella: An Anecdote and Some Reflections," 183n1. The echo of *The Portrait* is of the final section of Stephen's diary at the work's conclusion (*Portrait* 253).

48. Gerald Dawe praised "Nightwalker" as taking "the imagination into previously uncharted territory. The hostility and indifference of governmental offices and the political chambers are sites where, until Kinsella, Irish poetry had never been and had not a hope in hell of survival"; see his article "In the Violent Zone: Thomas Kinsella's *Nightwalker and Other Poems*," *Tracks* 7 (Spring 1987): 31.

49. According to the *Oxford English Dictionary*, in Ireland "Souper" is "a Protestant clergyman seeking to make proselytes by means of dispensing soup in charity" or "one converted to Protestantism by the receipt of soup or other charity."

Yet the protagonist's own comment upon Amergin's *rosc*—"A dying language echoes / Across a century's silence"—suggests no relief. Conscious of the mutilations that the Gaelic tradition has suffered, Kinsella offers no simplistic revivalism. Brother Burke in his Christian Brothers' school epitomizes that crude nationalism which, in its clericalism and censorship, perverted the ideals of the Easter Rising and is condemned no less than are de Valera and O'Higgins, the archbishop, the young minister in hunting pinks, and the other figures of the "new Ireland." Instead, Kinsella is bitingly ironic: "Adolescents, / Celibates, we offer up our vows / To God and Ireland in Her name, grateful / That by our studies here they may not lack / Civil servants in a state of grace." Joining Amergin, however, Joyce provides one more preferred alternative through his familiar Morse code tapping on the initials of his *Wake* protagonist, HCE, with whom this section closes: "*H*esitant, *c*ogitating, *e*xit" (my italics).

The mundane action of the protagonist's wife buttering bread indicates a further source of inspiration.[50] Like some latter-day and quotidian *aisling* figure, she offers him, who is "starved for speech," illumination in terms that point to the subsequent long poem "Phoenix Park": "I believe now that love is half persistence, / A medium in which, from change to change, / Understanding may be gathered" (67). Now the several female figures merge: the wife-muse gives way to the Virgin Mary, hailed for new and threatening attributes ("moon of my dismay, / Quiet as oil, enormous in her shaggy pool"), and capable of consuming the protagonist's sight. Such a moon goddess takes the form also of Queen Victoria in a conflation we have seen in the previous section and offering a wisdom that provokes "faint terror" in the protagonist. Kinsella's treatment is characteristically ironic: Victoria, during her visit to Ireland "to take the waters," recognizes the terrible nature of Ireland's sufferings from the Great Famine and articulates the poet's own ethic of endurance, imaged as the draining of the ordeal cup, but offers a teleology the poet dismisses wryly as "meaningful" and "soothing":

> When I drank
> I felt my patience and trust coming back.
> From time to time it seems that everything

50. Kinsella has acknowledged borrowing the image, "Her dear shadow on the blind," from Goethe; see O'Driscoll, "Interview," 63.

Is breaking down; but we must never despair.
There are times it is all part of a meaningful drama
That begins in the grey mists of antiquity
And reaches through the years to unknown goals
In the consciousness of man, which is very soothing.
(68)

Wife, muse, and Queen Victoria—all epitomize the moon goddess ruling over the ocean and influencing the protagonist in a combination of control and oppression:

Our mother
Rules on high, queenlike, pale with control.
Hatcher of peoples!
Incline from your darkness into mine!
I stand at the ocean's edge, my head fallen back
Heavy with your control, and oppressed!
(68)

The lunar experience with which the poem closes is thus the climactic consequence to which the poem leads and which follows from another reading of the "meaningful drama." For the experience serves as one more initiation into endurance, into recognition not simply of Ireland's failure and its decline into a land of the dead, but also of the individual spiritual ordeal that must be pursued. The experience parallels and is likely indebted to Jung's account of his descent into his unconscious, in which he seemed "at the edge of a cosmic abyss. It was like a voyage to the moon, or a descent into empty space. First came the image of a crater, and I had the feeling that I was in the land of the dead."[51] Such a possible source is reinforced by Kinsella's subsequent explicit use of Jung's account of childhood in *Song of the Night* (1978). Amid the lunar "Sea of Disappointment,"[52] Kinsella's protagonist is thus granted an infernal vision of a scene that might have come from Dante or from Eliot's *Waste Land*, captured in distinctive Kinsellan imagery of appetite and scuttling, squatting figures:

51. C. G. Jung, *Memories, Dreams, Reflections*, rev. ed., ed. Aniela Jaffé, trans. Richard Winston and Clara Winston (New York: Pantheon Books, 1973), 181.

52. Kinsella categorized the post-Holocaust world as a source not only of horror but of disappointment, the "realisation" of which he regards as "the most significant thing in contemporary poetry" and resulting in a "feeling of precariousness"; see "The Divided Mind," 215.

> A true desert, naked
> To every peril. The shadows are alive:
> They scuttle and flicker among the rock needles,
> Squat and suck the dry juice, inspect
> The eggs of shadow beneath the surface, twitching
> Madly in their cells.
>
> (69)

The poet offers no "soothing" relief: urging us to "take the waters," he notes their taste is "a human taste, but sterile" and is of "Massed human wills." Yet Kinsella has rejected the charge of nihilism: the poem's final section stresses understanding and, as the poet has noted, "the impulse is important, even if it's of no avail."[53] Moreover, understanding is to be gained not by transcending time but by submitting to change, disorder, and incoherence. Relief will come elsewhere, through the alternatives offered in "Phoenix Park" of art and love and on an individual rather than a societal scale.

The two long poems "Nightwalker" and "Phoenix Park" are linked by a third, "Ritual of Departure" (71–72), a moving description of "A man at the moment of departure." The man's feelings are vividly caught as he "treasures some stick of furniture / With slowly blazing eyes," unties a set of antique silver spoons, and recalls Dublin under the Georges. Related to his previous eye imagery, such "blazing eyes" indicate illumination—attributed to Joyce at Sandycove, for example, (*N* 63–64) and later, in *A Technical Supplement* (1976), sought after ("let our gaze blaze," *One* 33), as reflecting the comprehensive vision of understanding. Spiritual myopia, the antithesis of illumination, is correspondingly imaged by blank or dead eyes. Another image in the poem, reminiscent of James Malton's *Picturesque and Descriptive View of the City of Dublin* (1799), suggests the street scenes that appear later in *St. Catherine's Clock* (1987): "A portico, beggars moving on the steps— / A horserider locked in soundless greeting, / Bowed among the dogs and dung; the panelled vista / Closing on pleasant smoke-blue far-off hills." Such parallels with subsequent volumes reinforce the unity and coherence sought by the poet and the sense of recurrent preoccupations around which his protagonists perpetually circle. But more than either treasured belongings or vista, it is the land that constitutes the most disturbing element in the man's departure as, in the act of digging up potatoes, he is made aware of both past and

53. *Viewpoints*, ed. Haffenden, 111.

future. The "Landscape with ancestral figures" is more immediately that of Kinsella's own family, but also by extension that of Ireland's rural people suffering their own nineteenth-century diaspora and, like the Kinsellas, cut off from their inheritance and identity as a consequence of moving to Dublin to seek employment. The protagonist's scooping action thus becomes a last and holy contact with the land. Any future now requires the all-too-familiar Irish exile and the inevitable and painful tearing of roots: "I scoop at the earth, and sense famine, a first / Sourness in the clay. The roots tear softly." At the same time, such contact with the land is one more "sour encounter" the self must experience in its progression toward wholeness, and, while the roots tear, they do so "softly," offering little resistance to an inevitable and necessary process.

The Kinsellas' departure for the United States in 1965 provoked both "Ritual of Departure" and "Phoenix Park." Both poems, together with "Nightwalker," involve sustained self-evaluation and honest scrutiny of one's life achievement. The scope of "Nightwalker" encourages comparison with *The Waste Land*: personal experience provides the basis by which the poet diagnoses a society's spiritual ills. However, both the linking poem, "Ritual of Departure," and "Phoenix Park" are more explicitly autobiographical, although their scope goes beyond the personal to fuse family and national history. The dispersal of family from rural Wicklow to Dublin is now extended further, for Kinsella resigned from his Civil Service post and undertook an academic career in the United States. The change of both career and country is accompanied by an important development in Kinsella's writing. "Phoenix Park" focuses upon questions of love and art and, while such questions continue in subsequent volumes, they are expressed in a sharply different manner and refocused to concentrate upon rather different subjects. "Phoenix Park," then, represents a climax and a conclusion in the development of Kinsella's poetic achievement. Fine poem though it is—and at least one critic has described it as "one of the great love poems of the century"[54]—it nevertheless is the final statement of the first half of the poet's career, a farewell to the formal meditative poem and to the English poetic tradition.

It is not coincidental, therefore, that the epigraphs to the *Night-*

54. Conleth Ellis, "Above the Salt: The Early Peppercanisters," *Tracks* 7 (1987): 34.

walker volume ("Fair Eleanor, O Christ Thee Save") and to "Phoenix Park" (*"The Phaenix builds the Phaenix' nest. / Love's architecture is his own"*) both have English sources. The first is from "The Ballad of Lord Thomas and Fair Ellinor" in Bishop Percy's *Reliques of Ancient English Poetry*, the second is from Richard Crashaw's "In the Holy Nativity of Our Lord God."[55] No subsequent poem makes such explicit use of English poetic sources. Wholly characteristic, on the other hand, is the wry irony with which Kinsella plays upon the coincidence of names, those of the ballad's protagonists and his own and his wife's. The irony enables him to suggest parallels and continuities while avoiding pretentiousness. And, despite the epigraph from Percy, the shadow of English verse no longer falls heavily across his work and, like the phoenix, Kinsella seeks a rebirth of sorts, involving poetry as well as his husband-self. Although both the cadence and the stanza unit appear traditional, lacking the more adventurous experimentalism of "Nightwalker," the poem opens with parodic acknowledgment of T. S. Eliot, whose *Four Quartets* he had earlier admired:[56] "One stays or leaves. The one who returns is not / The one, etcetera. And we are leaving." Again, the landscape is distinctively Irish, with strong personal, literary, political, and historical connections. For Phoenix Park is close to Kinsella's childhood home in Phoenix Street; St. Mary's Hospital in the park is the tuberculosis sanatorium where Eleanor Kinsella had been a patient in the early fifties; and the park provides the setting for another of the poem's vignettes, that involving their first child Sara after her First Communion. The historical and political, unlike in "Nightwalker," do not surface, but the inevitable symbolism of phoenix and rebirth, which Joyce made central to the *Wake* and pursued through the landscape of Phoenix Park, is implicit here. For it is the path to regeneration through love and poetry that Kinsella explores, and at the center of that process is the wife-muse figure. Likewise, the poet's impending departure for the United States leads, by the poem's end, in good Celtic and Joycean fashion, back upon one's self, following a coiling, labyrinthine path back to the sources of one's self and creativity. The

55. Bishop Percy, *Reliques of Ancient English Poetry*, 4 vols. 6th ed. (London: Richards, 1823), 3:341–44; *Carmen Deo Nostro, The Poems, English, Latin, and Greek, of Richard Crashaw*, ed. L. C. Martin (Oxford: Clarendon Press, 1957), 249.

56. "You are not the same people who left that station / Or who will arrive at any terminus"; see "The Dry Salvages," *Four Quartets* (London: Faber and Faber, 1944), 30.

poem is thus both a celebratory acknowledgment of the past and a venturing forward into the future, with the latter made possible only through the strength and understanding gained from the past and from the love shared by poet and wife.

The journey, through the park to Lucan and back through Inchicore to Dublin, provokes memories and self-scrutiny, during which prosaic events take on symbolic significance:

> A twig with two damp leaves drops on the bonnet
> From the upper world, trembling: shows us its clean
> Fracture and vanishes, snatched off by the wind:
> Droplets of moisture shudder on the windscreen.
>
> —You start at the suddenness, as though it were
> Your own delicate distinct flesh that had snapped.
> (74)

Likewise, the young poet visiting his future wife in the hospital, takes "the twisting paths / To find you by the way of hesitation." Both paths and progress suggest a dialectic to be pursued, although it is tempting, given the Phoenix Park setting, to read political implications in the term "hesitation."[57] Yet it is upon love and the understanding gained from love rather than upon political history that Kinsella focuses, that which he calls "the one positive dream," known through appetite which in turn is at the heart of all things:

> I stooped and tasted your life until you woke,
> And your body's fever leaped out at my mind.
> There's a fever now that eats everything,
> —Everything but the one positive dream.
> (74)

Experience and appetite thus merge to form taste, the basis for illumination, known, as the wife-muse knows everything, "bodily." What follows are experiences of appetite, whether remembering as a young child eating mushrooms, characteristically seen as "Death-pallor in their dry flesh, the taste of death," or in adulthood in deep

57. In an attempt to discredit Charles Stewart Parnell, Richard Piggott forged a letter in Parnell's handwriting condoning the Phoenix Park murders and had it printed in the London *Times*. The forgery was uncovered through Piggott's misspelling of "hesitency." See Lyons, *Ireland since the Famine*, 192–93. Joyce in the *Wake* played with the misspelling ("Hesitency was clearly to be evitated," *FW* 35:20).

depression offering himself up to such deathly process, "*Take me, / I am nothing*," or again as the woman driven "in vague hunger" to prostitution, or poet and wife in the present, drinking in a pub at Lucan. Understanding has, nevertheless, been gained; their union has produced their firstborn, remembered "in her Communion finery," and the poet's discovery of "Laws of order." While appetite, with "The ordeal-cup" that must be drained, provides the generating force, so the contrary impulse toward structure, epitomized by crystal, captures the self's other important force. For crystal suggests beauty, preciousness, clarity, and strength, qualities more readily associated, as we have seen, with the transcendent, set off against the temporal and organic. As one critic has rightly noted, the crystal forming in the ordeal cup reinforces "the phoenix as symbol for reconciliation of opposites." Hence crystal here grows, is "the live crystal," and "represents light opposed to darkness, life opposed to death, order opposed to chaos, and the unseeing vision of knowledge opposed to intellection."[58] "*The dream*" thus describes a process that encompasses the self, growth, and, by extension, all things. The process generates the dialectical tension between chaos and order, appetite and spirit, and brings knowledge gained bodily or through will and reason. Kinsella's polarities bear comparison with Yeats's Blood and Moon, and indeed Kinsellan man also runs his ancestral race between these extremities. The dream retraces the path identified in the prose address to the beloved in "Wormwood" and draws upon the poet's recurrent imagery of ordeal cup, tissue, mirror, crystal, garden, shade or shadow, woman, hands, and heart. It is a measure of Kinsella's achievement that such imagery now acquires the resonance and complexity of poetic myth.

"Look into the cup," the poet requires, "the tissues of order / Form under your stare. The living surfaces / Mirror each other, gather everything / Into their crystalline world" (77). The figures in the dream include a child plucking and tasting death, a "shade, made flesh," stumbling on "understanding," "women-shapes . . . / . . . full of knowledge," and the crystal's subsequent formation. The process is toward understanding, the crystalline vision revealed through the wife-muse and founded in the dialectical and the temporal:

58. Peggy F. Broder, "Breaking the Shell of Solitude: Some Poems of Thomas Kinsella," *Eire-Ireland* 14 (Summer 1979): 88.

Laws of order I find I have discovered
Mainly at your hands . . . of failure and increase,
The stagger and recovery of spirit:
That life is hunger, hunger is for order,
And hunger satisfied brings on new hunger

Till there's nothing to come;—let the crystal crack
On some insoluble matter, then its heart
Shudders and accepts the flaw, adjusts on it
Taking new strength—given the positive dream;
Given, with your permission, undying love . . .
(77)

The dream world is inhabited by shadowy figures, some recognizable (women or child), others suggestive less of growth than of threat and death. All participate in a process enabling the tissue to form, an embryonic self moving toward structure, shape, or order, and gaining understanding through stumbling—the action parallels Yeats's myth of tragic failure—just as "the crystal . . . increases, / Eliciting in its substance from the dark / The slowly forming laws it increases by" or heart, in accepting and adjusting to flaw, takes "new strength." The dream, he insists, is "positive," although progress entails further descent into darkness, confrontation with phantasmal figures, further appetite so that "this live world is emptied of its hunger / While the crystal world, undying, crowds with light, / Filling the cup" (78). Yet transcendence, immortality, or integration of self within time are all withheld: the "one last phantom," "aching to plant one kiss / In the live crystal as it aches with fullness," is denied, "The final / Kiss ungiveable." The process, while it may lead to understanding, is by definition endless, although, thanks to the love of poet and wife, he knows "undying love."

Unlike his wife, whose knowledge is gained "bodily," the poet-narrator knows such things only intellectually, as "mere idea," but he knows with Yeats that fulfillment comes only through hunger for the apple most out of reach, Dante's face made hollow out of love and banishment ("Ego Dominus Tuus"). Hence, draining his glass in the Lucan pub—an ironic mundane equivalent—the poet is led to echo the ballad of "The Lord Thomas and Fair Ellinor" and later to include the Crashaw, to indicate awareness of their own mortality and threat to their love. His stress, however, is upon choice, upon the willed exercise of appetite, upon suffering endured, upon the conscious striving after order and the corresponding growth of tissue into a self. Failure of will and of choice lead to "a hungerless no dream"; ironically, it is to the very "*Fragility*" of temporal finiteness and moral weakness that the poet appeals, a fragility that brings its own ultimate reward in spiritual fulfillment. Once more it is organic life, for all its imperfections, that proves preferable to transcendence:

Fragility echoing fragilities
From whom I have had every distinctness
Accommodate me still, where—folded in peace
And undergoing with ghostly gaiety
Inner immolation, shallowly breathing—

You approach the centre by its own sweet light.
I consign my designing will stonily
To your flames. Wrapped in that rosy fleece, two lives
Burn down around one love, one flickering-eyed
Stone self becomes more patient than its own stone.
(80)

Such Rosicrucian imagery reveals its Yeatsian origins, as does the imagery of the lovers' union as one: we have seen similar parallels earlier in the volume ("Wormwood," N 30). Such inheritance is now carried casually, with Yeats joining a host of other literary ghosts in the poem to take his place within Kinsella's own myth. That Kinsella has distanced himself from earlier exemplars may also be evidenced in his parodic tone: "The road divides and we can take either way, / Etcetera." Parody, after all, entails the questioning of authority and encourages choice; it is also "an important way for modern artists to come to terms with the past."[59]

On the drive back to the city Dublin offers a contrary organic "green world," "An eighteenth century prospect to the sea" but also, in antithesis to such ordered structure, the more Joycean "umpteenth city of confusion." Kinsella's criticism here of contemporary Dublin is as savage as anything in "Nightwalker," Swiftian in pitch and intensity and anticipating *One Fond Embrace* (*FCC* 1–10):

A theatre for the quick articulate,
The agonized genteel, their artful watchers . . .

59. Linda Hutcheon, *A Theory of Parody: The Teachings of Twentieth-Century Art Forms* (London: Methuen, 1985), 101.

Malice as entertainment. Asinine feast
Of sowthistles and brambles! And there dead men,
Half hindered by dead men, tear down dead beauty.
(81)

The return drive provokes not only such hostile social criticism but personal memories and self-examination: "where we smiled and passed," "where we roamed at night," "where naked by firelight / We stood and rested," and above all "That room," Kinsella's flat in Baggot Street, already significant in "Baggot Street Deserta." Indeed, the earlier poem is explicitly acknowledged as the poet recalls his life before marriage and "The shapes of tiredness" that threatened depression:

One midnight at the starlit sill I let them
Draw near. Loneliness drew into order:
A thought of fires in the hearts of darknesses,
A darkness at the heart of every fire,
Darkness, fire, darkness, threaded on each other—

The orders of stars fixed in abstract darkness,
Darknesses of worlds sheltering in their light;
World darkness harbouring orders of cities,
Whose light at midnight harbours human darkness;
The human dark pierced by solitary fires . . .
(82)

Restored, however, by appetite, albeit of a muse in haglike shape ("hunger / Came with gaping kiss over terrible wastes"), the poet is granted revelation, insight into his own self, his ancestral past, into the very process of life itself:

Attracted from the night by my wakefulness
Certain half-dissolved—half-formed—beings loomed close:
A child with eaten features eating something—
Another, with unfinished features, in white—
They hold hands. A shadow bends to protect them.

The shadow tries to speak, but its tongue stumbles.
A snake out of the void moves in my mouth, sucks
At triple darkness. A few ancient faces
Detach and begin to circle. Deeper still,
Delicate distinct tissue begins to form.
(82)

The concluding four lines serve as epigraph to the next volume, *Notes from the Land of the Dead* (1972), where the revelation that the lines suggest is explored further. While Kinsella's work has previously been inhabited by shadows motivated by appetite and has traced the growth of the self as tissue forming, the myth has shown only occasionally Irish origins and the self-examination has remained within the realms of conscious experience. What distinguishes the next stage in Kinsella's development is the increasingly Irish character of his myth and the pursuit of understanding and self-knowledge by descent into the unconscious. As the imagery of mouth and tongue makes clear in these concluding lines, poetry requires appetite and darkness for its articulation, with the muse now taking the more ominous form of "A snake out of the void." Knowledge of self requires contact with older, primordial forces operating at the very sources of the life process itself. The direction then must be downward, toward levels of darkness hitherto not penetrated in Kinsella's work, and, as the title of his next volume, *Notes from the Land of the Dead*, suggests, requiring courage, honesty, and perseverance against fearful odds. Finding a balance in the violent zone, however necessary to progress, makes serious demands upon both poet and reader. What is clear, on the other hand, is the subsequent major poetic achievement for which such balance serves as preparation.

four

Imaginative Bedrock

Between *Downstream* (1962) and *Nightwalker* (1968) Kinsella's work underwent considerable changes; the sharp contrast between the first and final versions of "Downstream" illustrates that purging of style which, in Kinsella's case, went hand in hand with his emerging poetic majority. Changes in Kinsella's writing were matched by changes in his personal life and career. In 1963 he made his first visit to the United States; two years later he resigned from the Civil Service after deciding to devote himself to writing and teaching, and moved with his family to Carbondale, Illinois. It is tempting to argue that the Kinsellas' voluntary exile from Ireland provoked the poet to turn to more intrinsically Irish sources; "Ritual for Departure" and "Phoenix Park" are sufficient proof that the move to the United States was undertaken with a mixture of reluctance, pain, and uncertainty. Yet Kinsella had concerned himself from the outset of his writing career with producing translations from the Irish. Indeed, it was thought appropriate to collect these with his own poetry to date in *Poems and Translations* (1961), although the most impressive single translation came eight years later with his influential and internationally acclaimed version of the *Táin*. Other major translations have continued to appear: in *An Duanaire, 1600–1900: Poems of the Dis-*

possessed (1981), his collaborative volume with Seán Ó Tuama, and in his edition of the *New Oxford Book of Irish Verse* (1986).

While departure for the United States may have provoked the kind of self-examination described in "Phoenix Park" and may have made him more conscious of both personal and national histories, it would be misleading to regard Kinsella's commitment to Irish sources as entirely new. We have seen that he employed the Deirdre myth in "Death of a Queen" *(AS)* and that he made use of the Ferriters, Pierce and Sybil, in *Downstream*. At the same time, what is evident, according to his own account, is that Kinsella rediscovered Gaelic literature and the Irish tradition, seeing it, for all his writing in English, as a vital part of his inheritance. This Gaelic inheritance served as an effective means by which the Irish poet might avoid the double shadow of Yeats and English verse. For while Yeats too had drawn upon the ancient myths, legends, and sagas, and shown their relevance to the twentieth-century Irish poet writing in English, Kinsella, with Catholic upbringing, early schooling in Irish, and closer contact with the myths' original Gaelic, could recognize an ancestral inheritance from which Yeats, by birth and language, was to a greater extent removed. Furthermore, while Yeats promoted the eighteenth-century Protestant Ascendancy as a golden age, with luminaries like Swift, Goldsmith, Berkeley, and Burke, Kinsella became increasingly committed to another Ireland, one older, tribal, Catholic, and Gaelic-speaking. Although Swift continues to affect him, as in his late volume *Blood and Family* (1988), Kinsella's eighteenth century is notable less for Yeats's Ascendancy than for Brian Merriman, Aogán Ó Rathaille, Eoghan Rua Ó Súilleabháin, and Eibhlín Dhubh ní Chonaill. Consequently, in 1972 he saw Yeats as "*isolated*" (his italics) within the Irish tradition,[1] although at the same time he did not abjure what he termed ten years later as "the English element in the Irish inheritance."[2] Nevertheless, intent on overcoming "the Gaelic League mentality" and "the old dividing idiocies," Kinsella described himself at that later date as "a late-awakened convert . . . [to] the two-tongued Irish tradition." In such "an act of self-scrutiny and re-

1. Kinsella, "The Divided Mind," 210.

2. "Another Country . . . ," in *The Pleasures of Gaelic Poetry*, ed. Mac Réamoinn, 178. Kinsella's *The Dual Tradition: An Essay in Poetry and Politics in Ireland* (Manchester: Carcanet, 1995), appeared too late for consideration in my study. An extract, "from *The Dual Tradition*," appeared on *Krino* 14 (Winter 1993): 30–32.

definition," the poet's goal is, as one might expect, "greater understanding."[3]

Not a native speaker himself nor able to write poetry in Irish, Kinsella is inclined to refer to his translation work as "a hobby."[4] Such modesty is misleading, especially since the work has gained significance not just in its own right but for its profound effect upon Kinsella's own poetry. As he himself attested, it has been "an act of responsibility. It's ours, Irish, and it deserved a new currency." "It's a commitment to tradition; an understanding of them [the *An Duanaire* poems], as part of *our* past, is an understanding of our totality. . . . The *Táin* is part of our imaginative bedrock, and my translation was an act of loyalty to that part of one's own past, not necessarily to the quality of that particular work."[5] It was not until after the publication of the *Táin* that Kinsella's mining of that "imaginative bedrock" affected his own poetry to any significant degree. His translation of the *Táin* "had been self-contained and antiquarian enough not to have aroused, by itself, broad questions about its relevance to my own poetry."[6] The same cannot be said for his subsequent use of *Lebor Gabála Érenn (The Book of Invasions)*. Moreover, as Seamus Heaney has recently argued, translation from Irish by an English-speaking Irish writer is an act with more than literary implications.[7] Yet the revived interest in early Irish literature in translation, to which poets like Heaney and John Montague have also contributed significantly, may, in retrospect, be seen to be much indebted to Kinsella's example and in turn to the receptivity of Liam Miller and the Dolmen Press.

The impact such translation work has had upon Kinsella's own work occurred, in crucial Kinsella fashion, coincidentally; chance as much as choice has a central role in his myth and, as in Yeats, the two pursue an appropriately dialectical path:

3. Ibid.

4. Conversation with Brian John, Dublin, 3 May 1982. Kinsella applied the same term to his own writing; see *The Poet Speaks*, ed. Orr, 109.

5. *Viewpoints*, ed. Haffenden, 112. Cf. "An act of repossession," as Ó Tuama and Kinsella described *An Duanaire* in their preface (*Duanaire*, vii). Cf. Eiléan Ní Chuilleanáin, who notes that the "*duanaire* or poem book kept by great families is the reason for the survival of so much bardic verse"; see "Love and Friendship," in *The Pleasures of Gaelic Poetry*, ed. Mac Réamoinn, 51.

6. Kinsella, "Another Country . . . ," 177.

7. Heaney, "Earning a Rhyme," *Poetry Ireland Review* 25 (Spring 1989): 95.

> It was late in my literary career, when things were firmly committed, that I looked seriously for the first time at Gaelic literature and at the tradition and culture that produced it. It seems in retrospect a long dereliction or blindness, yet I was shaken from it only by a series of accidents.[8]

One such "accident" was his address to the annual Modern Language Association (MLA) meeting in December 1966 on "The Irish Writer," in which he spoke movingly of his sense of a mutilated past and of his translations as "an offering to the past from which I feel separated."[9] A few years later, in a Radio Eireann Thomas Davis Lecture in August 1971, he focused upon "the 'divided mind' of the modern Irish poet."[10] What seemed previously to be a handicap now becomes transformed; the division, discontinuity, and mutilation from which the Irish literary tradition has suffered denote in turn the predicament of the quintessentially modern writer:

> [E]very writer in the modern world, since he can't be in all the literary traditions at once, is the inheritor of a gapped, discontinuous, polyglot tradition. But any tradition will do: if one function of tradition is to link us with the significant past, this is done as well by a broken tradition as by a whole one—however painful, humanly speaking, it may be. What matters for poetry . . . is the quality of the response.[11]

Kinsella offers what Richard Kearney has called "a hermeneutics of discontinuity" as distinguished from "a hermeneutics of continuity" offered by Vivian Mercier and Frank O'Connor.[12] Continuity, Kinsella argues, in itself has no great value, nor is discontinuity necessarily calamitous: "[T]here is nothing ruinous for poetry in all this."[13] Rather, what is important above all is the self and its ordeal. According to Kinsella, "For any writer there is also the relationship with other literatures, with the present, with the 'human predicament,'

8. Kinsella, "Another Country . . . ," 177.

9. Kinsella, "The Irish Writer," in *Davis, Mangan, Ferguson?*, 60.

10. Kinsella, "The Divided Mind," 208–18.

11. Ibid., 216–17.

12. Kearney, ed., "Introduction" to *The Irish Mind: Exploring Intellectual Traditions* (Dublin: Wolfhound Press, 1985), 34. Kearney notes that "[t]he archetypes of mythic memory are invoked [by Kinsella] to cope with nausea, not nostalgia," and that "[h]is use of the mythological past is one of homelessness and dispossession"; see his "Poetry and Myth: Kinsella, Montague, Kennelly," in *Myth, History, and Literary Tradition* (Dundalk: Dundalk Arts Publications, 1989), 20.

13. This and subsequent quotations are from Kinsella, "The Divided Mind," 208–18.

with the self. This last may be the most important of all, for certain gaps in ourselves can swallow up all the potentiality in the world." While he may mourn the "broken" nature of the Irish tradition, Kinsella nevertheless stresses the "link . . . with the significant past" and "what matters for poetry." At no time has he practiced or advocated provincialism or the second rate: "the quality of the response" is more important than any break between Gaelic Irish and English Irish while, significantly, his judgment upon nineteenth-century Irish poetry in English is more severe ("dullness" and "waste") than that of Yeats. Instead, his advice to the Irish writer hinges upon cultivating discrimination but, equally distinctively, upon "a willingness and determination to investigate one's self and one's world, to make relentless comparisons, and to remain open at all costs to the teaching that life inflicts upon us all." Kinsella's next book of poems, *Notes from the Land of the Dead*, shows him following his own advice and embarking on his most accomplished phase to date. The judgment of one reviewer—"Ireland's best living poet has brooded himself to pieces"[14]—seems in retrospect remarkably inappropriate.

I

Notes from the Land of the Dead appeared in three different versions, first in the Cuala Press limited edition in March 1972, followed by the U.S. edition by Knopf in 1973, and finally under the title of *New Poems* by Dolmen Press in the same year. Apart from several minor variants in individual poems, the most significant differences concern the inclusion of a long "Invocation" only in the Cuala edition—the poem has never been reprinted; the inclusion in the Knopf edition of nine "Other Poems" together with the first two Peppercanister pamphlets, *Butcher's Dozen* and *A Selected Life*; and the inclusion in *New Poems* of all the Knopf poems except *Butcher's Dozen*. The Peppercanisters point, in familiar Kinsella fashion, to the next stage in his writing, the poems that form the two substantial collections of the 1970s, *One* and *Fifteen Dead* (both 1979). My focus, then, will be upon those poems grouped under the volume's title and upon the "Other Poems."

Linking *Notes from the Land of the Dead* with its immediate ancestor, *Nightwalker*, is the epigraph taken from the concluding lines of

14. Calvin Bedient, quoted in Johnston, *Irish Poetry after Joyce*, 104.

"Phoenix Park." The reader is thus made aware of a continuous, evolving process, tracing the self's emergence into fullness but also establishing a coherent unity within Kinsella's total oeuvre. Implicit in the epigraph and recurrent in his later poetry is the image of the coil or spiral, an image that captures the dialectical antitheses of opposites, the energy or field of force that drives those opposites, and the torsion that keeps them irrevocably married to each other, but also, in its labyrinthine pattern, the tracing of a path or way through. The image indicates continuity and repetition, and, when taking the form of a serpent, suggests less evil than transformation, the shedding of skins. The way through entails the self's regeneration. The imagery is archetypal, primordial, Jungian, whether it is found in early Celtic decoration or in the evolutionary theories of Teilhard de Chardin.[15] And, not coincidentally, Kinsella employs such coils and spirals with increasing regularity as he incorporates material from early Irish literature. Such imagery serves in part also to explain parallel features of his practice in the later work: for example, to leave poems open—in some cases, quite literally so, with no final punctuation—and so allow further development; but, similarly, to include lines from previous poems, to quote from himself and so create resonances within his work. He told one interviewer that he saw "Tear" as a poem that "doesn't close and still has the potential for development," and other poems being echoed in later ones, a process of "gathering up" yet still moving forward.[16] Indeed, Kinsella's increasingly frequent habit of quoting from himself constitutes part of the evolution he sees both in his own work and in the world itself. For his is "Work in Progress," to return to Seamus Deane's description,[17] for which the most appropriate parallel must be Joyce. Moreover, writing on another occasion of both Joyce and Beckett, Deane distinguishes the two writers thus:

15. Pierre Teilhard de Chardin wrote of the coiling movement of the evolutionary process: "[W]e find the Universe from top to bottom brought within a single, immense coiling movement generating nuclei, atoms, molecules, cells and metazoa"; see his "Turmoil or Genesis?" (1948), in *The Future of Man*, trans. Norman Denny (London: Collins, 1964), 217.

16. *Viewpoints*, ed. Haffenden, 105.

17. Deane, "The Music of Kinsella's Poetry," 34, 38. Cf. Maurice Harmon, reviewing *Out of Ireland* and *St. Catherine's Clock* (in "Nutrient Waters," *Poetry Ireland Review* 21 [Spring 1988]: 21): "These poems are glosses on the larger manuscript of Kinsella's reinvigorating recovery of things past."

> Where Joyce's writing is heavy with the weight of history, Beckett's is weightless. But both of them include in their works the history of their own texts. Both consciously rewrote their texts in relation to earlier ones. Both insisted on the right to pillage and repeat earlier writings. Translation [of one's own work] is only the most pronounced form of this kind of repetition.[18]

Kinsella aligns himself more particularly with Joyce than with Beckett, sharing "the weight of history" and exercising his powers of translation upon earlier Irish ancestors rather than upon his own work. However, his pillaging of his previous work, like his translating, serves to focus attention upon continuity and repetition, while at the same time permitting redefinition and repossession. Not coincidentally, his collection of translations *An Duanaire* is subtitled *Poems of the Dispossessed:* the dispossession is of language and culture as well as of land, and therefore ultimately of that most precious possession, identity. Kinsella's device of quoting from previous poems, like his translations, thus becomes an act of repossession, a way by which history is reshaped and meaning gained. Repossession goes beyond reclamation of property: the poet strives for coherence and unity within and without, while at the same time being fully conscious of the powerful forces pulling toward incoherence and disunity. The shaping spirit of his imagination thus takes up the challenge of the world's disorder. He is driven on, like any Beckett protagonist, by the compulsive nature of his search, despite knowing, again like Beckett's figures, that he is likely to fail. At the same time he shares Joyce's faith in the process of gestation, believing that, however unknowable and incoherent life may be, there remains the implicit meaning and coherence to which the embryonic self is committed in its struggle to develop. In the last resort, however, Kinsella's teleology is more Darwinian than Christian, and any purpose behind the process remains enigmatic.

The epigraph to *Notes from the Land of the Dead* undergoes subtle but significant change in its transfer from *Nightwalker*. The lines' italicization signifies their new status as epigraph, and the lines now remain open. Punctuating only with a comma, Kinsella signals through nonclosure that the poems that follow are a direct product of

18. Deane, *Celtic Revivals*, 131. Richard Kearney notes that "the entire Beckettian corpus constitutes a cross-textual play of traces where each text refers to a predecessor"; see his "Beckett: The End of the Story?," in *Transitions: Narratives in Modern Irish Culture* (Manchester: Manchester University Press, 1988), 79.

the process captured in the epigraph; that the process is essentially of evolution of self as tissue, coiling like the archetypal snake, circling like the ancient faces; and that, as both snake and circling movement indicate, the process depends upon the omphalos and involves eternal return. Likewise, Kinsella creates the sense of an extended narrative, in which individual poems form part of a sequence, the meaning of which is being gradually revealed. It may be that such gradual revelation adds to the drama being enacted, but the procedure also embodies the very nature of experience itself. Meaning is attained through accumulation, synthesis rather than analysis, and the sequence, like the coil imagery, proves eminently suitable. Whatever strength his previous work possessed, Kinsella emerges in *Notes* and subsequent volumes as a major Irish poet of international stature, creating a sustained body of writing unsurpassed in accomplishment, seriousness, and scope since the death of Yeats. Furthermore, whatever previous handicap Yeats's shadow might have represented has been finally overcome, not the least with the help of Joyce whose HCE is once more acknowledged in the prefatory poem's opening line, "*h*esitate, *c*ease to *e*xist, glitter again" (my emphases).

The main body of poems constituting *Notes* is structured around three sections, "an egg of being," "a single drop," and "nightnothing." The narrative of the prefatory poem, "hesitate, cease to exist, glitter again," provides the focus and direction as well as the imagery with which the volume is concerned. The focus is upon the self, the direction is downward and inward, the imagery is of enclosure (room, pot, cauldron), of instruments (key), of origins (egg and zero), and of journeys into darkness. The driving force of appetite increasingly takes the form of an infernal digestion, a fearful ravenous hunger at work within a cosmic soup with biological and psychological implications. The scope, however, extends to embrace both the creation of a self and the self's creativity, with self and artistic act coming together so that the poems that follow bear upon their mysterious conjunction. The "*delicate distinct tissue begins to form*": it is a process in itself dialectical as the opening lines indicate, continuing the epigraph's syntax, to

> hesitate, cease to exist, glitter again,
> dither in and out of a mother liquid
> on the turn, welling up from God knows what hole.
>
> (*NLD* 3)

The deliberately flippant phrasing ("dither," "mother liquid," "on the turn," and "God knows what") is a familiar Kinsella ploy to undercut potential pretentiousness. Likewise, the protagonist recollects his original "disarray," a formlessness matched by other lacks—"How artless, / how loveless I was then!"—using a mocking, ironic tone and self-scrutiny reminiscent of W. H. Auden.[19] Kinsella may have learned from both Auden and Joyce how mundane details might acquire symbolic significance, but both the myth and symbols that follow have their origins as archetypes. Moreover, the techniques are recognizably Kinsellan: the use of broken syntax—

> The key, though I hardly knew it,
> already in my fist.
> Falling. Mind darkening.
> Toward a ring of mouths.
> Flushed
> Time, distance,
> meaning nothing.
> No matter.
>
> (4)

—or the distinctive context as the self emerges in a dark, fetid, but ultimately positive landscape:

> So sunless.
> That sour coolness . . . So far from the world and earth . . .
> No bliss, no pain; dullness after pain.
> A cistern-hiss . . . A thick tunnel stench
> rose to meet me. Frightful. Dark nutrient waves.
> And I knew no more.
>
> (4)

The unlikely image "nutrient" works admirably to suggest a process involving embryo and fertility; it is as if we were at the level of genetic forces or spermatozoa on their journey to the womb. The "wavery albumen bodies / each burdened with an eye," "our red protein eyes" —once more a significant image—follow the shaping of an egg, the creation of a self. The journey the protagonist has undertaken is to the very roots of life itself, with the mental and the physical reinforc-

19. Cf. W. H. Auden, "Letter to a Wound," *The Orators*, in *The English Auden: Poems, Essays, and Dramatic Writings*, 1927–1939, ed. Edward Mendelson (London: Faber and Faber, 1977), 71–73.

ing one another, and given meaning by way of archetypal imagery, of journey, cauldron, and prize. Exploration of the self thus entails tunneling underground, like some early passage-grave builder, or descending into an abyss, a traditional image found in a Kinsella exemplar at this time, Teilhard de Chardin:

> I took the lamp and, leaving the zone of everyday occupations and relationships where everything seems clear, I went down into my inmost self, to the deep abyss whence I feel dimly that my power of action emanates. But as I moved further and further from the conventional certainties by which social life is superficially illuminated, I became aware that I was losing contact with myself. At each step of the descent a new person was disclosed within me of whose name I was no longer sure, and who no longer obeyed me. And when I had to stop my exploration because the path faded from beneath my steps, I found a bottomless abyss at my feet, and out of it came—arising I know not from where—the current which I dare call my life.[20]

While the direction, the self-scrutiny, and the imagery are Dantean in turn, Kinsella's distinction lies in part in taking such traditional imagery and giving it contemporary application, for example, with the "stale abyss" (*NLD* 15) of his grandmother or musky smells in dingy back rooms, with family history and Dublin streets and subterranean streams. His myth, in effect, has taken on the shape and archetypal details of what Joseph Campbell, using Joyce's term, called the "monomyth."[21] The "prize" is the "egg of being" as it is shaped into existence through the experiences described in that section's six poems.

Kinsella's sequence thus begins to pursue an overall "plot," with origins both in the poet's childhood experiences and in archetypal, particularly Irish, myth. The "plot" traces the evolution of the creative self or poetic consciousness within a context that is at the same time personal and national, contemporary and primordial. The imagery of uroboric snake and "triple darkness," strengthened by subsequent imagery of woman, shell, egg, key, and pomegranate, all point to the more infernal aspect of the archetypal Great Mother Goddess, known

20. Quoted in Émile Rideau, *Teilhard de Chardin: A Guide to His Thought*, trans. René Hague (London: Collins, 1967), 109–10.

21. Joseph Campbell, *The Hero with a Thousand Faces* (1949; New York: World, 1969), 30n35. Cf. *FW* 581:24.

as the Terrible Mother and taking the form of Hecate.[22] Presiding over the underworld, Hecate merges also with the figure of Proserpina and with the muse, thus accounting for all art, creativity, and fertility, and maintaining the world in constant flux and process, of creation, destruction, and rebirth. While infernal and related to witchcraft, Hecate is neither diabolic nor evil. Rather, her presence indicates the extent to which the creative self has its origins in and is sustained by contact with the underworld/unconscious. Kinsella's preoccupation with these myths thus expresses his concern with origins, with ancestry and inheritance, and with the evolution of the creative self. As for Teilhard de Chardin, that preoccupation entails a willingness to confront the abyss of the self; to cross the hinterland between light and darkness, order and disorder, consciousness and unconsciousness; and to reach down to know the matrix, the very life force of existence. The rape of Proserpina and her subsequent life for part of the year in the underworld is thus only one classical expression of the self's experiencing that abyss. However, more significantly and more positively, Proserpina (with Demeter, her mother, and Hecate) completes the triad of goddesses who together constitute the Great Mother.

The Proserpina myth is more directly referred to in "Invocation."[23] The protagonist wakes "in a moist / wood, a narrow place," in a "night sweat" and "dragged rude upright," imagery explicitly sexual, as are the seductive voice calling "*Come*" and the protagonist's penetration into the dark wood. The "bright being," however, is both classical and Irish, Proserpina and the *aisling* sky-woman/muse. Led along archetypal paths through a familiar wood to equally archetypal springs and his "seventh heaven," the poet-protagonist paints a deliberately deflationary self-portrait—"I throw my hands / up in wonder, and break into / a modest run across the dew . . ."—and even engages in a pun: "There is something that is forever / taking a little of the spring / out of a person's step." Proserpina's rape did indeed bring winter to the world, but it also made possible the advent of spring. Thus a

22. For Hecate, uroboros, and related imagery, see Jung, *Symbols of Transformation*, 369–71; also see Neumann, *The Great Mother*, 169–70, 275, and *The Origins and History of Consciousness*, trans. R. F. C. Hull, Bollingen Series, vol. 42 (Princeton, N.J.: Princeton University Press, 1954), 10ff, 83, 162.

23. A version of the poem was completed by 12 November 1967, when it formed part of Kinsella's Peacock Theatre, Dublin, poetry reading and was described in a program note as "a new poem" (Freyer Collection, Trinity College, Dublin).

descent into the underworld initiated the revolution of the seasons. A similar progress is set in motion as the initial "coil of light is torn / tenderly out of its humblest recess," a progress in which the poet traces the creation of a self, with tissue, cells, and anatomized parts fusing in a version of the Creation story:

> Certain fierce lights appear in the depths,
> ascending like snow. Flakes of fiery tissue
> burn on the surface: living particles—
> cells: eyes: tongues—drifting out
> in a cloud toward either bank, to meet
> the living blossoms clustering down in answer
> to the current
>   —cells of ruby blood, jewels
> to kiss and melt; crystal eyes
> to fasten against, fluttering; pink tongues
> to cling lingering among—
>   then loosen,
> gold-plashy and smiling, dew-bedabbled
> and refreshed, sinking dove-pale
> and bewildered with blood back under the depths,
> through the clouds that rise swirling to replace them,
> mingling their paths . . .
>
> (*NLD Cuala* 13–14)

Such creation is made possible through the powers of the regenerative water, which is suitably dialectical and contrary—"youth-dew, / toil-sweat, Christ-blood, death-sweat"—and involves the self's descent into the interior. This descent is analogous to the river's subterranean passage in Coleridge's "Kubla Khan": "Farther than the eye can follow / the river runs. / Into the interior, beyond telling, / it vanishes." As we have seen, the process likewise involves love and sexual appetite, an analogy Kinsella has pursued previously in "Phoenix Park" and earlier poems. And in characteristic fashion love goes hand in hand with "purgatorial whispers," "suffering," a "dying in your arms," "a great determination / . . . and pity, / and contrition" before the poet-self is led to swear allegiance: "*Yes*! / *Yes*! *Tomorrow: you'll see!*" The commitment is to the muse and the creation of poetry but, in Kinsella's own description, "is actually a kind of put-off, and not much of a guarantee."[24] The poem remains indeed an "invocation."

24. Letter to Brian John, 1 February 1986.

The volume's subsequent poems substantiate the poet's commitment, telling of crucial experiences drawn from his childhood when personal, archetypal, and ancestral lives merge to form a numinous whole.

"The psyche," Jung tells us,[25] "is not of today; its ancestry goes back many millions of years," while the individuation process bringing fulfillment and wholeness of self involves "integrating the unconscious, in bringing together 'conscious' and 'unconscious.' " Moreover, "the unconscious corresponds to the mythic land of the dead, the land of the ancestors."[26] Kinsella's material is the archetypal, whether Jungian or Irish in origin, and the parallel with Ted Hughes, which Edna Longley has suggested, seems inappropriate: "The sequence reads like an attempt to outcrow *Crow*."[27] Certainly Kinsella's myth is enacted in an underworld in which primordial figures and forces appear dark, sometimes ferocious, often threatening or at least unsettling, and, while on occasion it parallels the Creation story, the myth is not offered in the manner of *Crow* as a black Bible. Rather, Kinsella takes us back, by way of his storytelling, to the formation of the self, more particularly of his self, in certain numinous experiences and involving, above all, a latter-day Hecate in the fearful figure of his own grandmother. The archetype of the Triple or Great Mother, of whom Hecate is only one form, is primordial and universal, but also distinctively Irish:[28] the parallels in early Irish mythology and history are manifold, whether in the form of the three goddesses representing Ireland, Ériu, Banba, and Fotla, greeting the Sons of Mil; the triple figure of Brigid; the three Machas; or the triune fearful war goddess, the Morrígna. Robert Graves's White Goddess assumes similarly triplicate shape and, as his "historical grammar of poetic myth" reveals, she is also the muse. In her more threatening and infernal form she is Hecate, the dominant figure in the opening section of *Notes*.

In "Hen Woman" she presides over the mystery of the creation of an egg. The experience in itself is common enough, and is drawn

25. Jung, *Symbols of Transformation*, xxiv, 301.

26. Jung, *Memories, Dreams, Reflections*, 191.

27. Longley, "Spinning through the Void," 1446.

28. Rees and Rees, *Celtic Heritage*, 30–36; Anne Ross, *Pagan Celtic Britain: Studies in Iconography and Tradition* (London: Routledge and Kegan Paul/New York: Columbia University Press, 1967), 73–78, 204–33; Neumann, *The Great Mother*, 228–29.

here from personal childhood recollection. An earlier, looser, and longer version appeared in the *Irish Press.*[29] Although the poem in its essentials is evident in that earlier version, the specific identification of Mrs Delaney as the hen woman; the straightforward, less elliptical narrative; and the excessively personal details—all are eventually dispensed with in order to focus upon the emblematic nature of the act. The original opening eighteen lines, finally reduced to ten in *Notes*, will suffice to illustrate the significance of Kinsella's revision. They also indicate the extent to which revision, even at this relatively late stage in his career, was needed.

> One day of midsummer,
>   when I was ten years old,
> the noon stillness seemed heavier
>   than I had ever known it.
> The silent heat
>   smelled of dryness and coming thunder.
> Mrs Delaney's cottage door was open
>   like a black cave-mouth
> in a whitewashed wall so bright
>   the eyes narrowed.
> In the middle of the yard
>   near the shore a hen scratched
> and picked at the cement.
>   The brooding silence seemed to say "Hush!"
> Inside, a clock murmured "Gong . . ."
>   (To this day that sound will bring it back to me:
> the hot cement around the iron grating,
>   the stale cool breath from the underworld.)
>
> (*New Irish Writing* 1, 77)

Apart from occasional phrases in these eighteen lines, only two lines (ll. 9 and 15 above) in their entirety are retained in the final version.

As a clock strikes and the egg appears in the sphincter, so "time stood still," as chicken, woman, and boy all stand with mouths agape. The details neatly parallel each other: the egg is also "an egg of being," the very life process itself, but at the same time it is the poet's self initiated into mystery; its "torsion"—a distinctive and recurrent late

29. The *Irish Press* (1968) version was collected in *New Irish Writing: An Anthology from "The Irish Press" Series*, ed. David Marcus (Dublin: Dolmen Press, 1970), 77–80.

Kinsella term—is part of the dialectical tension of opposites, the source of energies and generation; the appetite serves in turn as a similarly creative–destructive and therefore dialectical force, the driving force toward life and consciousness, structure but also consumption, whether animal or creative hunger. Such parallels enable the poet to comment quite matter of factly upon the self's search for "structure" (another form of "landing place") in which it may wake:

> I feed upon it still, as you see;
> there is no end to that which,
> not understood, may yet be noted
> and hoarded in the imagination,
> in the yolk of one's being, so to speak,
> there to undergo its (quite animal) growth,
> dividing blindly,
> twitching, packed with will,
> searching in its own tissue
> for the structure
> in which it may wake.
>
> (*NLD* 11)

Similarly crucial is another experience with a beetle struggling to carry a ball of dung—another circle or whole, another shaping and enduring—for in this way the child discovers the scarab,[30] the ancient Egyptian symbol for renewal and rebirth. Apparently ordinary experience is thus made extraordinarily seminal; the child is initiated into the mystery of creation and the marriage of opposites essential to that mystery. The dropped egg and the hen woman's reaction likewise take on symbolic meaning. The egg is lost in a grating,[31] that parallels the grill through which the protagonist in the prefatory poem (*NLD* 5) must travel with his prize; the woman's cry of resignation—"It's all the one. / There's plenty more where that came from!"—may point in turn to the hen's fertility, but the poet's punning comment, "*Hen to pan*!" also expresses the inclusive pan-vision to which the child has been introduced. The Greek for "one in all," "*Hen tō pan*" is the ancient alchemical formula, as Kinsella would have learned from

30. Cf. *New Larousse Encyclopedia of Mythology*, introduction by Robert Graves (London: Prometheus Press, 1973), 10, 13, 15; also see Jung, *Memories, Dreams, Reflections*, 179.

31. "Shore" (ll. 3, 50) is a variant on "sewer" *(OED)* for which there is a "grating" (l. 74).

Jung: "Its symbol is the uroboros, the tail-eating serpent."[32] Like all good myths, Kinsella's is gaining in complexity and scope, reaching out in time and space, as here in "Hen Woman," to take on universal significance.

The subsequent poems follow a similar path. In "A Hand of Solo" the local experience is of Kinsella's grandparents, an uncle, and a friend playing cards. However, as the poem's title suggests, the experience contributes to the self's evolution into a "solo" or "one," just as the scene in the Dublin shop kept by the grandmother takes on mythological significance through the portrayal of the old woman as a Hecate figure, presiding over her underworld. When the young child approaches her, she calls out ominously to him:[33]

> "Shut the kitchen door, child of grace.
> Come here to me.
> Come here to your old grandmother."
>
> Strings of jet beads wreathed her neck
> and hissed on the black taffeta
> and crept on my hair.
>
> ". . . You'd think I had three heads!"
> My eyes were squeezed shut against the key
> in the pocket of her apron. Her stale abyss . . .
>
> (14–15)

From her high stool in the shop, she offers the boy a pomegranate which, with the reference to "three heads," beads hissing like a Medusa head of snakes, the key, and sense of abyss or underworld, completes the imagery identifying her as Hecate. The child's choice of fruit, as Kinsella has insisted,[34] is based on fact, but he admits to the convenience of the symbolism. The scene is preceded by a delicately lyrical section in which the poet appeals for the muse's aid: "Woman throat song / help my head / back to you sweet." The blatantly sexual conclusion to the poem—"I drove my tongue among them"—as the child ravages the fruit, should thus be seen as evidencing Kinsella's

32. Jung, *Psyche and Symbol*, 178–79. Kinsella acknowledged the Greek source in his Project Arts Theatre poetry reading, Dublin, 26 March 1982.

33. A similar initiation is offered by the mother to her grown-up son in "Dura Mater" (*FCC* 23), a poem that also echoes "Tear" (*NLD* 20–23) in the son's withheld kiss given only after the mother's death.

34. *Viewpoints*, ed. Haffenden, 108–9.

recurrent theme of appetite, the child's participation in a process as old as the rape of Proserpina, and his throat experiencing a bloody communion in its necessary initiation into those mysteries that will enable it to sing of them at some later stage.

In "The High Road" the departing boy is offered a mandoline-shaped candy by his grandmother and, like the dropped egg or pomegranate, the experience continues to reverberate, this time as a profound sense of loss. Despite the golden balls of dung dropped by Padno Carty's carthorse (reminiscent of the scarab earlier) and Mrs. Fullerton's sqawking parrot (the local equivalent of Hecate's owl), the Robbers' Den[35] into which the boy finally ventures proves disappointingly mundane and no archetypal matrix or womb of rebirth. Taking "the high road" must be replaced by descending into the abyss, and the child is instinctively "pulled downward by a queer feeling." The mandoline candy is a poor substitute for Proserpina's pomegranate that had brought him such rich initiation. Instead, only in the subsequent poems "Ancestor" (19) and "Tear" (20–23) is the boy brought, through his experiences of his grandmother, closer to the abyss, to taste—a characteristic Kinsella means to experience and wisdom—the suffering in the old woman's dying and in his own father's tears years before over the death of an infant daughter.

The grandmother epitomizes some dark temptation, as she lies in bed, her hair spread out, Medusa-like, her body drying into "mud" (21), but also some ancestral wisdom, giving voice to love and understanding and passing them on to the young boy. Such communication is effected by way of mouth, appetite, and heart's consumption. It may be that the conjunction of heart and mouth is characteristic of Kinsella—"How I tasted it now—/ her heart beating in my mouth!" (22)—but its ancestry surely lies with Yeats ("Two Songs from a Play")[36] and, further back, with Dante, the Christian symbolism of communion, and pagan ritual sacrifice. As one critic describes the grandmother figure, "She has always known what he does not want to know. Her loosened hair symbolizes openness to the dark unconscious, the secrets of the greedy emotions, not accountable to reason,

35. Austin Clarke referred to "the Robbers' Cave / Beyond Kilmainham, above the coach-road," in *Mnemosyne Lay in Dust*, IX (1966), *Poems 1955–1966*, ed. Miller, 340.

36. See Brian John, " 'To Hunger Fiercely after Truth': Daimonic Man and Yeats's Insatiable Appetite," *Eire-Ireland* 11 (Spring 1974): 90–103.

at once terrifying and the source of life."[37] Certainly in "Ancestor" the grandmother is given a profile "dark like a hunting bird's," a "black heart," and a "smell, musky and queer," all suggesting a primeval, infernal quality, as derived from the Terrible Mother. At the same time we must remember that Hecate or the Terrible Mother is only one aspect of the Great Mother, who is also the muse, and that birds are traditionally a means of divination, as illustrated by the ancient Irish poet-priest-shaman who wore a cloak of feathers. The Suibhne myth bears closely upon this association of bird, flight, and the imagination.[38] Similar imagery might again be found in Yeats—in the famous discipline expressed in "Two Songs from a Play"—but once more the reader is made aware of Kinsella's distinctive expression. Not Yeats but Joyce is whom the reader is most reminded of, not only through the description of the child's relationship with the old woman but through the everyday rhythms and language of the poem, at far remove from Yeats's hieratic rhetoric:

> How I tasted it now—
> her heart beating in my mouth!
>
> She drew an uncertain breath
> and pushed at the clothes
> and shuddered tiredly.
> I broke free
>
> and left the room
> promising myself
> when she was really dead
> I would really kiss.
>
> (22)

II

In the second section of *Notes* two poems in particular, "Nuchal" and "Survivor," point in the direction Kinsella will take in his next volume, *One*, toward marrying his experience of the abyss, the land of the dead, or the unconscious with Irish myth. "Nuchal,"

37. Broder, "Images of the Feminine," 95.

38. Cf. Brian John, "Contemporary Irish Poetry and the Matter of Ireland—Thomas Kinsella, John Montague, and Seamus Heaney," in *Medieval and Modern Ireland*, ed. Richard Wall (Gerrards Cross, U.K.: Colin Smythe, 1988), 52–57.

for example, is named in *Lebor Gabála Érenn* (LGE)[39] as the source of the four rivers of Eden. Like Diana, the moon goddess in the next poem, "Endymion," the woman figure here is in the tradition of the Great Mother archetype, a maternal matrix, source of creation and creativity. The four rivers of Paradise flow from the woman's fingers trailing in the water and, appropriately, the poem finishes in midsentence, with the incomplete syntax and lack of closure reflecting the continuing flux of being. The woman with trailing fingers is Kinsella's own invention, but *LGE* (paragraphs 28–29 and Poem VI) certainly provided him with the name "Nuchal," the four rivers, the four cardinal points, even the imagery of bdellium, onyx, pearl, and gold (though not amethyst).

"Survivor" (30–33) relies even more upon *LGE* (section 3), for it reenacts the escape of Fintan from the sexually predatory expedition of Cessair, female leader of the first and predominantly female invasion of Ireland before the Flood. The expedition consisted of three males and fifty females, but, with the deaths of two men, Fintan was left to satisfy the sexual appetite of the whole contingent. He escaped both the women and the Flood by hiding in a cave and, while assuming different shapes (salmon, eagle, hawk), witnessed the subsequent invasions down to the coming of the Sons of Mil.[40] Kinsella's Fintan, whose experiences he takes over as emblematic of his own exploration of the land of the dead, survives through suffering endurance, nourished by rock, protected by the cave. There is considerable irony in his having run away from a sexual death in the wombs of Cessair and her women, to survive through his spiritual death in the womblike cave. The speaker remembers their flight from Paradise—"we were all thieves" (*NLD* 31)—and their search for a "fair beginning," "an entire new world" in the newly discovered island. For, according to the *LGE* account, Cessair's expedition to Ireland proved necessary because Noe (Noah) refused them admittance to his ark ("this ship is no ship of robbers and no den of thieves," paragraph 179). When the expedition members fall sick and die, however, Ireland becomes no alternative paradise but "A land of the dead." Instead of the beautiful

39. *Lebor Gabála Érenn: The Book of the Taking of Ireland*, 5 vols., ed. and trans. R. A. Stewart Macalister (Dublin: Irish Texts Society, 1938–56), vol. 1, ch. 2, para. 28, and Poem VI; hereafter abbreviated as *LGE*, followed by volume and paragraph number. The work is usually translated as *The Book of Invasions*, the title used here.

40. For Cessair's invasion, see *LGE*, vol. 2, sec. 3; also see Rees and Rees, *Celtic Heritage*, 28.

goddess figure of "Nuchal," Fintan experiences an infernal *cailleach* (old woman or hag) in familiar Kinsella squatting position, with her mouth distorted into a "muzzle," her vision only of nothingness. "The Hag: squatting on the water, / her muzzle staring up at nothing" (32). The Great Mother has become the Terrible Mother, creation transformed into destruction, and the poem concludes with Fintan striving to remember and explain, falling into a fearful broken staccato, and finally seeking the relief of death:

> There is nothing here for sustenance.
>   Unbroken sleep were best.
> Hairs. Claws. Grey.
>   Naked. Wretch. Wither.
>
> (33)

As we have seen previously, however, such withering includes a pun upon the adverb "whither," for Fintan's future direction will depend upon his capacity to achieve spiritual negation. Another version of the same myth of Fintan appears in John Montague's *Mount Eagle* (1988), under the same title, "Survivor." However, while Kinsella drives his Fintan to an elemental, dislocated state, as intense and nihilistic as any Beckettian survivor, Montague concentrates more optimistically upon Fintan's eventual transformation into a salmon by way of which he survives the Flood and achieves regeneration. Kinsella's poem provides a free-flowing narrative with unrhymed lines of varying stresses; Montague's is a sonnet. Such differences, however, illustrate less the superiority of one version over another—each is an impressive poem in its own right—than the distinctive characteristics of the two poets and their ways of looking at the world.

None of the remaining poems in "a single drop" draws so explicitly upon Irish sources. Nevertheless, even in "Endymion" (29), where Kinsella draws upon the classical myth of Diana and Endymion, the transformation from "nothing" to the "single drop" is effected through an *aisling* illumination (the light "blazed") and through the moon goddess's role as muse-Hecate, associated with her traditional owl ("—great raw wings, curled—a huge owlet-stare—/ as a single drop echoed in the depths"). In "At the Crossroads" Kinsella employs the archetypal and also Irish image of crossroads to symbolize a dialectical synthesis. As we have seen, the ford in "A Country Walk" (*D* 45–49) possessed such significance, granting the poet insight into his ancestral past and into the creative–destructive nature of existence. "At the

Crossroads" (*NLD* 34–35) offers a similar illumination under a moonlit sky, whether in the dog's mutilated body, the protagonist's ghostly experiences, or the appetite he is made aware of through imagery of mouth, stomach, and torn meat. The moon too is one such mouth, appearing before him like the prostitute in "Phoenix Park" or the grandmother in "Tear," tempting, offering herself as muse to her poet. The same destructive hunger drives the "white ghost" of an owl, one more appearance of the muse in her Hecate form and representing the choice the self must confront between appetite and reason, a crossroads where the unconscious and intellection interact:

> A white ghost flickered into being
> and disappeared near the tree tops.
> An owl in silent scrutiny
> with blackness in her heart. She
> who succeeds from afar . . .
>   The choice—
> the drop with deadened wing-beats; some creature
> torn and swallowed; her brain, afterward,
> staring among the rafters in the dark
> until hunger returns.
>
> (35)

In "nightnothing," the final section of *Notes*, located more explicitly in Dublin, the poet returns to his Irish sources. "All Is Emptiness, and I Must Spin" recollects fragments of experiences known to the dislocated self, existing in "vacancy," the darkness of nothing that must be experienced if growth is to be achieved. While Kinsella's account appears wholly divorced from the Matter of Ireland, his reader is encouraged through the echo of Amergin's *rosc* to see the inheritance passed on to the contemporary poet: "I have been in places . . ." (41). Like Amergin, Kinsella's protagonist must descend into nothing, journeying through the land of the dead, knowing and suffering all as an Irish Tiresias. The result is the skillful interweaving of voices and experiences in "Ely Place," all pointing to appetite and savage tongues; the contrast in "Touching the River" between the "stopped brown water" experienced by the nude in the painting and the flux known to the protagonist's "unstopped / flesh and senses" (45); the Christmas spent amid the snow and cold in "The Liffey Hill"; and in "Good Night" the experience of "nightnothing" in one more Kinsella room, while confronting the darkness:

and the sounds of the house are all
flowing into one another and turning
in one soft-booming, slowly swallowing
vertige most soothing and pleasant
down this suddenly live
brinegullet
                    to a drowned pit
clasping the astonished spectre of
the psyche in its sweet wet.

(48)

"Vertige," like torsion and the appetitive "brinegullet," brings experience of antitheses and leads not to submergence of but to emergence of self. It may be "where monsters . . . / . . . feed us / and feed in us, and coil / and uncoil in our substance," just as the Camac articulates the same endless flux, "Camacamacamac. . . ." The river, which flows through Kinsella's childhood territory of Bow Lane, Kilmainham, and Inchicore, is in part subterranean and the elision of its name captures the uroboric process exactly. Yet the conclusion is indeed "a Good Night, smiling" (50). Kinsella, learning from Joyce, recognizes how readily the quotidian, especially that of Dublin and of his own experiences, takes on mythic dimensions. He has gone beyond the vision of a latter-day necropolis (*N* 58) and descended into a land of the dead, where childhood experiences and landscapes merge with ancestral figures and events out of Ireland's mythic past to enable him to bring back to the world the "notes" we can ill afford to do without.

III

The nine "Other Poems" vary in subject matter, length, and significance. The first, "The Route of the Táin" (53–54), illustrates Kinsella's narrative accomplishment as he describes fluently and vividly the manner in which he and his friends trace the route through the Cooley Peninsula, scene of the *Táin Bó Cuailnge*, and discover in the course of their journey that ancient saga and modern landscape correspond. Such correspondence indicates that continuity, in good Irish *dinnseanchas* (lore of places) tradition, is, albeit with difficulty, maintained: literature and life (or landscape) coincide, despite the broken nature of the Irish tradition, despite the need for translation. "We should have trusted our book," the protagonist insists as the features of the present landscape reveal the ancient route described in the *Táin*. More than that, however, the experience highlights the process itself by which insight is gained:

> the process, the whole tedious
> enabling ritual! Flux brought to fullness
> —saturated—the clouding over—dissatisfaction
> spreading slowly like an ache: something
> reduced shivering suddenly into meaning
> along new boundaries

Not coincidentally, then, the poem's conclusion describes the travelers journeying "toward these hills that seemed to grow / darker as we drove nearer," when their own mortality and finitude are highlighted and dismissed ("joking together in growing illness / or age or fat"). For the route taken by the *Táin*, and now traced by these latter-day participants, is also toward tragedy and death, the darkness to which all things are ultimately brought.

Other poems focus upon landscapes far removed from Ireland—"St Paul's Rocks: 16 February 1832," "Crab Orchard Sanctuary: Late October," and "Wyncote, Pennsylvania: A Gloss"—yet again point to the nature of life's process. The setting in the last two is explicitly the United States to which the poet had moved. The first is set in the South Atlantic and derives from Darwin's account in the *Voyage of the Beagle*. As Rita Kelly has shown,[41] Kinsella works closely with Darwin, in both details and in verbal echoes, although he typically diverges from the Victorian by placing the rocks in even greater isolation (Kinsella's are a thousand miles from land as opposed to Darwin's three hundred and fifty) and by exchanging its equatorial, tropical climate for an "eternal grey" (63) more fitting to his own vision. For regardless of its Darwinian source, Kinsella's poem is very much his own, evidencing appetite and elemental forces amid dung and squalor. Much the same vision is offered in "Crab Orchard Sanctuary" (69–70) for all its alternative heat, house, woodpeckers, and cardinals. Instead, the insect husks ("stiff little Fuseli devil bodies") and the "myriad / leather seed-cases [which] lie in wait / nourishing curled worms of white fat" catch his attention.

"Wyncote, Pennsylvania: A Gloss" (71) offers a beautiful mocking-

41. While showing convincingly the poet's use of Darwin's material, Kelly is surely wrong in attributing to Kinsella "an endemic disgust of life" and a "gnawing contempt"; see her "Darwin and Mr. Kinsella," *Belle* 1 (Autumn 1978): 64–69.

bird and colorful description but no less appetite and threat as the bird swallows a berry and a thunderstorm advances. Yet precisely that conjunction of beauty and threat, appetite both creative and destructive, casts upon the poet's papers a "luminous" quality. Nor is this an exclusive phenomenon; indeed, as the subtitle also indicates, the poem is a contemporary equivalent, despite its Pennsylvanian setting, of those glosses appearing in the medieval manuscripts of Irish monastic scribes.[42] Medieval scribe and contemporary poet share experiences —such an analogy Kinsella develops in a later volume, *Out of Ireland* (1987)—although instead of the medieval affirmation "God is good!" (*TNOBIV* 30), Kinsella emphasizes the numinous, known through appetite and suffering, and his renewed commitment to his art. At the same time he is capable of concluding with a pun: the care he takes will indeed be "painstaking," an epithet that ironically captures the connection between, on the one side, assiduity and accomplishment and, on the other, the experience of pain:

> A mocking-bird on a branch
> outside the window, where I write,
> gulps down a wet crimson berry,
> shakes off a few bright drops
> from his wing and is gone
> into a thundery sky.
>
> Another storm is coming.
> Under that copper light
> my papers seem luminous.
> And over them I will take
> ever more painstaking care.
> (*NLD* 71)

These poems are given firm concrete locations, yet "The Clearing" (62) reminds the reader of Kinsella's persistent attention to the self and its interior landscapes. This clearing, for example, is as much in the head as in an external world. Indeed, such distinction of internal–external Kinsella constantly breaks down. And, appropriately enough, what constitutes clarity of perception is the self's awareness of appetite, in both the internal and the external worlds: "The eyes grow sharper /

42. Cf. Dennis O'Driscoll, "Remembering the Past (Reply to John Hill)," *Crane Bag* 3 (1979): 90. Such medieval glosses Kinsella translated in *TNOBIV* 30.

—and the teeth!" The "troubled figure," moving about the frontier "between the fire and the gloom" and whose "brainworm will not sleep / squirming behind the eyes," is in fact both hunter and hunted, and "the great ease" experienced after a successful hunt is misleading and only temporary. For what the protagonist experiences in his "clearing" is what in the subsequent poem, "St Paul's Rocks," is described in the Darwinian term "symbiosis" (63), or in "Good Night" is known as monsters who "feed us / and feed in us, and coil / and uncoil in our substance . . ." (49). In the biological world the process is of Darwinian evolution; in Kinsella's psychic world, the gestation is of the self, as conscious and unconscious come together in necessary, if painful, contact, leading ultimately to the deliverance of full consciousness.

The most ambitious of these "Other Poems," however, is "Worker in Mirror, at His Bench" (55–59) the longest poem in the volume with the exception of the Peppercanister sequences which properly belong to the next volumes, *One* and *Fifteen Dead*. It is also among the most demanding, with abrupt transitions marking shifts between the worker, his external and internal voices, and his shop customers, and with a bare style in which syntax, pace, spacing, and tone all contribute to the poem's meaning. Commenting upon the charge of obscurity, Kinsella has described his poems as "constructs rather than statements, of themes operating together. And they assume that the act of reading is a dynamic one, the completion of an act of communication, not an inert listening to something sweet or interesting or even informative." His poems are meant "to embody a construct of significant elements."[43] "Worker in Mirror, at His Bench" functions in precisely such a manner to explore central Kinsella themes: the nature of the creative self and its operation in the artistic act.

The poem, consisting of three sections, first has the artist provide ironic titles for the work he is creating. Kinsella regularly applies such deflationary irony against himself, deflecting criticism of portentousness and excessive grimness. Here the title on which the worker settles deliberately invites criticism:[44]

43. Deane, "A Conversation," 88.

44. Such invitation is part of Kinsella's relationship with his reader, requiring the reader's active engagement, participation, and choice; see Deane, "A Conversation," 88.

Silent rapt surfaces
assemble glittering
among themselves.

A few more pieces.

What to call it . . .
                    Bright Assembly?
Foundations for a Tower?
Open Trap? Circular-Tending
Self-Reflecting Abstraction . . .

(55)

His medium (mirror) points to a recurrent Kinsella image and preoccupation, the self-reflection he satirizes here. But a past master may be another target of his satire: "Foundations for a Tower" is surely directed at W. B. Yeats.

The middle and longest section takes on a more dramatic character, for the action involves the intrusion of some customers upon the worker at his shop bench, their negative reactions, and the worker's responses. Given both the spoken and the unspoken responses of the artist, the reader is privy to his interior drama, to his resentment of the intruders ("the way they mess / with everything"), the dislikeable male customer, but also the artist's recognition of his own limitations. Moreover, such drama relates to Kinsella's practice of having the reader participate in and choose between positions in a search for understanding. In the course of explaining his work the artist articulates familiar Kinsella concerns:

No, it has no practical application.
I am simply trying to understand something
—states of peace nursed out of wreckage.
The peace of fullness, not emptiness.

(56)

As Kinsella told John Haffenden in 1979–1980,[45] he could no longer write a poem like "Nightwalker," "that sort of full-throated outcry"; rather than teaching people how to behave, he now saw that the artist's prime duty is to understand. While the trope, "states of peace nursed out of wreckage," has the same resonance as the famous

45. *Viewpoints*, ed. Haffenden, 106–7.

concluding line from "Downstream" ("Searching the darkness for a landing place"), in both cases Kinsella's emphasis has been lost, his focus obscured by the excessive attention readers have given to the "darkness" or "wreckage." The landing place is not just a safe harbor, a retreat from the painful search for understanding; the "peace nursed out of wreckage" does not entail suspension of the temporal flux, the suffering of the dialectic overcome in transcendence. It is, as the artist insists here, "The peace of fullness, not emptiness." Thus those attributing nihilism to Kinsella need to recognize what is implied here, that "fullness" and "emptiness" are both necessary poles in his dialectic, and that the self needs to undertake the awful descent into the land of the dead, into the unconscious, if fulfillment and "The peace of fullness" are to be achieved. The search for "the guardian structure" involves precisely the medium, mirror, in which the artist works, capable of revealing "random / persistent coherences." Chance is ever-present; the coherences are "random"; but at the same time the artist's function, as Yeats affirmed, is to bring choice and chance together, to shape chaos into structure. While the artist proceeds to deny his own affirmation—"We all are vile" and "Emptiness, / is that not peace?"—such denials are in part put-downs. By the first he intends more to rid himself of intrusive customers than to assert any Jansenism; by the second, he suggests a nihilism that is at once answered. The section thus ends with the artist commenting upon his own statements and pursuing an appropriately contrary path:

> Conceal, and permit . . .
> —pursuit at its most delicate,
> truth as tinkering,
> easing the particular of its litter,
> bending attention on the remaining depths
> as though questions had never been . . .
>
> (57)

As the worker bends over his creation, like many a Kinsella prowler in the night, his senses "reach out . . . / to the four corners of their own wilderness," in explicit movement through states of gold, silver, bronze, and finally iron. The first three are all "Forgotten" states in which the self has fallen from innocence into increasing pain and eventual evil. The last, not yet a forgotten state and evidenced in one more instance of fratricide, we are urged to "Forget!"

Dark as iron.
All the light hammered
into two blazing eyes;
all the darkness
into one wolf-muzzle.
Resist!
An unholy tongue laps, tastes
brothers' thick blood.
Forget!

(59)

Kinsella once summed up the poem in these terms: "The act of understanding initiated by the worker, as observer, when he looks into the construct he has made, ends in an understanding of what lies in wait for unreasonable hope. This realization 'dawns' on him."[46] The eyes blaze with illumination—a recurrent Kinsella image, as we have seen—in this instance an illumination revealing the darkness intrinsic to all things and captured in fratricidal appetite and the face transformed into "wolf-muzzle." But as the worker "straightens up, unseeing"—an action that corresponds to the vertical or upright imagery upon which Kinsella will increasingly depend—he recognizes the necessity for further descent, to practice "the stare inward / to the four corners of / what foul continuum." That the process is necessary and continuous is indicated by the poem's conclusion, which is open-ended, unpunctuated, and lacking even ellipses, where the poet suggests that the self must be receptive to further exploration:

blackness—all matter
in one light-devouring
polished cliff-face
hurtling rigid
from zenith to pit
through dead

46. Quoted in Daniel O'Hara, review of *Song of the Night* and *The Messenger*, *Eire-Ireland* 14 (Spring 1979): 133.

five

Seeing How the Whole Thing Works

I

Fifteen Dead (1979) collects the first four works published by Peppercanister, Kinsella's own press. *Butcher's Dozen* (April 1972) was written as a consequence of the publication of the Widgery Report, which detailed the findings of the judicial tribunal established to investigate the events of Bloody Sunday (30 January 1972); *A Selected Life* (July 1972) and *Vertical Man* (August 1973) serve as elegies for the recently dead Seán Ó Riada; and the fourth Peppercanister volume, *The Good Fight* (November 1973), was written for the tenth anniversary of the assassination of John F. Kennedy. Of the Peppercanister series, Kinsella has commented to John F. Deane about its origin and its effect upon his writing:

> It began in 1972 with the quick publication of *Butcher's Dozen*, but it existed as an idea long before that. It was a basic irritant which brought it into being: the dislike of poetry being used in journals between articles, stories etc.—poetry as a space-filler. Peppercanister is primarily a substitute for magazine publication. It has a secondary effect in giving me another look at the work before publication—a final draft in published form. Interim publication gives a distancing effect, and helps toward clearing things. . . . The books are no longer random gatherings of poems, or

> merely occasional poems. I have started writing books of poems as units. The Peppercanister books in the beginning were quite short, consisting even of a single poem, something like the couple of poems I wrote soon after Seán Ó Riada's death. The two Peppercanister books I have just got ready for publication [*Out of Ireland* and *St. Catherine's Clock*] make full books of 28 and 32 pages. They are full-scale undertakings.[1]

The establishment of the Peppercanister series thus served Kinsella's larger search for the forms and expressions most suitably fitted to embody experience. What is striking about the transition from Peppercanister to trade edition, of which the poet makes no mention, is that, increasingly, the earlier version needs little revision. "Things" have already been clarified, with Kinsella in possession of his own voice and in control of his own form. In fact, his volumes have never been "random gatherings," although the first four Peppercanisters may quite accurately be called "occasional poems," in that they originated in specific events. Such "occasional" poetry, Kinsella has claimed, has a distinctively Irish character: in English, the term suggests a poetry in which the poet's "full seriousness is not engaged"; in Irish, such poems "set the tone and are the masterpieces" because "poetry played a much more direct part in the spending of people's lives."[2] Given such origins—and in the first instance, *Butcher's Dozen*, the poem was written in great haste and heat, within a week—all four works nevertheless cohere and find their appropriate place in Kinsella's canon. Indeed, the transition from "Worker in Mirror, at His Bench" (*NLD* 55–59) to *The Good Fight* is not as considerable as might at first sight appear. Kinsella himself has noted that he began the latter poem "after Kennedy's assassination," an event that had killed the "foolish expectations and assumptions" he had experienced during the Kennedy administration. He went on to say, "But the poem jammed and allowed time for the foolishness to digest. A great deal of foreign matter was lifted from it, and developed into a separate poem, 'Worker in Mirror, at His Bench' " (*FD* 74).

This aside, all four Peppercanisters not only have their source in the deaths of particular individuals but explore the central Kinsella themes of humanity's potential for evil and the artist's relationship to his community. The first theme has universal, ethical, and philosophic relevance; the second bears particularly, in Kinsella's case,

1. Deane, "A Conversation," 87.
2. Kinsella, "Another Country . . . ," 179.

upon Ireland. The same social sense that provoked "Nightwalker" functions in the first and fourth Peppercanisters, *Butcher's Dozen* and *The Good Fight*, and may also be traced operating beneath the surface of the two Ó Riada elegies. For just as Kinsella's quest poems extend beyond individual self to touch upon matters that concern us all, so too his work, with the exception of his earliest volumes, has upheld the artist's responsibility. For while he might acknowledge in *Another September* a "lack of public concern," asserting instead that "little is relevant but the dignity of the isolated person, whose conscious or unconscious bargainings with time insist, like those of a condemned or dying man, that they be respected,"[3] *Downstream* contains in varying degrees political poems ("Old Harry," "A Country Walk," and "Downstream") written from the perspective of social critic. Two decades later he rejected the titles of "moralist" or "spoiled romantic," and preferred to describe his work as evidencing "responsibility toward actuality" while at the same time avoiding didacticism.[4] Such a sense of responsibility led him in *Butcher's Dozen* to address the inflammatory, because intrinsically political, subject of the British military presence in Northern Ireland. The subject continues to provoke discussion and the poem has been criticized in turn for being crudely partisan, or at least politically biased, and therefore aesthetically flawed.

The poem was written in response not to Bloody Sunday itself, when British paratroopers shot and killed thirteen civil rights demonstrators in Derry on 30 January 1972, much as Kinsella may deplore the killings, but to the publication of the Widgery Tribunal's findings in April that year.

> Witnesses before Lord Widgery included people who had been present at the demonstrations, ballistics and explosives experts and the paratroopers who had done the shooting—in their case with a dreadful comedy, as they were bundled in and out of the building to give their orchestrated, anonymous testimony. Their evidence was not fully reported in British newspapers at the time, but it was published in great detail in Ireland, and accumulated into a clear indictment of the British troops and their officers. The Tribunal, after a brief consideration, exonerated the troops more or less, and managed to leave a suspicion of conspiracy and covert violence hanging over some of the victims. (*FD* 54)

3. Kinsella, *Poetry Book Society Bulletin* 17 (March 1958).
4. *Viewpoints*, ed. Haffenden, 102.

Kinsella himself has listed the various criticisms raised against his poem: that it omitted mention of the civil rights campaign in the North; that it did not lament the Protestant dead or note the Catholic Church's bigotry; that it commented upon Northern Ireland's affairs, which, because he lived in the Republic, he had no right to do; that it offended against aesthetic as well as political attitudes, that "it was not poetry at all" (58). A particularly virulent attack was published by the British and Irish Communist Organization in a parodic rewriting of the poem. There Kinsella is dismissed as "the Southern establishment poet," possessed of "anti-British emotions," and, predictably, serving "the interests of the bourgeoisie."[5] However, the more considerable literary critic, Edna Longley, also objected to the poem's "Republican cast" and while she tolerated the appropriateness of the "Broadsheet doggerel," she regarded "the ghoulish way in which the dead speakers are introduced" as a technique that destroyed "their dignity."[6] On an earlier occasion she accused Kinsella of putting "a fascist hysteria" into the mouths of the victims and, equally injudiciously, judged *Kinsella's Oversight* "a political corrective to the attitudes of the poem."[7]

The poem continues to divide Kinsella's critics. Moreover, even sympathetic readers, like Conleth Ellis and W. J. McCormack, when commenting upon the poem's form, have failed to see the distinctively Irish model on which the poem is based: Ellis sees "no obvious model for the form," although he rightly recognizes ancestors in Kinsella's own work; McCormack sees the poem as "an oddity in the modern canon, even in Kinsella's personal canon."[8] It has taken Kinsella himself to point out his use of the eighteenth-century *aisling* form and, more particularly, of Brian Merriman's tribunal in *The Midnight Court*. At the same time he has acknowledged the poem's peculiar

5. "Introduction" to *Kinsella's Oversight: A Reply to "The Butcher's Dozen"* (Belfast: British and Irish Communist Organisation, n.d.), 1–2. The "Introduction" is dated January 1973.

6. Longley, "Spinning through the Void," 1446. Denis Donoghue criticized the poem's "crudity" and its derivation from "the primitive demand, the insistence upon immediate rage"; see "The Literature of Trouble," in *We Irish: Essays on Irish Literature and Society* (New York: Knopf, 1986), 187. Cf. "Together," in *We Irish*, 149. Macdara Woods, on the other hand, has compared *BD* with Patrick Kavanagh's *The Great Hunger* because both poems were written "at white heat" and "in the teeth of the anti-life brigade"; see *Cyphers* 11 (Winter 1979): 52–53.

7. Longley, "Searching the Darkness," 136–37.

8. Ellis, "Above the Salt," 35; McCormack, "Politics or Community," 66.

position in his work: "One changed one's standards, chose the doggerel route, and charged" (*FD* 58). More recently, while remarking that "[t]he ballad cauterised the wound," Gerald Dawe nevertheless saw Kinsella's poem as "in places, perilously close to the caricature of a sort that cuts art down."[9] Seamus Heaney, on the other hand, has more favorably compared what he calls the "rage and certitude" of Kinsella's poem with "the swell of political energy" in poems by Ó Bruadair and Ó Rathaille included in *An Duanaire: Poems of the Dispossessed, 1600–1900*.[10] Given Kinsella's use of the eighteenth-century *aisling* and of Ó Rathaille as an enabling voice and exemplar, the comparison is clearly appropriate.

"Violence is terrible," Kinsella argues in his Commentary, "but it is not inhuman" (*FD* 56). The qualification indicates the poem's larger scope: more than simple Republican protest, *Butcher's Dozen* focuses upon injustice (here perpetrated, with terrible irony, by a judicial system, headed by the Lord Chief Justice, the Rt. Hon. Lord Widgery) but also, by extension, upon the human propensity for evil. It would be wrong to claim that Kinsella is politically neutral—he was deeply moved by the events of Bloody Sunday and is scathing in his condemnation[11]—but the poem, rather than being eccentric to his recurrent preoccupations, takes its proper place within the canon of his work. It is one further instance in his quest for understanding, in which he weighs in the balance principles like truth, justice, and purgatorial suffering. To condemn with Swiftian "savage indignation" —another Irish model—the killing of civilians by a military force does not in itself entail partisanship, although to point out that the civilians were unarmed and the military foreign and British would, in some quarters at least, indicate Republican sympathies. The poem focuses instead, to use Kinsella's terms describing "Old Harry," upon "the possibility of the monstrous choice in the human brain."[12] For it is not the killing that is Kinsella's prime subject but instead "the evil real causes" of violence in the North:

9. Dawe, "In the Violent Zone," 27. Declan Kiberd has also argued that, when Irish poets like Kinsella address "social conditions," "in becoming 'political' they virtually cease to be poets"; see "Irish Literature and Irish History," in *The Oxford Illustrated History of Ireland*, ed. R. F. Foster (Oxford: Oxford University Press, 1989), 331.

10. Heaney, "The Poems of the Dispossessed Repossessed," 32.

11. McCormack described Kinsella's visit to Derry shortly after Bloody Sunday and his conducting the poet through the march route; see "Politics or Community," 70–71.

12. *The Poet Speaks*, ed. Orr, 107.

> *Butcher's Dozen* was not written in response to the shooting of the thirteen dead in Derry. There are too many dead, on all sides, and it is no use pitting them hideously against one another. The poem was written in response to the Report of the Widgery Tribunal. In Lord Widgery's cold putting aside of truth, the *n*th in a historic series of expedient falsehoods —with Injustice literally wigged out as Justice—it was evident to me that we were suddenly very close to the operations of the evil real causes. (*FD* 57)

The title itself signifies the heavy irony functioning in the poem: instead of the proverbial "baker's dozen," the number referring to the thirteen demonstrators killed, "butcher" bitterly replaces "baker." The subtitle—"A Lesson for the Octave of Widgery"—reinforces that irony: in one sense the "octave" refers to the eight days during which the poem was composed, but within Catholic practice the term refers also to a week of devotion and spiritual preparation (as in the octave of Pentecost or of the Epiphany). In this second sense the term, together with its related "lesson," highlights the moral turpitude and crass cover-up Kinsella sees in the Widgery Tribunal's report.[13] Certainly, as the poem opens, the charge of murder is explicitly made:

> I went with Anger at my heel
> Through Bogside of the bitter zeal
> —Jesus pity!—on a day
> Of cold and drizzle and decay.
> A month had passed. Yet there remained
> A murder smell that stung and stained.
> (13)

Furthermore, instances of British Army culpability are scornfully detailed by the phantoms inhabiting the scene:

> "A bomber I. I travelled light
> —Four pounds of nails and gelignite
> About my person, hid so well
> They seemed to vanish where I fell."
> (14)

13. For analysis of the report, see Samuel Dash, *Justice Denied: A Challenge to Lord Widgery's Report on "Bloody Sunday"* (New York: The Defence and Education Fund of the International League for the Rights of Man/National Council for Civil Liberties, 1972). Kinsella quotes from Dash in his own Commentary, *FD* 54–55.

Kinsella scores his satirical hits—"Careful bullets in the back / Stopped our terrorist attack, / And so three dangerous lives are done"—in traditional fashion, through ironic emphasis gained from the adjectives "careful," "terrorist," and "dangerous." When "The truth will out," the adjectives will be redistributed: the British Army will be seen to constitute the real danger to life and liberty. For while the phantoms' accounts differ radically from those of the British Army and of Widgery, they are substantiated by "All not blinded by your smoke," including photographers and priests. Their conclusion was that British paratroopers planted arms on the dead to justify their unlawful killing, and that among the dead were those shot in the back and left to suffocate in an armored car.

The travesty of justice—Kinsella's main focus—is the subject of another phantom's biting scorn, articulated through familiar Augustan caesuras and couplets which balance, with effective irony, the reality against the appearance:

> "The shame is theirs, in word and deed,
> Who prate of Justice, practise greed,
> And act in ignorant fury—then,
> Officers and gentlemen,
> Send to their Courts for the Most High
> To tell us did we really die!
> Does it need recourse to law
> To tell ten thousand what they saw?
> * * * * * * * * * * * * * * *
> Where's the law that can't be changed?
> The news is out. The troops were kind.
> Impartial justice has to find
> We'd be alive and well today
> If we had let them have their way."
>
> (14–15)

Others, however, berate Unionist and Orange Order sectarianism or British imperialism, argue for violence (" 'England, the way to your respect / Is via murderous force, it seems' "), or simply curse:

> "My curse on the cunning and the bland,
> On gentlemen who loot a land
> They do not care to understand;
> Who keep the natives on their paws
> With ready lash and rotten laws."
>
> (17)

As he momentarily adopts the position of "sympathetic politicians" who ascribe to the Irish an intrinsic violence and excessive preoccupation with the past, the narrator also undercuts himself:

> It seemed the moment to explain
> That sympathetic politicians
> Say our violent traditions,
> Backward looks and bitterness
> Keep us in this dire distress.
> We must forget, and look ahead,
> Nurse the living, not the dead.
> My words died out.
>
> (16)

In all this Kinsella's nationalist sympathies are clearly engaged, just as in his Commentary he notes, "Amid the swirling evils, miseries and stupidities in the North there are a few certainties: . . . Northern Ireland is a state founded in injustice"; "It is a state maintained in injustice"; and British army withdrawal is necessary (56). Yet the poem cannot be dismissed as simply nationalist rant: it is too varied in tone and, like its model, *The Midnight Court*, too parodic and ironic. For while in part it articulates the anger, hatred, and resentment of the Catholic community both North and South, it also notes the sectarian tribalism dividing Protestant and Catholic. A particularly virulent attack upon the Orange Order is thus answered by the final and thirteenth phantom, who pleads, not without fierce irony at times, for pity and understanding between the communities:

> though there's reason for alarm
> In dourness and a lack of charm
> Their cursed plight calls out for patience.
> They, even they, with other nations
> Have a place, if we can find it.
> Love our changeling! Guard and mind it.
> Doomed from birth, a cursed heir,
> Theirs is the hardest lot to bear,
> Yet not impossible, I swear,
> If England would but clear the air
> And brood at home on her disgrace . . .
>
> (19)

Moreover, while humanity may inherit and practice evil, in the last resort evil is the product of human choice: "Good men everyday inherit / Father's foulness with the spirit, / Purge the filth and do not stir it." Calling for British evacuation and reconciliation between the two communities, the thirteenth phantom notes the heterogeneous nature of all societies and asks, " 'What nation's not / Where any stranger hung his hat / And seized a lover where she sat?' " "The gentle rainfall" in the poem's conclusion, however, offers only distillation of "silent grief" rather than a more positive regeneration.

Nearly three decades later Kinsella still describes *Butcher's Dozen* as offering "a reasonable view. My view of the social and political realities of the thirty-two counties and of the six counties hasn't changed. Northern Ireland is an unjust society and I see nothing unreasonable about saying this, on one of its most brutal occasions. The idea of the poem being in support of terrorism or that kind of thing is a misreading, probably a deliberate one."[14]

The artist in "The Worker in Mirror, at His Bench" rejects any "practical application": "I am simply trying to understand something / —states of peace nursed out of wreckage." *Butcher's Dozen* was written too much out of anger for one to claim that it seeks only understanding, although, as Kinsella has argued, British distortion of the events of Bloody Sunday is yet another instance of the human propensity for violence and evil. At the same time, it is not coincidental that in the U.S. edition of *Notes from the Land of the Dead* the volume concludes with *Butcher's Dozen:* Kinsella shapes his volumes too carefully for that inclusion to have no purpose other than to pad out the volume. In part, *Butcher's Dozen* leads into what eventually became *Fifteen Dead*, but it also underlines the connection between *Butcher's Dozen*, the two elegies to Ó Riada, and the Kennedy poem, *The Good Fight*.

In all four Peppercanisters Kinsella mourns the deaths of his heroes, the "fifteen dead" of the sequence's title. While both J. F. Kennedy and the dead of Bloody Sunday were unknown to him, Seán Ó Riada was a close personal friend. Furthermore, "he was Ireland's foremost composer and musician" (*FD* 59), a fellow artist whose work with traditional Irish music, despite Kinsella's comments to the contrary,[15] paralleled in many ways the poet's own translations and in-

14. O'Driscoll, "Interview," 64. In the 1992 reissue of *Butcher's Dozen*, on the twentieth anniversary of the Widgery Report, Kinsella confirmed his original view, now borne out, he believed, by subsequent recent events in which British justice had been shown to be flawed and original convictions overturned.

15. O'Driscoll, "Interview," 62–63.

creasing preoccupation with the Gaelic tradition. Indeed, the work of each was profoundly influenced by the joint holiday they and their families took in the Dingle Peninsula in 1959. As we have already seen, Kinsella's fine elegy, "The Shoals Returning" (*N* 37–42), mourns the death of Gerry Flaherty, the Dingle fisherman whose *sean nós* singing impressed both poet and composer. "For Reidy [Ó Riada] it was all a swift liberation" (*FD* 69), as Kinsella has since described it, taking shape in "his unabated new drive towards Irish music. It was a recovery, in fact: he had only to become conscious of it to realize that he was already in possession of it, from the time he played the traditional fiddle as a young boy growing up in Bruff, County Limerick" (70–71). A similar "recovery" or repossession Kinsella practiced himself in his own involvement with the Irish Gaelic literary tradition, as revealed in his own work from the mid-1960s onward. Moreover, motivated equally by a sense of the artist's social responsibility, Ó Riada sought to escape "the traditional 'European' relationship between the composer and a select audience" and undertook a "revival of the old native relationship between Irish traditional music and the Irish community, and his renovation of it for the twentieth century" (59). According to Kinsella, "His primary material was Ireland's rich store of traditional songs and dance tunes—the music of a sophisticated tradition, which he was always at pains to distinguish from folk music as usually understood" (59–60). Founding first the Ceoltóirí Chualann in Dublin and working later with the people of Coolea in West Cork, he sought a close "relationship between music and the community" (60). What, however, in the poet's eyes further marks Ó Riada's achievement is its tragic character: no other figure in Kinsella's work so movingly illustrates the creative–destructive aspects of the muse and the artist's experience of and submission to the world's appetite.

Whether focusing upon the dead in Derry in 1972 or Ó Riada or John F. Kennedy—all prematurely dead, it should be noted—Kinsella's concern is to arrive at a structure that will reveal meaning and harmony behind apparently meaningless and disharmonious events, and so reach understanding. While conceding that his early work was tragic and seemingly nihilistic, Kinsella has argued that any artistic response to that tragedy "makes it more acceptable," while the search to understand "counterbalances any notion of nihilism. The impulse is important, even if it's of no avail."[16] As we shall see, the

16. *Viewpoints*, ed. Haffenden, 107, 111.

elaboration of Kinsella's structure depends upon imagery appropriate to Ó Riada and, in turn, increasingly central to his own work: music, appetite, a room, darkness, and other supporting images.

A *Selected Life* (*FD* 23–27), the first of the two Ó Riada elegies, attends only briefly to the composer's life. Apart from the opening nine-line poem set in Galloping Green, Co. Dublin, May 1962, with the establishment of Ceoltóirí Chualann, Kinsella's elegy centers on the funeral and the graveyard. Yet the opening portrait of Ó Riada, "crouched forward, thin / as a beast of prey," beating the *bodhrán* (goatskin drum) "cruelly / with his nails" and provoking the drum's "answering arid bark," anticipates the ominous crow and the woman-animal vision in the sequence's second, third, and fourth poems. For the "woman-animal" figure in the fourth poem, *Vertical Man*, reminds us of the fearful aspect of the creative self, the muse who consumes as well as inspires. Furthermore, in Irish myth the Morrigan, the great war queen, often assumed the shape of a crow[17] and in this form perched on the shoulder of the dying Cuchulain. In the second poem the crow provides an ominous companion to the poet gathering with the dead man's family and friends at Coolea:

> A crow scuffled in the hedge
> and floated out with a dark groan
> into full view. It flapped up the field
> and lit on a rock, and scraped its beak.
> It croaked: a voice out of the rock
> carrying across the slope. Foretell.
>
> (23)

The crow's presence serves, in the manner of Irish myth, to announce the death of a hero but also, more particularly according to Kinsella's own system, to evidence the world's appetite. The crow, like Kinsella's owl in "At the Crossroads" (*NLD* 35), has "blackness in her heart" and is associated with that other ravenous bird, which is also Hecate's symbol. As if to epitomize darkness, both the world's and its own, the crow is caught picking at the body of a dead rat. With the death of Ó Riada the infernal or underworld is more readily evident:

> A rat lay on its side in the wet,
> the grey skin washed clean and fleshy,
> the little face wrinkled back in hatred,

17. Ross, *Pagan Celtic Britain*, 219, 220–22, 242ff.

> the back torn open. A pale string
> stretched on the gravel. Devil-martyr;
> your sad, mad meat . . .
>   I have interrupted
> some thing . . . You! Croaking
> on your wet stone. Flesh picker.
>   (24)

Such darkness and appetite may be part of the creative self but they have also brought about Ó Riada's premature death.

The second poem concludes with assorted details of the funeral: of the family mourners, "sundry musical effects," drinks, and the contralto (Bernadette Greevy) singing Mahler's *Das Lied von der Erde* ("Earth's autumnal angst"). As evening falls in the sequence's closing poem, the crows settle, their appetite satisfied, while the poet is torn by recollections of Ó Riada, now remembered as "Pierrot limping forward in the sun / out of Merrion Square, long ago, / in black overcoat and beret" (cf. *FD* 64) or lying in a London hospital, "Gold and still . . . / on his secondlast bed." Experiencing "His first buried night," the dead man lies in his final bed, "swallowed back" by the earth, its appetite fed like that of the crows. At least one critic[18] has complained that Kinsella's lines here are too bleak, despairing, and dismissive a summing-up of man's existence: "animus / brewed in clay, uttered / in brief meat and brains, flattened / back under our flowers." But the lines are not simply misanthropic; they might be put up against similarly bleak statements in, say, Shakespeare or Beckett. Moreover, while "animus" is synonymous with "rancor" or "enmity" (as in "animosity"), its meaning here includes the Latin one of "reason" or "intellect" or the spiritual principle, and the brief span allowed to humanity in which to develop one's intellectual or spiritual life. ("Animus" is given a similar ambiguity in a later poem, "Brothers in the Craft" [*FCC* 19].) Likewise, Kinsella makes plain the transforming nature of life within time: Ó Riada lies "Gold and still," a condition of refinement in sharp contrast to the brutal appetite he is subject to. Not the least, however, the lines express the poet's deeply felt grief at the loss, first, of a friend but, second, of a maestro whose health he pledges with a farewell drink. The Russian, "*Yob tvoyu mat'* " (Fuck your mother), may perhaps recall the drunken evening in Dublin shared by both men passing themselves off as "a pair of simple and

18. Longley, "Spinning through the Void," 1446.

lonely seamen from the Baltic" (*FD* 66) but it serves more as a defiantly unsentimental and mocking contrary to the final salutation, "Master, your health."

The sequel and fourth poem in the whole sequence, *Vertical Man* (28–33), pursues these images and dialectical experiences in the new environment of Philadelphia where, a year later, Kinsella moved into yet another fateful room and nighttime setting. "I was pouring a drink . . .": the poem's opening picks up the conclusion of *A Selected Life* in one of those circles that occur so frequently in Kinsella's work, linking experiences, shaping a structure, and drawing upon the sense of omphalos or eternal return, all of which lead to understanding of origins. Indeed, in the Peppercanister edition, *Vertical Man* has as its epigraph the final line from *A Selected Life*, "Master, your health." The experience that follows is not only startling and moving, expressing the close bond between poet and composer, but is convincingly numinous, a further instance of darkness shedding light and illuminating the poet. Before the "little altar" (*FD* 72) of Ó Riada's death mask, hand cast, and the sleeve of the composer's recording, *Vertical Man*, the poet experiences "Ó Riada's presence . . . in the room; for an extraordinary moment we drank together. It was a definite farewell" (72). The next two pages are seen as "offerings . . . made to the ghost, in propitiation" (72), pursuing further the evaluation of a man's life that the poet began in *A Selected Life*. Beginning, then, with phrases from Plato's *Laws*, a work he was studying and incorporating in *The Good Fight* (1973), Kinsella proceeds to apply Plato's "sour ancient phrases," assuming, like the philosopher's Athenian, that "mankind is worth considering." Again his conclusions are negative: "That the days pass, / that our tasks arise, dominate our energies, / are mastered with difficulty and some pleasure, / and are obsolete"; "That there can be a sweet stir . . ." that ends only in "The ugly rack"; "That you may startle the heart of a whole people"—Ó Riada's own achievement with his film score for *Mise Eire* (*FD* 60)—only to see that heart "soon beating to a coarse pulse / to glut fantasy and sentiment"; and "That for all you have done," only "a residue in the timidity, / a maturer unsureness," remains.

Against such negativism Kinsella affirms, first, the artistic act with its concomitant search for a structure, as he refers to his own creative struggle ("Only this morning . . ."). We have already seen the poet set both the artistic act and the search for structure as counterbalances against nihilism. Burying his face in his hands, "in self-devouring prayer," as Kinsella puts it, suddenly his "charts and notes come crawling to life again / under a Night seething with / soft incandescent bombardment." Instead of Plato's "sour ancient phrases" the poet is offered illumination, a vision of the Quincunx which is both given (and so the product of chance) but also chosen (the consequence of appetite, of self being devoured). The situation parallels once more that of Yeats in "Two Songs from a Play" where heart's consumption brings both defeat and triumph, death and rebirth. At least one critic, Arthur E. McGuinness,[19] writing sensibly of the Quincunx vision, has noted a further Yeats parallel, in this case of the phases of the moon. For the Quincunx reflects a "new self . . . shaped by primal female and male energies in a chthonic-solar union"; or again:

> "Quincunx" is a structure shaped like a Greek "chi" (X) having five points, the fifth being the centre. The structure can be observed on the cover of *Fifteen Dead*, where the Roman numerals for fifteen (XV) can also be read as quincunx and vertical man. A recent study of traditional symbols describes quincunx as "the Cosmic Centre, the four cardinal points meeting at the fifth point, the Centre; it is the meeting point of Heaven and Earth."

Suggesting the image's source in Plato's *Timaeus*, McGuinness overlooks a source closer to home, in the Irish tradition of the country's ancient division into five provinces. The fifth meets at the center, marked at the Hill of Uisneach, which Giraldus Cambrensis called "the navel of Ireland," by the Stone of the Divisions.[20] McGuinness is correct, however, in defining the Quincunx as "a cosmic structure symbolizing the creative tension, 'woman-animal,' that constitutes the self."[21] Kinsella's lines bring his reader back to the underworld experiences of *Notes from the Land of the Dead* and point in the direction of *One*, both of which volumes constitute significant expressions of the poet's search for structure and meaning, for understanding, the gaining of which in turn brings illumination and the formation of his new self. Surrounded by his "instruments" (charts, notes, paper, and pen) and engaged "in self-devouring prayer," the poet is

19. McGuinness, " 'Bright Quincunx Newly Risen,' " 106–7, 122.

20. Rees and Rees, *Celtic Heritage*, ch. 7, "The Centre." For "Uisneach," see Darragh Smyth, *A Guide to Irish Mythology* (Blackrock, Co. Dublin: Irish Academic Press, 1988), 156. Cf. Brendan Purcell, "In Search of Newgrange: Long Night's Journey into Day," in *The Irish Mind*, ed. Kearney, 44.

21. McGuinness, " 'Bright Quincunx Newly Risen,' " 123.

granted a vision of process: of light born out of darkness and forming itself into the Quincunx of a new self, shadowed by a sphinxlike "woman-animal," the familiar muse-earth goddess figure, who fades before a child's call, that of the emerging new self. Kinsella's expression of that process impresses in part because he manages to create a sense of origins, of psychic development given a mythic framework, but also because the experience's numinous quality is vividly and convincingly caught:

> At the dark zenith a pulse beat,
> a sperm of light separated wriggling
> and snaked in a slow beam down
> the curve of the sky, through faint
> structures and hierarchies
> of elements and things and beasts. It fell,
> a packed star, dividing
> and redividing until it was
> a multiple gold tear. It dropped
> toward the horizon, entered
> bright Quincunx newly risen,
> beat with a blinding flame and dis-
> appeared. I stared, duly blinded.
> An image burned on the brain
> —a woman-animal: scaled,
> pierced in paws and heart,
> ecstatically calm. It faded
> to a far-off desolate call,
>   a child's . . .
>
> (30)

Conceding that Ó Riada's ghost is "accustomed to / that dark" and therefore more capable of following that vision, Kinsella is brought back to his dead friend's presence; to their drinking together as the poet prepares to play Mahler's *Das Lied von der Erde*, a work to which Ó Riada introduced him; to his intensified sense of loss and "waste"; but also to Mahler's final song in that work, "Der Abschied" ("The Farewell"). There two friends drinking together undertake a moving farewell as one of them, a knight, prepares for his own death. That death is given meaning when seen against the eternal cycle or return, of life to its dark origins but also, as spring is born out of winter's deathliness, to regeneration. The drinking song Kinsella offers Ó Riada ("A drinking—a *drunken*—song / for the misery of this world") is his equivalent of the Hans Bethge text Mahler used for "Das Trinklied von Jammer der Erde," the opening song to *Das Lied von der Erde*. Kinsella's version includes as acknowledgment of Ó Riada an ironic echo ("Earth has not anything to show more fair") of Wordsworth's sonnet "Upon Westminster Bridge," a poem he remembers intoning in BBC voices with Ó Riada in his Baggot Street flat (65). The parallel with Mahler is pursued through the "queer vision" Kinsella shares with Ó Riada's ghost, of the apelike creature crouching and howling "accursed silent screams / into the fragrant Night. . . ." Bethge's poem concludes with precisely such an ape among the moonlit graves, its howling ringing out "amidst the sweet scent of life" —"In den süssen Duft des Lebens!" (73). And Kinsella's *Vertical Man* thus becomes his version of Bethge's "Drinking Song of Earth's Misery," offered in response to life's temporal nature and the inevitability of death, and so places Ó Riada's death in the context of life's processes. "It is time," indeed, as Kinsella notes—time for Ó Riada's departure, time which inevitably brings death in this world, but time also to gain the heroic status of vertical man. Thus Kinsella mourns "A black / bloody business" but concludes with three recollections of his friend, experiences he describes in his prose Commentary (65–66, 67–68, 70), and in one instance (of Flaherty's *sean nós*) quoting with only minor variation from his earlier poem, "The Shoals Returning." (Kinsella developed this intertextual practice in *Notes from the Land of the Dead*; it will reach its height in a late work, *Out of Ireland* (1987) collected in *Blood and Family*.) The experiences epitomize moments shared by the two friends and crucial to their artistic development. Such moments indeed are epiphanies, numinous in their intersection of the timeless with time, and prefaced with the same imagery of gold employed in *A Selected Life*—here, ironically, a glass of bourbon. It may be time for Ó Riada's final farewell, time which is the mortal condition, but it is also "more than time" as both this and previous epiphanies reveal. The poet's grief is by no means diminished —Ó Riada's death remains a personal and a national loss—but the experience of the Quincunx also endures, providing for reconciliation, understanding and further spiritual growth.

The Good Fight centers on another national loss, the assassination of John F. Kennedy and the destruction of people's hopes for a new and superior political era. It may be that those hopes were founded more upon illusion than reality; Kinsella acknowledges as much in his Commentary, where he also assumes the guilt of Lee Harvey

Oswald. Such details do not diminish his treatment of the larger issues with which the poem is concerned: once more the heroic figure suffers defeat, as the world's appetitive nature is confronted and endured; once more the conjunction of choice and chance proves crucial; and once more principles of justice and truth, together with the creation of an ideal society and the nurturing of an ideal ruler, come together. For the world's dialectical nature is paralleled in the creative tension of energies within the individual self, with macrocosm and microcosm bound in the same circling, coiling, labyrinthine dance. In considering Kennedy's "philosophic nature," the poem thus concludes by praising his "balance" (50), suggesting the musical analogy of pitch. Kinsella, it should be remembered, had praised Ó Riada for possessing "absolute intelligence" (67) and had referred to Ó Riada's "claim to absolute pitch" (63). The relation between the Ó Riada elegies and *The Good Fight* thus comes clearer, as similar claims are made for the dead president:

> (His "philosophic nature"
> —balance, you will remember;
> apportionment, as between Mind and Body!
> Harmony, and proper pitch!
> The Dance!)
>
> (50)

The association of the dance image with Ó Riada is continued in two poems ("The Dance" and "Exit") in *Out of Ireland.* Moreover, the relation also with *Butcher's Dozen* is established at the outset of *The Good Fight,* where appetite and justice coincide in the presidential candidate. Hence the poet refers to "the human mouth / tasting Justice or a favourite soup / with equal relish" (37) and to Kennedy wiping his lips in the cabin of his campaign plane (another Kinsella room). The lines draw heavily upon details in Theodore H. White's *The Making of the President 1960*; indeed, the whole elegy employs an intricate weaving or montage of phrases and images from White and other contemporary accounts of the Kennedy years, together with sentences from Plato's *The Republic* and *The Laws.* The montage techniques, learnt from exemplars such as Ezra Pound and Thomas Mann, effectively embody the poet's search for structure, meaning, and harmony.

Yet the poem begins with a more ominous instance of appetite that serves as commentary upon the Kennedy years, with people's hopes dashed by assassination and the dream of an ideal society eliminated by the existential tension of energies, of "life and doom." The storybook phrasing of the opening lines suggests not just the narrator's fictive function but an age-old process, archetypal and primordial. It also acknowledges the extent to which the fairy-tale character of Kennedy's Camelot is a fiction with aesthetic as well as political relevance:

> Once upon a time a certain phantom
> took to certain red-smelling corridors
> in sore need. It met, with a flush of pleasure,
> the smell of seed and swallowed
> life and doom in the same animal action.
>
> (37)

That same compulsive, devouring appetite appears later in the narrative as "the Jaw," as we learn of Kennedy's campaign and the fearful physical effects, akin to stigmata, it has upon the candidate:

> Once, he rolled up his sleeve
> and looked at the calloused, scratched arm:
> "Ohio did that to me."
> (One day in Philadelphia
> his hand *burst* with blood.)
>
> (38)

"He held out his inflamed right hand / for the Jaw to grip. The sinews winced" (39). In antithesis to such appetite Kennedy epitomizes reason: in answer to Plato's doubting query, "*Can we believe it possible . . . ?*" Kinsella poses Kennedy, "His hands flexed. / All reasonable things are possible." The quest, while political, is analogous to Kinsella's aesthetic and philosophic concerns: in all instances the search is for understanding through the structuring of contrary energies, and Kinsella's description of the presidential cabinet "with all kinds of precision instruments" (41) reminds us that similar instruments have been (since at least *Notes from the Land of the Dead* 3–6), the necessary equipment for his poets and questing selves. Against reason and precision, however, lies the beast; against chance is posed choice ("The accident that brought our people together / out of blind necessities /—embrace it!—explosive—to our bodies" (39)). At times Kinsella's language harks back to "The Worker in Mirror, at His Bench" (*NLD*), and it becomes easier to see how that poem was originally part of *The Good Fight*:

(It sounds as though it could go on for ever,
yet there is a shape to it—Appropriate
Performance. Another almost perfect
working model . . . But it gets harder.
The concepts jerk and wrestle, back to back.

The finer the idea the harder it is
to assemble lifelike. It adopts hardnesses
and inflexibilities, knots, impossible joints
made possible only by stress,
and good for very little afterward.)

(39–40)

That same striving to shape a structure for the world's dialectic is paralleled in the individual: in Kennedy's words, " 'Welcome challenge, that can stretch / the two sinews of the Soul, / Body and Mind, to a pure pitch' "; " '—Let us make ourselves vessels of decision! / We are not here to curse the darkness. / The old order changes!' " (40). The echo of the last words of Tennyson's King Arthur to the knight Bedivere ("Morte d'Arthur") comments ironically upon the popular media image of Kennedy's White House as Camelot. A further irony exists in the posing of Kennedy's fine words against "The swaying mass" of the American people. The reader is again made acutely aware of the need for balance, particularly in the light of Plato's own pessimistic queries in *The Republic* (6: 492, 494), postulating how philosophical natures might be corrupted: "*(Where is a young man's heart in such a scene? / Who would not be stunned by the beast's opinion? / Nor think wisdom control of the beast's moods? / What schooling will resist, and not be swamped / and swept downstream? . . .)*" (40–41). Kinsella's protagonists have for some time been "*swept downstream*": learning to endure the world's appetitive nature and to balance body and mind, choice and chance, order and chaos, have constituted his major discipline since at least the early sixties.

Against the various rooms Kennedy inhabits (the airplane cabin, the campaign room, the Oval Office) Kinsella posits "A lonely room" inhabited by the eventual assassin. "His cell hangs in the night" : the imagery possesses fearful ironies, as we are made aware of Oswald's alienation from society, his awful loneliness which imprisons him as in a cell, his driven nature compulsively committed to "savagery."

Whether inhabiting room or cell, Oswald is as much a nighttime prowler as other Kinsella figures have been, as much torn by choice and chance, by appetite, and in search of meaning. Indeed, the portrait of Lee Harvey Oswald, which takes up the second section of the poem and focuses upon his private, alienated self, is a good deal more convincing than that of Kennedy the public man. Instead of the impersonal "He" describing the president, the reader identifies with Oswald through the intimacy of the first-person pronoun, "I." Such identification is reinforced by the pathos aroused for the man driven by hunger into such separateness that he stands outside himself as if another "thing":

> I have seen myself, a "thing"
> in my own eyes, lifting
> my hand empty and opening
> and closing my mouth
> in senseless mimicry
> and wondered why I am alive
> or why a man can live in this way.
> (44)

The second section closes with Oswald's doodling deconstruction of the words "man" and "beast": from "man" through "(d)amn," from "mean" to "team" to "meat," from "beast" through "best" to "b^{r}a^{i}ns," and with his postulating opposition to a whole people, land, and society. Such utter alienation, however, posits Oswald as the necessary and inevitable antithesis to Kennedy, the contemporary philosopher-king. Man and beast similarly experience appetite, and the extended dialogue or counterpoint, achieved through Kinsella's quotations from Plato, with his own brief, querying, and exclamatory commentary, serves only to remind us of that correlation of man/beast and humanity's persistent potentiality for evil. The quotations in heavy type ask to be read first and the brief phrases in the left-hand column only afterward. Such dialogue is in itself a dialectic, another version of the choices confronting the self. Hence Plato reminds us that the rule of the philosopher-king is undermined when "*honour*" replaces "justice"; that "*Passion, ignorance and concupiscence are obscurities clouding the soul's natural judgment. They are the origin of crime.*" His late work, *The Laws,* which provides expert advice from the Academy to the government, much as Kennedy drew upon his Harvard advisers, stresses the need for understanding.[22] In *The Good Fight* the Platonic vision darkens, moving from "*the fitting penalty*" to "*the abyss*" and "*Images of evil in a foul pasture*" (45). While in *The Republic* Plato might insist, "We would not have our Guardians grow up among representations of moral deformity, as in some foul pasture" (3:401), Kinsella uses the final phrase to signify humanity's capacity for evil. He may also remind us, if only obliquely, that his conception of music and poetry differs radically from that of Plato: Kinsella's own work contains its quota of "representations of moral deformity," and it is wholly appropriate that the particular image he associates with such deformity—the squatting figure—surfaces also in Plato's account of human depravity, elevating "*Greed and Money*" and making "*Reason and Spirit squat on the floor under it* . . ." (45).

The poem's third section, prosaic and the least successful, describes the effect upon people of Kennedy's death, of the abnormal reaction of "Things . . . exalted / altogether out of proportion" and the "surprising swiftness" with which "matters settled down" (48). Yet such prosaicness proves eminently suited to the poet's purpose: the shock to the system is assimilated and life's processes continue, as if some evolutionary change, however major, had been absorbed.

The poem ends with Robert Frost in apparent "disarray" as he fumbles with his papers to speak at Kennedy's funeral. In fact he pursues precisely that same dialectical quest for understanding that Kinsella's figures, particularly his poets, engage in, and he emulates in his interweaving of phrases from earlier sections of *The Good Fight* precisely that Poundian technique the poem itself practices. He comes, Frost declares,

> Not in judgment, and not
> in acceptance either.
>   Uncertain.
> For if all you wish to do
> is curse the world and your place in it
> —well then . . .
>   But some appetite
> is not satisfied
> with that, is dissatisfied unless—
>
> (49)

22. Clinias defined virtue as consisting of four parts, "But the chief of them all is understanding"; see *The Laws of Plato,* trans. A. E. Taylor (London: Dent, 1934), 12:358.

The lines' fragmentary nature reproduces the poet's quest for understanding, his rejection of plain pessimism ("curse the world and your place in it"), and his essential openness. Of "the cross-weaving," as he calls it, of Kennedy and Oswald, both "vessels of decision," Kinsella has Frost declare in favor of the dialectical process: "You have to / wear them down against each other / to get any purchase, / and then there is this / strain." Any "purchase" (gain, attainment, or profitable return) is achieved through the counterpoint of contraries. Kinsella's final image is also helpful, for in its musical sense "strain" points to the harmony and dissonance running through the poem, whether in the characters of Kennedy and Oswald or in the world itself; it points also to the "musical" nature of the poem's technique; and, in another sense, it includes the burden (another musical term) or responsibility the self must endure. The "strain," in effect, is a version of Murphy's Law, "That all *un*reasonable things / are possible. *Everything* / that can happen will happen"—a position that acknowledges irrationality in a world striving for reason and meaning, but also acknowledges the infinite potentiality—for good as well as evil—within the self. Moreover, Kinsella has Frost turn the reader's attention back upon the aesthetic implications of the poem by addressing his fellow poets: "My brothers, huddled in wait, / feeble warriors, self-chosen, / in our secondary world. . . ." The term "secondary" reminds us of Plato's views on poetry and music, but also of Kinsella's own poem and work which effectively deny the Platonic conception of Art as at a double remove from the Real. Art may remain a fiction, but for Kinsella, as for Coleridge and his theory of the Secondary Imagination,[23] it constitutes an important quest for understanding. Similarly, his poet is "self-chosen"; this phrase points to two fundamental elements in any successful quest—the arena of self and the primacy of choice—while at the same time suggesting the further element of obsession or appetite, of being driven by self into the self. Consequently, Kinsella-Frost concludes with an appropriate defense of the poet and his requisite openness to experience which brings understanding, another expression of the philosophic nature:

> it is we, letting things *be*,
> who might come at understanding.

23. S. T. Coleridge, *Biographia Literaria*, 2 vols., ed. J. Shawcross (1907; London: Oxford University Press, 1967), 1:202.

That is the source of our patience.
Reliable first in the direction
and finally in the particulars of our response,
fumbling from doubt to doubt,
one day we might knock
our papers together, and elevate them
(with a certain self-abasement)
—their gleaming razors
mirroring a primary world
where power also is a source of patience
for a while before the just flesh
falls back in black dissolution in its box.

(50)

II

With the publication of *One* (1979) Kinsella's poetry enters its most substantial phase to date: his work from *Poems* (1956) onward has shown impressive development both in vision and technique, so making possible the achievement of *Nightwalker* and *Notes from the Land of the Dead*. But the later volumes—*One*, *Blood and Family* (1988), and *From Centre City* (1994)—mark off Kinsella as a major Irish poet whose oeuvre takes on even larger dimensions, prompting comparison with Yeats and Joyce. Yet if compared with Seamus Heaney, another major Irish contemporary, it must be admitted that Kinsella has not been granted the same degree of recognition. It may be that, in sharp contrast to both Heaney and John Montague, the only two Irish poets whose achievement might be said to rival his in scope and substance, Kinsella's dark vision and free-form narratives make him less accessible and accommodating. Certainly he continues to make considerable demands upon his readers. Yet few poets, Irish or otherwise, writing in English over the last twenty-five years can match the formidably sustained performance Kinsella has given, from *Nightwalker* to *From Centre City*. He has perfected his voice and language, honed his instruments, and set out a vision of self and world that both moves and convinces. In the course of developing that vision Kinsella has progressed from the moralistic, didactic position of his earlier work, critical of humanity's propensity for evil, and from his inclination to impose order and structure, to a greater awareness and tolerance of the complexity of self and world. No less struck by the dark potentialities within existence and persisting in his search for structure and meaning, he is more particularly concerned now with seeing "how the whole thing / works" (*One* 33).

Kinsella admitted in 1979–1980 to having gone beyond the moral stance of "Nightwalker," and conceded also that that poem attacked "easy targets." The artist's duty, as he now saw it, was not to make people behave better but to understand.[24] Hence he has described *A Technical Supplement* (1976), the middle volume in the sequence *One*, as "a plunge of a different kind into the nature of things—how objectionable and how pleasant, how rewarding and how diabolical—without being committed to any particular point of view except that of dynamic response to whatever happens."[25] As Jung, an increasing presence in Kinsella's work, has argued, "We must be able to let things happen in the psyche." "Consciousness is forever interfering, helping, correcting, and negating, and never leaving the simple growth of the psychic processes in peace."[26] Kinsella adopts a similar approach. The result is a greater openness to experience, a greater inclusiveness of vision matched by increased freedom of language, form, and technique. Such development is of a piece with his desire for an enabling voice, to permit poetry to do or say anything. It says something for the conservatism of Irish poets after Yeats that in 1985 one transatlantic critic[27] regarded Kinsella's recent volumes as the only "avant garde" Irish writing before Paul Muldoon's *Quoof* (1983). Yet in reaching forward toward new ground and expression Kinsella has turned back to the oldest material—the Matter of Ireland, that rich body of early Irish literature—to explore the essential energies within self and world. The early Irish material we have seen already in *Nightwalker* and *Notes from the Land of the Dead*; it reaches its finest expression in *One and Other Poems*, where it gives the poetry complexity and depth that go beyond such distinctively Irish origins to enable the poet to speak of universal matters, of reality and justice, to use Yeats's famous terms.[28] There can be no higher aim.

One and Other Poems is made up of three smaller sequences published by Peppercanister: *One* (September 1974), *A Technical Supple-*

24. *Viewpoints*, ed. Haffenden, 106.

25. Ibid., 111.

26. Jung, "Commentary on the Secret of the Golden Flower," *Psyche and Symbol*, ed. de Laszlo, 313.

27. Johnston, *Irish Poetry after Joyce*, 263.

28. W. B. Yeats, *A Vision* (London: Macmillan, 1937), 25.

ment (May 1976), and *Song of the Night* (June 1978). The volume is the natural outcome of *Notes from the Land of the Dead*, where the questing self, in search of origins and understanding, proceeds downward and inward, into the darkness of the underworld, the realm of the self's unconscious or shadow, and draws upon the oldest material available to the Irish poet. This mythic material is given prominence at the outset: *One* is prefaced by a ten-line poem in italics[29]—a favorite Kinsella device in the entire sequence and one he has used previously, with similar effect, in *Notes from the Land of the Dead*. Indeed, the first sequence, *One*, both begins and ends with italicized poems. However, the prefatory poem here (*One* 8) serves to set the sequence at one further remove by focusing upon the persona of "*the storyteller*," so that the subsequent poems constitute the storyteller's narrative. Kinsella adopts the oldest role of the *seanchaí* (Gaelic storyteller) honing his knife before the fire and recounting "*the Voyage of the First Kindred*." The ease with which Kinsella's imagery (of knife, fire, voyage) merges with the earliest forms is impressive. For his reader undertakes one more voyage in the long line in his work of *immrama*—another instance in which ancient and modern marry without difficulty or awkwardness. That "*Voyage of the First Kindred*" may have origins in Indian myth,[30] so illustrating a relevance and scope beyond the Irish to the universal, but the *seanchaí* has returned to the most ancient of Irish settings, to tell of Bith. Bith was the son of Noah, the father of Cessair, and one of the three men who took part in the otherwise female invasion of Ireland. We are back with the origins of the Irish world—indeed, Bith's name means, literally, "world"[31]—back with the first of the seven invasions of Ireland that culminated in the establishment of the Gael. The sun's appetite creates movement and process and, as such, is paralleled in all living things: the world "waltzes," for example, in that dance in which we have seen already Ó Riada and J. F. Kennedy participating, and in which in a future volume, *Out of Ireland*, Kinsella himself will participate. Likewise, the protagonist in *One* coils and sheds skins, serpentlike, and achieves transformation. Furthermore, journeys begin, paradoxically, at the end of the world ("Finistère") but con-

29. The poem appeared first in *One and Other Poems* (Dublin: Dolmen Press, 1979) and was absent from the earlier Peppercanister 5 of the first sequence, *One* (1974).

30. Rees and Rees, *Celtic Heritage*, 107.

31. Ibid., 115. Cf. *LGE*, vol. 2, sec. 3, Introduction, 172.

clude, equally paradoxically and symbolically, around Phoenix Park where Kinsella grew up. Subsequent parts of the sequence move outward to Chicago, Philadelphia, and Carraroe, Connemara, and take on Diderot and Jung as guides. The sun, moreover, "*tunneled*" in its appetitive drive; the image is particularly significant because Kinsella relates it to the Boyne Valley passage-grave builders of the third century B.C. and in turn to the poet-self, tunneling into his unconscious and ancestral self. According to Ross, "The burial mound was regarded in Celtic belief as one of the entrances to the otherworld of which the Celts were so conscious."[32] Again, to quote Jung, "Even now I can do no more than tell stories—'mythologize' "[33]: the roles of poet-storyteller and analyst thus bear closely upon one another.

With a characteristic Kinsellan sense of paradox, the introductory poem (9–10), which constitutes the storyteller's first narrative, moves in the opposite direction, not tunneling underground but rising upward, toward the vertical and consciousness, but driven no less by appetite:

> *Up and awake. Up straight*
> *in absolute hunger*
> *out of this black lair, and eat!*

The "*furryfeathery bundles*" prove "*whimswift,*" "*Snapdelicious,*" "*Throbflutter*": such compounds possess a surreal quality; later compounds like "Hisshorror" (21) reveal their origins in a Bosch-like world. Moreover, any evolution seems motivated by such compounds forming a dialectic: "*The ache . . . The ease!*" as "*The two energies approach and come to terms, / balance somehow, grow still.*" Such balance we have seen earlier in *Fifteen Dead* attributed to both Ó Riada and Kennedy and constituting the Quincunx vision. A similar equipoise or unity of being the protagonist experiences in his dream: "*In the third part of the dream I saw /—I* was *two discs of light in the heavens / trembling in momentary balance.*" Kinsella's source is likely the creation story in the *Book of Invasions*: "And God made two bright and great lights: He made the greater light that it might take over the day, and the lesser light in the night" (*LGE* para. 23). Kinsella's dreaming self experiences their momentary balance, a synthesis the

32. Ross, *Pagan Celtic Britain*, 39.
33. Jung, *Memories, Dreams, Reflections*, 299.

visionary nature of which Yeats spoke in "The Tower" when sun and moon become "One inextricable beam" (*Collected Poems* 220). Kinsella's imagery includes also the shedding of skins and a coiling into sleep, both associated with the uroboric serpent.[34] Anne Yeats's striking line drawings of a coiling serpent in the Peppercanister edition of *One* reinforce the poet's point superbly. Such actions evidence process, transformation, synthesis, and cyclic return. We are not far, in fact, from the characteristically Celtic spiral motif which, while certainly decorative, is, more importantly, a magical symbol. (At Newgrange, in the Boyne Valley, for example, at both winter and summer solstices, the first rays of sunlight penetrate to the inner chamber of the passage-grave and strike a distinctively decorated three-spiral stone.) The reader has been introduced to the land of the self and undertakes journeys through dreams and the unconscious to the self's origins, all of which are set off against the Irish mythological account of the First People. The introductory poem thus opens with movement upward into consciousness but, by its conclusion, proceeds to sink downward into sleep. The two poles must be known and held in necessary and fruitful tension, and the reader is instructed, with fine irony, to "*Sleep on these things.*" Such friendly advice also illustrates that these matters are discoverable only at psychic depths, below consciousness, surfacing only in dreams.

"The Entire Fabric" (11–12) offers another introduction to the volume, presenting the whole as theatrical, a fabrication, a "making" in the best sense, with a curious mixture of Greek tragedy and London's Royal Court tableaux. The mockery of the quack-alchemist is surely self-directed, with the parody serving to defend the collation of personal and mythic. The poem also redirects the reader to recognize the aesthetic relevance of Kinsella's quest: that what follows is a fiction, a construction of the self in which it finds itself, a structure or "mechanism" that enables the poet to reveal meaning, the source of which is the rich matrix of the self. For the poet's search for origins and meaning has brought him back to the earliest surviving expressions of the Irish self, to a landscape of cairns, dolmens, souterrains, and passage-graves, to poetry written according to strict bardic meters and rhymes, and to enigmatic riddles, all of which were the province of bards like Amergin, the first Irish poet. Indeed, Kinsella makes bold

34. Neumann, *Origins and History of Consciousness*, 10ff.

and successful use of Amergin's famous poem in *LGE* (para. 387, Poem LXIX).[35] On one level the reader is provided with concrete descriptions of night-sea journeys, ocean currents and breezes, landings and, in "The Oldest Place," eventual establishment of a social structure. But the reader is also reminded of the relevance of all this to the self, to the exploration of the unconscious, to the tested, dividing, suffering, enduring self and its much sought-after fulfillment and wholeness. The order of the invasions, as given in *LGE*—from that of Cessair to the finally successful one of the Gaedil, the Sons of Mil—is significantly reversed in the ordering of Kinsella's poems. "Finistère," for example, which recounts the latest invasion, by the Sons of Mil, precedes "The Oldest Place," which deals for the most part with an even earlier invasion. Kinsella's progress is backward increasingly into the past as well as downward into the unconscious realms of the self, to the origins of being.

Hence, "Finistère" (*One* 12–16) opens with the Roman numeral I, printed in extravagantly large size, suggesting both a numerical progression and the first-person pronoun, and, further, the upright vertical to which the self, Milesian or modern, strives. Likewise, "one" is both cardinal number and indefinite pronoun, so reflecting at the same time unity and imperfection. In similarly paradoxical fashion, consciousness of self is achieved by descent into the unconscious, by proceeding backward to points of origin, the zero of being. The protagonist of "Finistère" is Amergin, the first poet of Ireland, and it is he who, in Kinsella's account, "From a bald boulder on the cairn top / . . . spied out the horizon to the northwest / and sensed that minute imperfection again." Ireland appears as a "minute imperfection," "A point of light" in the midst of increasing darkness. Again, however, Kinsella is prepared to adapt his sources: in *LGE* it is Ith who first spies Ireland from a tall watchtower in Spain, and only when Ith is slain by the Tuatha Dé Danann do the Sons of Mil, including Amergin, undertake their successful invasion as revenge for Ith's murder. Similarly, the Finistère (world's end) from which Kinsella's invaders and passage-grave builders come is in Brittany rather than Spain: the waves of invaders and the several accounts begin to merge.

Yet the same hunger driving the Sons of Mil to invade Ireland drives on the creative self; one is reminded of Kinsella's concession in

35. Cf. Maurice Harmon, *The Poetry of Thomas Kinsella*, 103.

"Phoenix Park" to his wife's superiority because she knows things "bodily" as opposed to the male "mere idea" (*N* 79). The Sons of Mil, catching sight of "A point of light" amid encroaching darkness, thus undertake a journey to Ireland, to a new land of the self, to go beyond their previous boundaries to found a new world. They are thought-adventurers whose expedition is fundamentally psychic in its implications.

> A maggot of the possible
> wriggled out of the spine
> into the brain.
>
> (O 12)

The same vision, captured in early Irish stone markings and echoed in the tight internal rhyming, alliteration, and assonance of early Irish poetry, motivates the poet in turn. And at the heart of that vision is the Irish *Magna mater* to whom the invading Sons of Mil pray.

Kinsella's articulation of their prayer goes beyond mere imitation of early Irish poetic techniques: he has skillfully adapted those techniques to express his own distinctive purpose and view, and at the same time he has captured expression that seems ageless and the root of a primary world. The internal rhyming of the opening lines—for example, "ill"/"well," "mild"/"wild"—establish the antitheses within which the people exist, but the lines' assonance and alliteration, as the sounds proceed from the tight, closed vowel "i" to the open "e," manage further to suggest the very movement of the antithetical process itself. The intricate rhyming patterns, in the manner of early Irish syllabic meters, shape the vowels and consonants into a highly structured sound: "ill" and "well," positioned appropriately, open and close the first line, but "wind" and "end" function equally significantly as, chiming across the caesura, they share their consonantal "nd" sound. Indeed, the rhythm and shortness of line help to embody that spiraling process that the prayer acknowledges, a spiraling that, like Yeats's winding stair, embraces the contraries, and to which the several antitheses refer ("peace"/"unrest"; "meet"/"unmeet"; "settle fulfilled and build"/"still unsettled"; "poolspirals"/"spiralpools"; "opening"/"closing"; "river"/"earth"; "sun"/"moon"). The "dances drilled in the rock" signify the dance of life itself, the dance the self must undertake to attain wholeness and knowledge:

—Ill wind end well
mild mother
on wild water pour peace

who gave us our unrest
whom we meet and unmeet
in whose yearning shadow
we erect our great uprights
and settle fulfilled
and build and are still
unsettled, whose goggle gaze
and holy howl we have scraped
speechless on slabs of stone
poolspirals opening on
closing spiralpools
and dances drilled in the rock
in coil zigzag angle and curl
river ripple earth ramp
suncircle moonloop . . .
(13–14)

The enigmatic rhetorical questions, posed in Amergin's *rosc* as he first stepped upon Ireland, are repeated by the twentieth-century poet-protagonist at the conclusion to "Finistère." Kinsella follows some of Amergin's details quite closely, including the wind, the wave, the "bull with seven scars," the salmon, the pool, and the incantation of questions. But he has avoided strict translation in order to draw attention to the parallel with his own questing protagonist-self. For the nature of Amergin's poem is such that it parallels the poet-maker: ". . . Amairgen on the ocean of non-existence embodies the primeval unity of all things. As such he has the power to bring a new world into being, and his poems are in the nature of creation incantations."[36] Kinsella now applies such power to bear on the journeying self, bent on descending to the lowest levels of the unconscious where poet and Milesian invader touch upon the same source. Amergin's questions do indeed constitute "creation incantations," while the new world he seeks to create, as the poem has shown all along, is of the self, that wholeness or integration of the personality to which all aspire. As poet, shaman, and bearer of news from the land of the dead, Amergin possesses a "craft" which, with fine Kinsella irony, is both literal boat and the craft of poetry. The landing place Amergin

36. Rees and Rees, *Celtic Heritage*, 99.

finds is but one of many sought in Kinsella's poetry, just as his vision and art constitute part of the contemporary poet's inheritance.

> When men meet on the hill
> dumb as the stones in the dark
>   (the craft knocked behind me)
> who is the jack of all light?
> Who goes in full into
> the moon's interesting conditions?
> Who fingers the sun's sink hole?
>   (I went forward, reaching out)
>
> (16)

The Sons of Mil, like the Israelites whose Exodus from captivity and progress to the Promised Land they parallel, are driven by "unrest" which, following the traditional account, is overcome by their discovery of eventual peace in Ireland. Over Kinsella's Milesians, however, rests a sense of doom and tragedy. And "The Oldest Place" (16–19) proceeds further back to tell of the First People who, with the exception of Fintan, were drowned in the Flood. Unlike the Sons of Mil, who are granted a sense of destiny, the First People are motivated by evil. As we have seen, Cessair and her company were refused admission to Noah's Ark because they were robbers and thieves. They were succeeded, incidentally, in the Second Invasion by Partholón, who fled to Ireland after killing his parents.

Kinsella has fused several elements of the different invasions into the one version of "The Oldest Place," just as the protagonist-narrator is at various times Amergin or an earlier invader, though always emblematic of Kinsella's questing creative self. Thus Kinsella has combined the second attempt at landing that characterizes the invasion by the Sons of Mil ("We approached the shore. Once more."); the sinfulness shared by both Cessair and Partholón; the establishment of an agricultural society (the clearing of plains undertaken by both Partholón and his successor, Nemed); the digging of a grave that becomes a lake and that occurs in both Partholón and Nemed tales (*LGE* paras 219, 250); and the infliction of plague, which overtakes Partholón in particular. By such mixing of elements and protagonists and by so violating the *LGE* accounts, Kinsella has indeed asserted the awful nature of "The Oldest Place" and its foundation in nightmare as much as in vision, in appetite that leads to both heroic questing and ravenous hunger. And Kinsella sees parallels in the modern self. The

First People's dreams are filled with creatures offering "clawfuls of dripping cloth / and gold and silver things," but "the withered plain of my own brain" belongs equally to first and latest Irish selves, a land of the dead that must be confronted and charted if the self is to grow in fullness and creativity.

Similarly, the Gothic experience, with which the poem concludes, centers upon the protagonist's dream of the standing stone and the ominous face emerging from the dark void. The description is deliberately imprecise: does he see a shawl that takes on the appearance of a face, or is the face shrouded by the shawl? What is clear, however, is that the experience emerges from the protagonist's unconscious and is of the hag/*cailleach* or Hecate, one further instance of the Terrible Mother. The torn forehead is inherited in later poems by similar faces before mirrors: Kinsella has progressed beyond the "dark exhausted eye" and "dry downturning mouth" of "Mirror in February" (*D* 63) and the "Too-bright eyes" of "The Serving Maid" (*N* 19–20), and in a short while will portray the more frightening vision in *A Technical Supplement*, Poem 22, and the wounding in "Self Renewal," "on a white brow crossed, / two ragged cuts; a wet mouth / held shut; eyes hurt and full" (*BF* 39). The mirror of the soul has darkened considerably; here the shawl-face is marked also for its tongue and its descent to earth signifies an inheritance—a combination of appetite and articulation—passed down from the First People:

> A shawl shifted on the top, dangled
> black and silver, a crumpled face
> with forehead torn crisscross, begging,
> with tongue flapping,
> and dropped to earth.
>
> (*One* 19)

The poems that follow apply the lines of origin more directly to the poet himself. In "38 Phoenix Street" (20–21) the poet provides four vignettes from his childhood recollections: of being a baby lifted up to confront the neighbor's baby similarly hoisted above the wall (another mirroring or paralleling of face); listening with the neighbor's son, Jimmy Cummins, on their gramophone to John McCormack; recollecting Jimmy's father's burial alive "for three days under a hill of dead" in the Dardanelles; and as a boy sleeping overnight next door "in a strange room." With the exception of the fearful wartime experience, each experience, while vividly described, is ordinary enough.

But with his extensive image patterns and thematic unities Kinsella is able to invest those experiences with profound significance. Even the street address (Phoenix Street) serves his purpose. The "wiry redgolden thing" (a centipede, reminiscent of Joyce's earwig with its reverberations of HCE) retreats to its hole, as much a symbol of rebirth as the scarab in "Hen Woman." Mr Cummins remains, like Fintan, "Sealed in his sad cave," risen physically from the dead but broken by his ordeal and scarred like so many of Kinsella's mirrored faces ("A black rubbery scar stuck on his white forehead"; "They noticed him by a thread of blood / glistening among the black crusts on his forehead"). The appearance of the Sacred Heart beating in the unfamiliar bedroom relates back to the "tongues of flame" in the kitchen lamp, to the color and the wriggling manner of the centipede and its dark womblike hole, and to the soldier's heart beating desperately in his struggle to survive. All, however, extend further Kinsella's awareness of that same struggle in all things and its positive contribution to spiritual growth.

As the burgeoning poet in "Minstrel" the young Kinsella appears "bent like a feeding thing / over my own source." As in Yeats, consummation of self involves the self's consumption; appetite here becomes self-devouring and reveals origins. Once again the lines of inheritance are traced: first, from the stereotyped minstrel figure of the opening lines, described in the language of sentimental Irish rebel songs ("A mist of tears lay still upon the land") to the young boy writing in his Inchicore kitchen, inhabited in turn by "A shadow" while, outside, heaven and earth are held in fundamental and antithetical conjunction:

> Outside, the heavens listened,
> a starless diaphragm
> stopped miles overhead
> to hear the remotest whisper
> of returning matter, missing
> an enormous black beat.
>
> The earth stretched out in answer.
> Little directionless instincts
> uncoiled from the wet mud-cracks,
> crept in wisps of purpose, and vanished
> leaving momentary traces
> of claw marks, breasts,
> ribs, feathery prints,

eyes shutting and opening
all over the surface.
A distant point of light
winked at the edge of nothing.
(22–23)

The landscape remains the intrinsically primordial one: the experience of origins moves out beyond the confines of the kitchen to include the world's elemental heartbeat, to recognize the antithetical forces of stillness and movement, light and darkness, totality and void. That "distant point of light" winking at the young boy is as much a beckoning to undertake the soul's essential journey as is the light the Sons of Mil spy in *LGE* and which results in their invasion of Ireland. The young boy is made aware of his more immediate ancestor when father and son confront each other through the dark night window, each a mirror of the other. The father's face emerges out of the darkness, much as the later memories surface, to illuminate the poet in his cave-room-womb and to suggest an awful inheritance that must be handed on.

The last of these autobiographical poems, "His Father's Hands," is perhaps the most inclusive in vision. The poem moves from a conversation over drinks between father and grown-up son; through reminiscences of the poet's grandfather cutting up pipe tobacco, mending the family's shoes, and playing the fiddle; to tracing family history; to racial memories hidden deep in the unconscious about the landing of the Gaels; and finally to the poet as a child emulating his grandfather. The imagery of hands, which is particularly dominant in the later volumes, establishes this train of association. For hands involve touch, sexual and otherwise; they communicate and enable exchanges of trust; and, like Kinsella's "body music" (71) in the volume's concluding poem or the bodily wisdom of woman (N 79), they lead beyond experience to understanding. In "His Father's Hands" the associations are vividly caught in the fragmentary sentences, the father's earnest voice, the grandfather whispering snatches of song as he plays the fiddle. Such associations embody the poem's thrust toward inheritance. It traces genetically the connecting lines of the past not because Kinsella indulges in sentimental nostalgia, but because he seeks to understand the process and its culmination in himself. *Blood and Family* (1988) continues the poet's exploration of what has been handed down to him, and there, as here, the narrative traces the intersection of family and national histories: "Your family, Thomas, met with and helped / many of the Croppies in hiding from the Yeos / or on their way home after the defeat / in south Wexford" (*One* 25). Blood lines soon begin to involve bloodshed, "dispersals and migrations," just as the grandfather's fiddle songs tell of heartbreak and loss. "Beyond that" and Kinsella's descent into the past takes on a starkly elemental character as he reaches back to the First People, the Mesolithic and Neolithic communities established after the last ice age, and to the megalith builders like those of the Boyne Valley:

> Littered uplands. Dense grass. Rocks everywhere,
> wet underneath, retaining memory of the long cold.
>
> First, a prow of land
> chosen, and webbed with tracks;
> then boulders chosen
> and sloped together, stabilized in menace.
> (25)

The experience unnerves, "feels evil," yet leads back ultimately "Through what evolutions or accidents / toward that peace and patience / by the fireside, that blocked gentleness. . . ."

> The blood advancing
> —gorging vessel after vessel—
> and altering in them
> one by one.
>
> Behold, that gentleness
> modulated twice, in others:
> to earnestness and iteration;
> to an offhandedness, repressing various impulses.
> (26)

Advance depends upon appetite ("gorging") and transmutation through vessels, in a literal sense, bloodvessels; as a central Jungian archetype, of womb or cave or alchemical instrument, the vessels enable transformation of self. Despite his sense of evil, the poet has been brought to peace, patience, and gentleness, which also constitute his inheritance and have molded his self. The climax comes with the poet's rediscovery of his childhood wooden block, which breaks open to issue forth "countless little nails / squirming and dropping out of it." Vividly resembling spermatozoa or embryonic cells in their first stages of evolution, the nails emerge out of the womblike block, reminding the poet of the continuing process. The nails scatter, like semen ejaculated, to proceed with their life cycle in a manner parallel to that of the poet, his family, and his ancestors, and to the coiling dialectical pattern of life itself. Like the hungry ravishing of the pomegranate in "A Hand of Solo" (*NLD* 15), the experience here is allegorical but founded on fact.[37] The sexual analogy points not only to the obvious biological evolution but to the psychological evolution of the self. For as Thomas Kilroy has reminded us, Kinsella belongs to "Our papish line," the "subject-matter" of which "is repression, sexual and intellectual, rather than political."[38] "His Father's Hands" traces the inheritance handed down in the process of generation and the release that accompanies the poet's tracing of blood lines.

The 1979 edition of *One* begins with the *seanchaí* but his tale is framed by dream poems that open and close the sequence. For the evolving process, which Kinsella traces throughout, seeing his own family descent against the larger ancestry of Ireland and its several invasions, is rooted in the self, unconscious and conscious, its dreams and nightmares, its intuited sources in darkness as well as light, and is centered on the Great Mother archetype of myth and Jungian analysis. The squirming spermatozoa-nails are thus transformed in the concluding dream to the first-person plural—"*We squirmed in expectation,*" "*our wriggling sheaves*"—and become subject, in "*The great cell of nightmare,*" to the Terrible Mother archetype. The Audenesque image of the cell[39] has undergone an evolution by way not only of Darwin and Kinsella's attention to Darwinian theory and embryonic development but also by way of Jung and his theory of archetypes. The cell is related in turn to Kinsella's preoccupation, particularly strong in *Notes from the Land of the Dead* and *One*, with numerology, proceeding from circular zero to the vertical I of the individual self. The "cell" now is of "*nightmare,*" which must be endured. At the same time, however, like the Terrible Mother, the cell is both prolific and devouring. Here the dominant image is of

37. "And the block did exactly that as far as actuality is concerned—not that it matters, except to me." As he said of his use of the pomegranate, "I would obey the facts"; see *Viewpoints*, ed. Haffenden, 112, 109.

38. Kilroy, "Thomas Kinsella: *Out of Ireland* and *St. Catherine's Clock*," *Krino* 5 (Spring 1988): 157.

39. "And each in the cell of himself is almost convinced of his freedom"; see W. H. Auden, "In Memory of W. B. Yeats" (l. 27). Cf. the subsequent image of "the prison of his days" (l. 76); see *Collected Poems*, ed. Edward Mendelson (London: Faber and Faber, 1977), 197–98.

apocalyptic harvesting: " '*Reap us!' we hissed, in praise.*" Both the hissing and the spread-out hair of the woman invoke the Medusa/ Hecate myth, and the hair, common among Jungian archetypes like the Medusa or Maya, symbolizes the net in which the masculine consciousness feels ensnared, preventing its growth toward light, individuation, and wholeness.[40] But the function of both dreams, as of Kinsella's *seanchaí*, is to bring these processes to light, to expression by the poetic word, and thus to our understanding. For the woman is also the Jungian anima who must be confronted, understood, and integrated if the self is to gain its essential totality and spiritual health. Wholly characteristically, however, such a Jungian reading is not without its Irish roots: as we have seen in previous work, Kinsella's Hecate figure merges also with his own formidable grandmother and in turn with the Irish *cailleach* or hag. Moreover, because within recent memory in rural Ireland the final stook in the harvest field was given particular attention and named the *cailleach*,[41] Kinsella's harvest imagery embraces biblical, mythic, and Irish significance in a totality that serves to confirm his meaning and to persuade his reader.

The second half of the concluding poem takes the form of abstract analysis. On one level, the process is clearly psychological in character, with reference to "*motherly warmth,*" "*Anxieties,*" "*nightmare-bearing tissue,*" "*the dawn-zone,*" and "*shadow.*" On another level, however, that process is also moral in significance: the descent into the unconscious, for example, is a "*fall,*" and Kinsella has perpetually used such descents to seek an understanding of evil, whether individual or cosmic. His self-exploration has been ruthlessly painful because of the painful nature of reality, of both world and self. As he remarked in 1971 of twentieth-century barbarism, "In the fifty short years since Yeats's prophetic poem 'The Second Coming,' that Second Coming has been accomplished; externally, in the physical chaos of extermination and race slaughter, internally in a sense of precariousness and disorder in the spirit." "It was no news that the human mind was an abyss, and that the will, just as much as the imagination, was capable of every evil. But it was something new that creatures out of Hierony-

40. Cf. Broder, "Images of the Feminine," 94–95.

41. E. Estyn Evans, *Irish Folk Ways* (1957; London: Routledge and Kegan Paul, 1979), 162–63; Kevin Danaher, *The Year in Ireland* (Cork: Mercier Press, 1972), 190–92, 198–99.

mus Bosch should have materialized in the world, formally inflicting and enduring suffering beyond all reason, in obedience to a diabolic logic. . . ."[42]

However, the "*nightmare-bearing tissue*" of *One* is not new, nor exclusively modern, nor unique; rather, it is primordial, primeval, known and experienced by the first invaders of Ireland, motivating them indeed on their voyages, both literal and spiritual. Kinsella's own parallels in *One* have illustrated that point vividly and forcefully. Moreover, because they also constitute his own ancestry, the cells of that tissue ultimately form a living thing, a "one" self replete with consciousness, having confronted the dark and articulated the wisdom gained from that confrontation. The prize in fairy tale, myth, or legend is often hidden, buried from sight, gained only after heroic questing and suffering. When given a Jungian archetypal interpretation, the prize consists of full consciousness or individuation, or, in Kinsella's term, understanding.[43]

The italicized poem prefatory to *A Technical Supplement* (*One* 31) traces the beginnings of that process by describing the action of a group of people. They may be early Irish invaders, survivors of a cosmic or nuclear disaster, or reassembling parts of a dismembered self. Kinsella is deliberately vague concerning their identity because all such meanings might be legitimate. Progression is possible, however, as individual members will themselves to movement, proceeding from inertia and malleability ("*No one did anything at first*"; "*Anyone could have done anything with us*") through the assertions of will ("*backbone*") and "*energy*" across the primeval, primordial "*mud.*" The narrator is the fourth and, with the emergence of a fifth, "*the whole world exploded behind us / and a golden light blasted us out.*" Given Kinsella's interest in numerology, it is particularly appropriate that five survive: as we have seen, the number has distinctly Irish relevance, as in the four provinces that intersect in the fifth, Meath; in the four peoples in the *Táin* from the four provinces known as

42. Kinsella, "The Divided Mind," 214–15. Bosch's "basic theme" is "the nightmare of human life"; see de Tolnay, *Hieronymus Bosch*, 202.

43. "The treasure which the hero fetches from the dark caverns is *life:* it is himself, new-born from the dark maternal cave of the unconscious"; see Jung, *Symbols of Transformation*, 374. Cf. "Every culture-hero has achieved a synthesis between consciousness and the creative unconscious," a synthesis which is the "hidden treasure" to be discovered; see Neumann, *Origins and History of Consciousness*, 212.

"fifths"; but also, behind such instances, in the Quincunx or principle of cosmic center or order. Moreover, while acknowledging Jung's contribution to his own use of numerology, Kinsella has also noted its nearly inevitable application to family: "It's very hard to work on profound personal and family matters without coming up numerological. One begins as zero, one develops into one, one meets another and becomes two; with luck, three emerges."[44] The scheme may be "a ridiculous reduction," as he calls it, but it enables him to show the five survivors on their necessary journey to wholeness or individuation, a journey that succeeding poems pursue.

Kinsella's moving prayer at the beginning of *A Technical Supplement*—"let our gaze blaze, we pray, / let us see how the whole thing / works" (*One* 33)—captures the positive and illuminating character of the poet's investigation and his persistent attention to process (or how a thing works). In this sequence he suggests a parallel with Diderot's *Encyclopédie*, a parallel continued in a later poem, *One Fond Embrace* (*FCC* 1–10). For both poet and philosopher, method remains crucial. Moreover, Diderot exemplifies those characteristic Kinsella virtues, will and endurance.[45] At the same time, Kinsella is mindful, like Diderot, of the forces within and without, pulling in the direction of disorder and incoherence. Above all, what distinguishes the poet's heroic protagonists and exemplars is their persistent, willed commitment to structure and meaning.

The parallel with Diderot and the Enlightenment succeeds because Kinsella's gaze is similarly encyclopedic, his scope is as wide as experience itself, and his honesty is equally ruthless and uncompromising. The fearful character of *A Technical Supplement*, highlighted in the Peppercanister edition with its vivid and fiercely exact illustrations from the *Encyclopédie*, is necessary rather than willful. It is the inevitable consequence of Kinsella's perpetual alliance of enlightenment and suffering, and of expansion of self through descent into nightmare. Furthermore, his attention to process has become increasingly internalized until, in *A Technical Supplement*, the psychological and moral shambles of the modern self is dreadfully paralleled in the

44. O'Driscoll, "Interview," 61.

45. See Kinsella's source, John Viscount Morley, *Diderot and the Encyclopaedists*, 2 vols. (London: Chapman and Hall, 1878), for the problems Diderot encountered with the *Encyclopédie*.

"shambles" (in the original sense of a butchery or slaughterhouse)[46] of Swift's slaughterhouse in Chicago. And the shambles of that slaughterhouse merge with the experience of another Swift, who, with his mind in shambles, spent his last years in a Dublin mental hospital. Like Diderot, Jonathan Swift epitomized enlightenment and understanding, pushing his vision and his mind to the limits. Once more history and place reveal uncomfortable parallels.

Yet it would be wrong to focus on the pain alone. The extraordinarily precise anatomical description (Poem II), for example, may pursue the knife's relentless peeling away of the human body's muscles so that they "drop away one by one writhing"—another instance in Kinsella's multitude of writhing, coiling figures—or dismiss the eyes as "dry staring buttons of muscle" (33) in an updated version of the "button-brown hard eyes" in "Soft Toy" (N 51). But it is torsion upon which the poet focuses: it was a key Kinsella image in *Notes from the Land of the Dead* (10, 30), one that described the stress within a field of energies intrinsic to process, evolution, and therefore existence itself, and it is a key image again here. The preferred image in *One* and subsequent volumes is the coil or spiral or writhing, wriggling figures. Kinsella's first two volumes, *Another September* and *Downstream*, look almost static or frozen in comparison: in "Brothers" (AS 61), for example, he approaches the later, more kinetic vision in describing a dog as "A model of sinews, fragile tissue and channelled blood," but the coiling formation of tissue comes only late in *Nightwalker*, in the conclusion to "Phoenix Park" which serves to preface *Notes from the Land of the Dead*. Here in *A Technical Supplement* the dialectical torsion holds the body together in a counterpointed balance broken by the dissecting knife:

> It would seem possible to peel the body asunder,
> to pick off the muscles and let them
> drop away one by one writhing
> until you had laid bare
> four or five simple bones at most.
> Except that at the first violation
> the body would rip into pieces and fly apart
> with terrible spasms.
>
> (*One* 33)

46. The description is founded upon personal experience of the Chicago slaughterhouse. Cf. Barrie Cooke's series of "much-debated carcass paintings" produced after a summer in Martinique; see John Montague, "The Painting of Barrie Cooke," *Dubliner* 3 (Spring 1964): 40.

The opposite is the "light architecture" of "No-stress against no-stress" (35) in the subsequent poem (III), set off against successive poems of anatomical dissection and fearful carnage in a slaughter-house (IV–VII). Appetite, the life force within such fields of stress, has turned monstrous. As Kinsella's knife or dissecting probe follows its path through tissue and cells to the roots of things, the reader is made conscious of his own bestiality and evil. Head and heart, mind and body are no longer held in unified balance but both are assaulted and rendered helpless; utterance is reduced to staccato and incredulous questioning:

> Vital spatterings. Excess.
> Make the mind creep. Play-blood
> bursting everywhere out of
> big chopped dolls: the stuff breaking copiously
> out of a slow, horrified head.
>
> Is it all right to do this?
> Is it an offence against justice
> when someone stumbles away helplessly
> and has to sit down
> until her sobbing stops?
>
> (39)

In similar fashion we are given the lizard, driven by natural instinct and appetite, seen not only as "A living thing swallowing another" but caught appropriately enough with "The head inside the mouth / and the little hands and feet and the tail / and the suddenly soft round belly / hanging down outside" (39). Justice plays no part in that natural instinctive action but both instinct and appetite are relevant to process. "The Breath, the Bite" (52) are irrevocably married in a conjunction that includes the essential "breath" of life and the inspiring breath, whether of the divine or of the muse—articulation and appetite are both made possible by the matrix of the mouth. Hence the poet confronts the muse as prowler on his landing, and as one who must be penetrated, to use the same sexual metaphor he provided earlier in "A Hand of Solo" (*NLD* 15). Kinsella's predatory animals or prowlers signify the imagination—in Yeats's phrase, "the stirring of the beast":[47]

47. Quoted in Seamus Heaney, "The Makings of a Music: Reflections on Wordsworth and Yeats," in *Preoccupations: Selected Prose, 1968–1978* (London: Faber and Faber, 1980), 72; also see "Lowell's Command," in *The Government of the Tongue*, 136.

The pen writhed. It moved
under my thumb!
It has sensed
that sad prowler on our landing again.

If she dares, come nearer, if she dares . . .
She and her "sudden and
peremptory incursions" . . .
I'll pierce her like
a soft fruit, a soft big seed!

(*One* 45)

Moments of peace (Poem X) or delight (Poem XVI) are likewise seriously qualified, and past and present in Poem XVII coalesce as the smell of homemade bread becomes associated with the discovery in the mid-nineteenth century of Viking remains at Islandbridge, close to Kinsella's childhood home: "Man-meat, spitted," the corpses preserve the Viking spearheads just as memory preserves the childhood experience of home-baked bread. Both involve appetite, which in turn destroys and preserves. In Poem XIX the *aisling* vision of the muse-woman offers a troubling darkness rather than comforting light:

I met a fair maid all shining
with hair all over her cheeks
and pearly tongue
who spoke to me and sighed
as if my own nervous nakedness
spoke to me and said:

My heart is a black fruit.
It is a piece of black coal.
When I laugh a black thing hovers.

(48)

Indeed, such darkness has long proved necessary as well as inevitable in Kinsella's world: "the years," he declares in poem XX, "propel themselves / onward on thickening scars, toward / new efforts of propulsion" (49). Torsion may provoke scarring, but suffering, like darkness, enables progress or movement within process, acting as a positive agent as well as a condition to be endured. The lesson is learnt when, in Poem XXII, the persona experiences torsion in the form of the dividing images as seen in a dressing-table triple mirror (a favorite Kinsella instrument and pose):

It began to separate, the head opening
like a rubbery fan . . .
The thin hair blurred and crept apart
widening from a deepening seam
as the forehead opened down the centre
and unfolded pale new detail
surfacing from within.

The eyes moved wider apart
and another eye surfaced between them and divided.
The nose divided and doubled and moved out
one to right and left.
The mouth stretched in a snarl
then split into two mouths, pursed.

(50–51)

Tormented and made uncertain by such multiplicity of vision, the persona is eventually reconciled thanks to the knowledge of further necessary multiplicity within the very nature of process itself:

Another ounce of impulse and
I might have driven my fist at the mirror
and abolished everything.
But the starred ruins
would only have started to divide and creep.

(51)

For all such torsion and appetite, however, the dominant image throughout the sequence is the knife or dissecting probe, accompanied in the Peppercanister edition with strikingly gruesome illustrations from Diderot's *Encyclopédie.* In the words of John Viscount Morley, whom Kinsella quotes in a concluding "Note on Illustrations" to that Peppercanister, "The animation of these folios of plates is prodigious." It is an "animation" that captures a world under torsion but also the response of Kinsella's questing protagonist in search of understanding and wholeness of self. For, as Morley proceeds, "To turn over volume after volume is like watching a splendid panorama of all the busy life of the time. Minute care is as striking in them as their comprehensiveness. The smallest tool, the knot in a thread, the ply in a cord, the curve of wrist or finger, each has special or proper delineation." Morley's description is peculiarly pertinent to Kinsella's sequence. His knife or probe functions both positively and negatively, in a creative–destructive dialectic that runs through the later poetry, exposing but also healing. It is the latter effect that the poet's critics have been slow to recognize. In fact, the visceral is kept in proper perspective by the parallel of Diderot, in search, like the poet, of encyclopedic understanding.

Yet it is to Jung and Ireland rather than to Diderot that Kinsella turns in the third and final sequence, *Song of the Night* (1978). One of the presiding figures is again the poet's father, as in the prologue poem where he carries his young son along the night street. Progress is marked by their dialectical movement from light to dark and on to further light, as they proceed past a succession of lampposts to the warmth and security of home and as the child suffers the contraries ("warm and chill, / homeward, abandoned" [54]). The father joins other male figures in Kinsella's poetry—Dick King, for example, or Gerry Flaherty, Ó Riada himself, and, in the next sequence, Gustav Mahler and Thomas Mann—all of whom provide a significant alternative to the long-standing importance of the woman-wife-muse. The other presiding male figure in *Song of the Night* is Jung, as we see in "C. G. Jung's 'First Years,' "

The details of Kinsella's poem are based upon Jung's account of his "First Years" in the opening chapter of his *Memories, Dreams, Reflections*. There Jung describes his earliest memories—of water and the Rhine Falls; of his nurse, whose ear, throat, and sallow skin he still remembers; of Jesus "eating" the dead; of his frightening experience of a Catholic priest, associated in his mind with Jesuits—and his dream. In Kinsella's words,

> A pillar of skin
> stared up dumb, enthroned
> in an underground room . . .
> (55)

The "dream . . . was to preoccupy me all my life," Jung wrote. Moreover, with even greater relevance to Kinsella's own poetic preoccupations, Jung commented further:

> Who spoke to me then? Who talked of problems far beyond my knowledge? Who brought the Above and Below together, and laid the foundation for everything that was to fill the second half of my life with stormiest passion? Who but that alien guest who came both from above and from below?
>
> Through this childhood dream I was initiated into the secrets of the earth. What happened then was a kind of burial in the earth, and many

years were to pass before I came out again. Today I know that it happened in order to bring the greatest possible amount of light into the darkness. It was an initiation into the realm of darkness. My intellectual life had its unconscious beginnings at that time.[48]

Just as Kinsella has incorporated the first invaders of Ireland and the early Irish myths into his poetry to express his own spiritual and psychological ancestry, so he has seen a further and crucial link with Jung. For Kinsella too has striven "to bring the greatest possible amount of light into the darkness," while the "burial in the earth" Jung underwent in his crucial dream corresponds to the several burials, tunnelings, and chartings of the land of the dead that Kinsella himself has undertaken. The early Irish builders of dolmens and passage graves were responding to more than a utilitarian need to dispose of their dead. Their spirals and zigzags express an ancient wisdom and lead down to the present, as the poet has acknowledged and as Jung would have appreciated. Moreover, the sexual basis of Jung's childhood dream is plain: what he sees is a giant "ritual phallus"[49] associated in his mind, through a remark of his mother, with the Lord Jesus as "his underground counterpart." The Irish pagan equivalent is the Lia Fáil, the stone penis on the Hill of Tara. But Jung's experience relates in turn to the persistent struggle on the part of Kinsella's protagonists to stand upright, a struggle analogous to the erection of dolmens. Once more we are reminded of the sexual character of Kinsella's own quest. Certainly dolmens have been so associated in myth and folklore: "The two pillars of the dolmen, covered with the transverse stone, are one of the earliest representations of the threefold Feminine, to which a fourth part is often added in the lone phallic pillar of the Masculine."[50] Indeed, the dolmen has been seen in ways peculiarly pertinent to Kinsella's vision, as "gate-womb, entrance to the underworld, and as sacrificial altar."[51] The consequence for Jung, as Kinsella's poem makes plain, is the assumption of "the throne," a kingship not of the political kind conferred by Tara's Lia Fáil but of a spiritual or psychic nature. It is a consummation of self that in turn depends, appropriately enough, upon appetite, upon the act of Communion:

48. Jung, *Memories, Dreams, Reflections,* 11, 15.
49. Ibid., 12.
50. Neumann, *The Great Mother,* 158.
51. Ibid.

Since when I have eaten Jesus . . .
and stepped onto the path
    long ago: my fingers stretched at the hill
    and a sleeve-winged terror
    shrank like a shadow and flapped away
    sailing over the dry grass;
    staring crumbs led up through the tree-darkness
    to a hollow, with bloody steps down . . .
and have assumed the throne.

(55–56)

A similar shadowy black bird figures as illustration in the Peppercanister edition and reappears in the volume's concluding and title poem, "Song of the Night," to accompany wholeness or unity of being to which the poet himself is brought.

This is not to argue that Kinsella's poems can be understood only if they are given a Jungian interpretation. That would be to exaggerate the debt and to limit the parallelism, since Jungian archetypes and Irish mythological literature, as we have seen, merge. Further, as "C. G. Jung's 'First Years' " is also meant to indicate, the autobiographical scope of Kinsella's work is irrevocably tied up in turn with both Jungian archetypes and Irish myth. Like La Tène handiwork or the intricate interlacings of works like *The Book of Kells*, both of which served Joyce earlier, the path Kinsella's poetry has followed has led him to discern the interrelatedness of things. The maze has been explored; the monstrous figures and beasts inhabiting the dark of the unconscious have been confronted, understood and, to that extent, overcome. The Terrible Mother has been shown to be also the Great Mother; the destructive evil, which brought depression and despair, has been from time to time transformed. The poet has proved a fit alchemist—another Jungian archetype—and his appetite suitably satisfied.

A similar interrelatedness is celebrated in the lovely triptych poem, "Tao and Unfitness at Inistiogue on the River Nore." The day is charted according to time ("Noon," "Afternoon," and "Nightfall"); the poet, on the other hand, is led to appreciate his own "unfitness" despite, in each section of the poem, a numinous experience, the Taoist equivalent of the intersection of the timeless with time. In sharp contrast to the black flies and cow dung, the poet is thus instructed: "Move, if you move, like water"; or conscious of punts knocking and trout rising, he learns: "Respond. Do not interfere.

Echo." Such enlightenment and freedom from didactic interference the poet has sought to practice since at least *Notes from the Land of the Dead*. The world at Inistiogue appears more idyllic that that of *A Technical Supplement*, yet appearances deceive: "Inistiogue itself is perfectly lovely, / like a typical English village, but a bit sullen." The emptiness of the square, the shops' lack of interest, the Protestant church guarded by a spastic retainer—nothing quite satisfies, just as the Tighe family's urge to shape their little world ultimately fails. The ravaging appetite of time is thus no less evident in the ruins of Woodstock, the Tighe family house; both house and countryside suffered during the War of Independence, and past and present come uncomfortably together:

> Black and Tan ghosts up there, at home
> on the Woodstock heights: an iron mouth
> scanning the Kilkenny road: the house
> gutted by the townspeople and burned to ruins . . .
>
> The little Ford we met, and inched past, full of men
> we had noticed along the river bank during the week,
> disappeared behind us into a fifty-year-old night.
> Even their caps and raincoats . . .
>
> (65–66)

Imagery of appetite persists, whether the "iron mouth" of military artillery or the townspeople gutting the house. The Tao advice offered —"Be still, as though pure," "Be subtle, as though not there"—thus constitutes a relationship with the world to which the protagonist may be drawn, but that advice in turn highlights his "unfitness."

Yet for all his awareness of the present's inadequacy (the sense of "ragged feeling, old angers and rumours" or the incongruous "mock-Austrian lodge" where the family stays), Kinsella emphasizes the life process at work, not the suspension of time in Taoist contemplation but life's fever:

> Down on the water . . . at eye level . . . in the little light
> remaining overhead . . . the mayfly passed in a loose drift,
> thick and frail, a hatch slow with sex,
> separate morsels trailing their slack filaments,
> olive, pale evening dun, imagoes, unseen eggs
> dropping from the air, subimagoes, the river filled
> with their nymphs ascending and excited trout.
>
> (66)

The language is both entomological and psychoanalytical at the same time[52] and describes an evolutionary process, a world driven by appetite and pursuing perpetual transformation. Likewise, what the poet admires is the poacher's ability to surface upon the fluctuating medium of the water and move effortlessly into the encroaching dark. He has made such accommodation with time that his landing place in the darkness, unlike that of the personae in "Downstream" earlier, is certain. It may be that the poet is made aware of his own "unfitness," but his commitment, for all his being drawn to Taoist stillness and order, is to the incoherent and destructive nature of the temporal world. As in numerous previous instances, the tension between contrary forces of order and disorder is acutely felt. The poacher is thus distinguished for his accomplishment, for he is capable of shaping the river's flux and of practicing precisely that Taoist perfection of which the protagonist remains in search. For Tao advocated during troubled times the imitation of water, since water always seeks the lowest place but can be very powerful. Furthermore, in Jung's terms, Tao is "the method or conscious way by which to unite what is separated." It involves "the realization of the opposite hidden in the unconscious," "the unity of . . . life and consciousness."[53] Hence Kinsella's poacher has become at one with his world; even his punt resembles "a fish, sinewing from side to side"; and the experience is almost religious in reflecting that oneness. Instead of Taoist light, however, Kinsella offers his own quintessential dark matrix as the source from which understanding comes:

> We were near the island—no more than a dark mass
> on a sheet of silver—when a man appeared in midriver
> quickly and with scarcely a sound, his paddle touching
> left and right of the prow, with a sack behind him.
> The flat cot's long body slid past effortless
> as a fish, sinewing from side to side,
> as he passed us and vanished.
>
> (67)

52. Jung defined the anima as "an imago," in "Commentary on the Secret of the Golden Flower," 334. In its entomological sense, "imago" is "[t]he final and perfect stage or form of an insect after it has undergone all its metamorphoses" *(OED)*. "Subimagoes" and "nymphs" are likewise entomological terms referring to different stages in an insect's development.

53. Jung, "Commentary on the Secret of the Golden Flower," 318, 322.

The vision prepares Kinsella's reader for the climax to the volume, in the title and concluding poem, "Song of the Night." For, as in the preceding poem at Inistiogue, the poet articulates a "song of the night" that places his preoccupation with darkness in its proper perspective. From the beginning he has offered his positives—love, understanding, imagination, or the creative self—and he has increasingly insisted upon the artist's function as revealing and embodying reality rather than imposing order or improving it. That reality reveals the interrelatedness of opposites, both positive and negative, in a tension that constitutes the basis for psychic growth.

Appropriately enough, the twin poles of Kinsella's recent life, of the United States and Ireland, provide the foci for his "Song of the Night," with the two boundaries of Philadelphia and Carraroe setting the limits of the Atlantic, the great primordial ocean that works away relentlessly, eternally, at each extreme while at the same time symbolizing rebirth. It is at Carraroe, in the Connemara Gaeltacht, where the numinous experience occurs. The occasion is a family camping expedition to Gorumna Island. At the end of the day parents and children proceed to the sea's edge to search for sand-eels. With the rich precedents of similar images in previous work, Kinsella achieves a maximum of symbolic meaning: "A cell of light hollowed around us / out of the night," a suitable answer to *"The great cell of nightmare"* in an earlier sequence (*One* 28) and made possible because the self has progressed beyond that dark, transforming it into a positive. Once more the experience takes place at the boundary—of both time (day-night) and space (the shoreline of land and sea, earth and water) —the liminal crossing over into the subliminal, and once more the woman figure (here the poet's wife) initiates the instinctive insight:

> She was standing in a sheltered angle,
> urgent and quiet.
> "Look back . . ."
>
> The great theatre of Connemara,
> dark. A cloud bank stretched in folds
> across the sky, luminous
> with inner activity.
>
> (70)

The music that the poet hears is both "new" and "That old / body music. *Schattenhaft*. SONG OF THE NIGHT. . . ." And indeed the music is elemental, like a heartbeat, and in this case emerges from the darkness, like shadows or shades *(shatten)*, the Jungian shadow that merges with the underworld shades of mythology. It is a "persistent / tympanum double-beat," which Kinsella will pick up again in *Her Vertical Smile* in the next volume and identify more particularly with the music of Gustav Mahler. Here the night's music is answered by another kind of music, the melancholy cry of the curlew, and again Jung provides an appropriate commentary, both upon this experience and upon Kinsella's long-standing preoccupation with the shadowy: "The shadow is unavoidable and man is incomplete without it."[54] Learning to live with one's shadow requires moral effort and acceptance of the self's dark side. At the same time, while the shadow may commonly be associated with evil and guilt, Jung has argued that "the unconscious man, that is, his shadow, does not consist only of morally reprehensible tendencies, but also displays a number of good qualities, such as normal instincts, appropriate reactions, realistic insights, creative impulses, etc."[55] For this is indeed how Kinsella has regarded his shadow and his charting of its chthonic existence in the land of the dead. Moreover, the curlew's name is derived etymologically from the French *courir*, "to run," and is associated with "courier" or "messenger." Certainly throughout Celtic mythology birds generally were regarded as messengers of the gods and, in English romantic poetry and as recently as Michael Hartnett's *A Necklace of Wrens* (1987), symbolize the muse or the craft of poetry. In a poem written twenty years earlier ("Baggot Street Deserta," *AS* 29), Kinsella characterized the bird's cry more explicitly as "A curlew's threadbare cry / Of common loss." The result here at Carraroe, where land and ocean meet, is numinous, and the black bird that flies off at the poem's close relates both to Hecate and to the muse, as not only the poet but also predecessors like Amergin have long known. The human condition itself (or "common loss") is the source, whether of darkness or of light, whether of division or of wholeness, and is celebrated through the poet's understanding:

> The bay—every inlet—lifted
> and glittered toward us in articulated light.
> The land, a pitch-black stage

54. Frieda Fordham, *An Introduction to Jung's Psychology* (1953; Harmondsworth, U.K.: Penguin, 1970), 50.

55. Jung, *Memories, Dreams, Reflections*, 399,

of boulder shapes and scalps of heaped weed,
inhaled.

A part of the mass
grated and tore, cranking harshly,
and detached and struggled upward
and beat past us along the rocks,
bat-black, heron-slow

(71)

It may be that Kinsella's vision is rooted in his experience of the "imaginative bedrock" of the Irish tradition, that Matter of Ireland which, from *Nightwalker* onward, has played an increasingly crucial role in his poetry. However, through the use of such early Irish material or through exemplars like James Joyce, Carl Gustav Jung, and others in later volumes, Kinsella has gained the authority and originality of a major poet. Moreover, it is an originality that, as the American poet, W. S. Merwin, defined the term, involves both origin and renewal:

> True originality has to do not with trying to be new but trying to come from the place from which all renewal comes. The meaning of originality has to do with origin, the place where something comes from, not the fact that it is different from everything else. You can't be different from everything else.[56]

In fact, Kinsella *has* made it new, as Pound recommended at the outset of the modernist movement, but he has done so by coming "from the place from which all renewal comes." His use of the Matter of Ireland, his several exemplars, his symbolic figures—not just the muse or Hecate but Seán Ó Riada too—his translations, and his descent into the self—all have helped to shape him into one of the most compelling and essential voices in contemporary poetry, as examination of his subsequent and, arguably, his most successful collection will reveal.

56. David L. Elliott, "An Interview with W. S. Merwin," *Contemporary Literature* 29 (Spring 1988): 18.

six

Reading the Ground

"One of the things that has disappeared" from his work, Kinsella recognized in 1989, "is the notion of a 'complete' poem, the idea that a poem can have a beginning, middle and end and be a satisfactory work of art thereby. The unity is a much bigger one than that. And it isn't a sequence, or a set of connected long poems. It's a totality that is happening, with the individual poem a contribution to something accumulating."[1] Volumes, no less than individual poems, must remain free of closure, open to further development, just as the self must remain receptive to further experience. The reader must read a person's writing in the light of the entire corpus, and like the poet must respond by accumulating readings of previous poems, and by synthesizing ever-expanding wholes. Meaning thus evolves organically, like cells joining together to form a larger nuclear whole, just as a poem is essentially an organism: anything less would be unfaithful to the "totality that is happening."

The coherent and complex nature of Kinsella's "totality" became more evident with the publication of *Blood and Family*, which collected the five Peppercanister editions that had appeared since 1979:

1. O'Driscoll, "Interview," 59.

The Messenger (June 1978), *Songs of the Psyche* and *Her Vertical Smile* (both 1985), *Out of Ireland* and *St. Catherine's Clock* (both 1987). We have seen how, from the beginning, Kinsella organized each volume, not only shaping themes and images into unities but fusing volume to volume, to the extent that by *Nightwalker* the concluding lines of "Phoenix Park" serve as an epigraph to the subsequent volume, *Notes from the Land of the Dead.* Coherence is achieved through repetition and accretion, in which the poet goes beyond the familiar method of establishing a body of recurrent images to convey personal meaning, to pursue his distinctive labyrinthine path of coils and spirals in which his past work, through the practice of intertextuality, is reassimilated in the new. As in the case of Yeats climbing the stairs of his Norman tower, the winding stair does more than repeat lower levels; it *includes* all previous meaning and reference in an ever-burgeoning whole. The climax for Kinsella, as for Yeats, is numinous vision, although their respective definitions of what constitutes that vision are starkly different. Nevertheless, Kinsella's more lyrical sequences, such as *Songs of the Psyche,* more closely resemble the last poems of Yeats, despite the fact that it is Joyce who has proved the more congenial artistic ancestor. Indeed, the larger structure and coherence of *Blood and Family* echo more particularly Joyce's method: patterns develop to embrace private, family, and national histories; Kinsella's protagonist walks through emblematic Dublin landscapes as through a labyrinth of the self; he sees the large cycles of history that make sense of both past and present and define identity, inheritance, and tradition; and the nature of the self is both freed from specific time and place and yet known through them. In brief, the reader, like the protagonist, "reads the ground."

In its own multiple and polyphonic use of the term "ground," the phrase "reading the ground" directs Kinsella's reader to the increasingly multiple or polyphonic character of his writing. For "ground" can mean earth or soil, a place for growth or burial; the more political "territory," that space upon which a person takes a stand; the bottom, the lowest limit or extremity; more positively, the foundation, the base or fundamental constituent; in painting, the surface providing the basis on which the artist works; and, in line with the volume's extensive musical analogues, the plainsong or melody against which the descant is sung. All such meanings bear upon *Blood and Family.* In "1740" (*BF* 85), the volume's concluding poem, the phrase describes Swift on the verge of decrepitude, with his mind and body at the end of their tether, suffering all and knowing all in that synthesis of purgatorial understanding or perception of fundamental constituents that Kinsella has long sought. Like Yeats, Kinsella has constantly drawn upon personal experience but, like Yeats again, he has transformed the private into the universal, writing indeed for the conscience of his race. His community and his tradition include Swift and Johannes Scotus Eriugena as well as his own family, and both community and tradition are structures by which meaning may be gained. Such structures enable the poet to shape chaos into order, to uncover a pattern among fragments, and to bring people, values, principles, and their antitheses—those shards of a time and culture that, separately, reflect only disharmony, alienation, and disorder—into a coherent and meaningful whole. Kinsella's methods of writing and of publication thus serve the same end that his vision seeks to express: an impressive hammering of thoughts into unity, as Yeats would have it, or, in more Kinsellan terms, the fit articulation of understanding.

The volume's very title, *Blood and Family*, provides an important sign to the reader: the two terms signify those emotional centers out of which much of Kinsella's poetry, particularly since *Nightwalker* and *Notes from the Land of the Dead*, has come. For "blood" is the medium, the dialectical element that is life giving, death bringing, and at the very heart of the process that makes life and movement possible. Its own rhythm or heartbeat reflects its dialectical nature. At the same time blood establishes continuity; it is one's inheritance, marking off a person into units, families, and tribes, and maintaining lines of descent. "History," as Seamus Deane puts it, "is personal."[2] Family is both the product of blood and the structure that enables blood to take direction, to have meaning and stability beyond the confines of a single self. The larger structures of community, tribe, society, and nation serve similar ends, providing security and relationship as well as containment, and are likewise maintained by blood lines. In the case of Ireland, whose history has been marked since earliest times by successive invasions, occupations, battles, bloodhed, and defeat, blood proves a particularly tragic and dark medium,

2. Deane, " 'Send War in Our Time, O Lord,' " in *History Lessons* (Dublin: Gallery Books, 1983), 12. Cf. "history never dies, / At any rate in Ireland"; see Louis MacNeice, "Valediction" (1934), *Collected Poems* (London: Faber and Faber, 1979), 52.

bringing also division and hatred and announcing only too emphatically the human propensity for evil. "Family" in Kinsella's case signifies much the same dialectic. The "ground" becomes anything but plain reading, and in characteristic fashion this latest volume to trace the poet's path to understanding begins with a death and a funeral.

I

The Messenger, written as an elegy for Kinsella's recently deceased father, traces the configuration of the father's life. Taking both the title and cover from *The Messenger of the Sacred Heart*, the popular Irish magazine for the Catholic faithful that is dedicated to the promotion of prayer and temperance,[3] the Peppercanister edition substitutes ironically antithetical images more appropriate to the father's faith: the famous Guinness label to acknowledge his employment at St. James's Gate; the plough and the stars to signify his union activities and lifelong commitment to socialism, particularly that of James Connolly and Jim Larkin; and, most prominently, the center figure of Hermes-Mercury, messenger of the gods, with caduceus and winged heels, surrounded by Celtic motifs of animal heads and interlacing.

Beginning and ending with the father's death, the poem offers successive vignettes of the man in characteristic poses and behaviors. As the poet-son proceeds to probe more deeply into his grief, he uncovers "more than mere Loss"; rather, "Something to discourage goodness," in which the father's death is related to the darkness implicit in all existence. Yet the italicized lines of the opening poem provide appropriate and more positive commentary:

> A *moist movement within*
> A *worm winds on its hoard.*
> A *rim of hide lifts like a lip.*
>
> A *dead egg glimmers—a pearl in muck*
> *glimpsed only as the muck settles.*
> *The belly settles and crawls tighter.*
> (*BF* 3)

3. Lyons, *Culture and Anarchy*, 80.

The reader is warned that the experiences to follow will be unsettling and will require investigation of "*muck*."[4] The image, like its corresponding "mud" (*N* 16; *NLD* 21; *One* 22, 31, 63, 66; *BF* 49) or "slime" (*BF* 11, 15), suggests a primeval point of origin, an evolutionary soup. On the other hand, in distinctive Kinsella fashion and following archetypal myth, the "*pearl*" of wisdom will be found in precisely that element of muck or earth, the element to which the dead father has now returned. That same cyclic process or origination completes the sequence, just as in the concluding poem the "*precious combination*" forms miraculously "A*n eye . . . in the dark*," an "*oddity [which] nestles in slime // functionless, in all its rarity / purifying nothing*" (15). Likewise, the dead man rolls out on his final set of "rubber tyres"—we have seen him in the preceding poem in his first job as messenger boy on a Post Office bicycle—and surrounded by the poet's "scattered tribe" of family. The "ragged band" of children in near-Blakean fashion possess a "lightness," a color and vivacity that place the poet's grief in proper perspective. The father's death has been both a regression and a progression. The blood lines have been maintained, the family sustained, and both time and history given shape and meaning. The death has provided a perspective that enables the poet to recognize the wisdom of the father-messenger, one more provider of notes from the land of the dead.

Blood finds expression also in the father's long-standing battles to form a trade union at the Guinness Brewery; to follow Connolly and Larkin in their socialist vision of a society characterized by equity, justice, and freedom; to oppose the conservative and hypocritical forces in Ireland, whether among the Catholic clergy or the newly arrived Catholic middle class, of Masons and Knights of Columbanus; or to improve himself and establish a better existence for his family. Twenty years earlier Kinsella had described his father as "a man of high and punishing ideals."[5] The struggle to stand upright, to gain wholeness of self and so become a "vertical man," is here described

4. "The female powers dwell not only in ponds, springs, streams and swamps but also in the earth, in mountains, hills, cliffs, and—along with the dead and the unborn—in the underworld. And above all, the mixture of the elements water and earth is primordially feminine; it is the swamp, the fertile muck in whose uroboric nature the water may equally well be experienced as male and engendering or female and birthgiving"; see Neumann, *The Great Mother*, 260.

5. Kinsella, *Poetry Book Society Bulletin* 17 (March 1958). Kinsella proceeded to describe his grandfather in similar terms: he "worked for most of his life in Guinness's

through a succession of scenes from the father's life that depict him fighting against changes in pension rights, walking a high beam in the brewery's racking shed, opposing the fascist Blueshirts in the thirties, and walking out of Mass in resentment at clerical interference, "telling every Catholic how to vote" (10). The priest's "white hair," "red face," and "black mouth" are set off against the father's hand—"He covered my hand with his"—an action reminiscent of Dick King in *Downstream* and allied to the poet's recurrent hand imagery.

Once more Kinsella returns to situations that previous poems have shown crucial to his own progression. For example, father and grandfather are shown repairing the family shoes:

> He reaches for a hammer,
> his jaw jutting as best it can
> with Marx, Engels, Larkin
>
> howling with upstretched arms into the teeth
> of Martin Murphy and the Church
> and a flourish of police batons,
>
> Connolly strapped in a chair
> regarding the guns
> that shall pronounce his name for ever.
>
> Baton struck,
>   gun spat,
> and Martin Murphy shall change his hat.
>
> Son and father, upright, right arms raised.
> Stretching a thread.
> Trying to strike right.
>
> (13)

The scene goes beyond simple naturalism to take on symbolic dimensions that embrace political and moral freedoms, national and personal events. For the actions of the poet's father and grandfather epitomize their commitment to the revolutionary socialist principles of James Connolly and the proclamation of the Irish Republic to which he was a signatory. The two men followed Connolly in seeking a more just and egalitarian Ireland, opposing the tyranny of capitalism

---

Brewery. . . . He was, at the same time, one of the original recruits to Father Matthew's Total Abstinence Association and resisted, until his death in 1947, all persuasion—even by his doctors—to take alcohol."

(in the person of Martin Murphy) and the authoritarianism of church and state (priest and police). Murphy, as a leader of the employers in the infamous Dublin Lockout of 1913, helped to break Jim Larkin's Irish Transport and General Workers' Union. As a wealthy industrialist and owner of several Dublin newspapers, Murphy spoke for the conservative Catholic middle class that was to be such a dominant influence in the new Free State after 1922. Kinsella thus ranges the heroism of Connolly, whose death by firing squad became part of Republican martyrology, against the hypocrisy and opportunism of Murphy. Father and grandfather in turn are "upright"—a crucial Kinsella term, as we have seen—and, with obvious irony, "Trying to strike right." W. J. McCormack distinguishes *The Messenger* from the previous sequences because it pursues the theme of rising as opposed to the previous one of falling, celebrating the father's "persistent, unsuccessful acts of rebellion."[6] Such lack of success may have its basis in biographical fact, but it also coincides with the poet's ethic of endurance and suffering. McCormack also notes pertinently that the Irish for "rebellion," *ais eirigh* or *eirigh amach*, is derived from the verb "to rise." Kinsella's imagery of "vertical" and "upright" thus takes on distinctly political overtones. The imagery indicates a principled life and is in turn associated with the archetypal status of both father and grandfather as "Wise Old Men."[7] Likewise, the jaw, more usually in Kinsella signifying fearful appetite, here evidences the determination and battling spirit of both father and grandfather.

Similarly, in another crucial scene the poet traces his origins back to the moment of his conception, heralded by the "gossamer ghost" of a dragonfly:

> A gossamer ghost arrows and hesitates
>
> out of the reeds, and stands in the air above them
> insect-shimmering, and settles on a bright
> inner upturn of her dress. The wings
>
> close up like palms. The body, a glass worm,
> is pulsing. The tail-tip winces and quivers:
>
> I *think* this is where I come in . . .
>
> (11)

6. McCormack, "Politics or Community," 68, 75.

7. Jung noted that the Wise Old Man is often represented by the grandfather figure and that in alchemy the pair of old greybeard and young boy is associated with Mercurius; see *Psyche and Symbol*, ed. de Laszlo, 70–71.

Kinsella's fine irony acts against any potential inflation in his narrative so that he can affirm playfully, "I am all egg!"

The poem's direction is, characteristically, backward in time and downward into the self, while the reader is made aware of the larger psychic development the poet traces, particularly as the self confronts pain and loss:

> Typically, there is a turning away.
> The Self is islanded in fog.
> It is meagre and plagued with wants
>
> but secure. Every positive matter
> that might endanger—but also enrich—
> is banished. The banished matter
>
> (a cyst, in effect, of the subject's aspirations
> painful with his many disappointments)
> absorbs into the psyche, where it sleeps.
>
> Intermittently, when disturbed, it wakes
> as a guardian—or "patron"—monster
> with characteristic conflicting emotional claims:
>
> appalling, appealing; exacting sympathy
> even as it threatens. (Our verb "to haunt"
> preserves the ambiguity exactly.)
>
> (7)

"The banished matter" is like "a cyst": the image is both medical (a growth) and archaeological (a grave or mound), and, absorbed into the psyche, makes suitably "conflicting emotional claims." A similar "haunting" is experienced by the poet as he comes to terms with his father's death by remembering childhood games played between father and son and instancing "*the beast*" that constitutes that "banished matter" in the psyche. Such games parallel the riddles of Amergin, the first Irish poet, whose work Kinsella has echoed previously (*One* 15–16), and reflect the ease with which the later poet can juxtapose early Irish and his own family experience. " 'Who'd like to know what *I* know?' / 'Who has a skeleton in *his* meat cupboard?' " The tempting voice focuses particularly upon appetite: " 'Guess who'd love to gobble *you* up . . . !' / Or 'Who'd like to see what *I* have?' " The poet-child's prompt answer, "*I* would," evidences his firm commitment to the father whose "pewtery heave of hindquarters" in explicit identification with the god, Mercury, he follows. And, in another action reminiscent of the young boy's squeezing the fingers of his neighbor-friend, Dick King, the poet reaches in his hand to relieve him of "something." Dick King was celebrated for teaching the young boy love, for being "upright," and for naming the famous neighborhood dead. A similar superior wisdom and inheritance are passed on here from father to son, in the form of a handing down and contact that the hand image signifies. For blood lines are being maintained, as the poet reaches in, as if to steal a treasure from the dead father. Just as Kinsella identifies his father, both here and on the cover illustration, with Mercury, the messenger of the gods, so too he draws upon the archetypal motif of treasure or prize that the hero carries off during his journey through the land of the dead and upon which his regeneration depends. Appropriately enough, in a myth of psychic development, the treasure is an "eggseed" or "pearl" (8, 9).[8] Rejecting the "supine" posture of the dead father, the son prefers to focus upon his uprightness:

> And have watched my hand reach in under
> after something, and felt it
> close upon it and ease him of it.
>
> The eggseed Goodness
> that is also called
> Decency.
>
> (8)

The several scenes that make up most of *The Messenger* thus reflect the father's goodness and decency, an inheritance passed on to his family of sons and grandchildren. Again the father's life, described in naturalistic detail, takes on symbolic character: as a Post Office messenger boy, in his first job, the father thus assumes his role as Mercury, later to bear news from the underworld to his poet-son:

> He is all excitement: arms akimbo,
> a thumb crooked by the telegram pouch,
> shoes polished, and a way to make in the world.
> * * * * * * * * * * * * * * *
> He unprops the great Post Office bicycle
> from the sewing machine and wheels it through the passage
> by odours of apron and cabbage-water and whitewashed damp

8. The child in the Jungian child motif often appears as something precious (jewel, chalice, golden egg or ball, pearl) and indicates the integrated self; see *Psyche and Symbol*, ed. de Laszlo, 122–23.

through the shop and into the street.
It faces uphill. The urchin mounts. I see
a flash of pedals! And a clean pair of heels!

(14)

Like Joyce before him, Kinsella has been quick to see the symbolic character of Dubliners and of Dublin life generally and also to see new and witty significance in tired clichés (the urchin Mercury's "clean pair of heels"). It is wholly appropriate, therefore, that the father, whose commitment to Connolly's socialism was firm, should begin work for the Post Office, the General Office of which was the scene of Connolly's engagement in the Easter Rising, and a building which, even today, bears atop its impressive classical façade three statues: of Fidelity, Hibernia, and Mercury. As Jung has put it, "we must *dream the myth onwards* and give it a modern dress."[9]

II

That "modern dress" continues in "Settings," the introductory section to *Songs of the Psyche,* with scenes from the poet's early education: rolling plasticine into snakelike coils; confronting decimals and declaring solemnly, "I am going to know / everything" (19); and being introduced to other crucial Kinsella concerns, " 'History . . !' " or divine judgment and retribution. Appropriately enough, the poet offers more images of appetite ("The taste / of ink off / the nib shrank your / mouth"[10]) and of the climbing of stairs to a landing and upstairs room, at home and at Bow Lane. Once again the grandmother makes an appearance: " 'What are you up to in there? / Always stuck in that old room' " (22). The young boy in fact is proceeding in his initiation into both self and world, and the sense of threat, of guilt about forbidden matters, as well as of continuity, is strong. That upstairs room proves an important matrix, providing initiation into the world's mystery; the room is a womb for the new self, and so gains symbolic status. Like the crossroads, the grandmother's shop, and the upper landing, such places provide illumination as significant and convincing as do Yeats's tower and winding stair:

9. Jung's italics; *Psyche and Symbol*, ed. de Laszlo, 123.

10. Joyce gave the Irish for "ink" as "*dubh*" or "black"; see *Smaller Social History of Ancient Ireland*, 203. The modern word is "*dúch*" which has helped to form "*dúchan*," meaning "blackening" or "blight." Once more a factual experience takes on symbolic status as the child-poet digests darkness or blight.

> I have climbed the narrow turn
> of the top stairs, holding
> the banisters draped with
> trousers and pullovers,
> and stood smelling the landing again.
>
> (21)

The corner cupboard, resembling Kinsella's mirror triptychs (as in Poem XX, *One* 50–51; and "Self Renewal," *BF* 39), serves as his father's "dark nest," a further instance of the poet's bird imagery:

> And I have opened the black-stained
> double doors of the triangular
> press up in the corner,
> and his dark nest
> stirred with promises.
>
> (21)

Such "promises" include the father's efforts at self-education ("Ruskin and Engels and Carlyle; / Shakespeare in tiny print"), his insurance book, and "a brown photograph // with four young men / dressed up together / and leaning together in laughter." The details prove discreetly moving, capturing the promise of early manhood but implying the inevitability of disappointment and loss. In the upstairs room, at his grandmother's in Bow Lane, he explores a wardrobe that provides a darker initiation, when he finds his dead uncle's painting. The young boy even shares the dead man's name—a deathly inheritance indeed:

> They kept Uncle Tom's painting
> hanging in there, in a black frame
> —a steamer with three funnels,
> and TK painted on the foam.
>
> He died in here in 1916
> of cancer of the colon. My father heard him
> whispering to himself: "Jesus,
> Jesus, let me off." But nothing worked.
>
> (22)

Promise has given way to suffering, death, and questioning of divine succor. The naturalism of these "settings" involves Kinsella's distinctive symbolism. The Christian meaning of suffering is caught also in the epigraph to the Peppercanister edition, dropped from the *Blood and Family* volume, where the poet also quotes from an earlier poem (*NLD* 6): "By the five wounds of Christ / I struggle toward / I had never been / so *deeply* uplifted . . ." (*SPsyche* 6). The paradox of the last line indicates what Kinsella has frequently shown and which constitutes his own account of suffering: uplift requires descent into the unconscious in order that the contraries of self might unite and be reconciled both to themselves and to life itself. In place of the Christian myth Kinsella relies upon the primordial figure of the Great Mother, to whom he offers his "Invocation":

> Sweet mother, sweet muscle,
> predatrix,
>
> always in the midst
> yet walking to one side
>
> silent, reticent, rarely seen
> yet persistent,
>
> we implore—the subsequent
> bustling in the previous:
>
> Judge not.
> But judge.
>
> (*BF* 23)

The figure is at the same time maternal ("Sweet mother"), sexual ("sweet muscle"), and destructive ("predatrix"), with her three faces reflecting the triple aspect of the Great Mother. Indeed, in an earlier Peppercanister version the personae offering up this invocation more particularly resemble spermatozoa, minute life, or embryonic selves: "as we bob and strike / with a wriggle of our tails // in the glum-green shallows / for our mud-green feed" (*SPsyche* 17).

The poems make severe demands upon the reader as Kinsella's method becomes increasingly elliptical and symbolic; as his language becomes more spare, elemental, and reminiscent of recent Eastern European poetry; and as his focus bears even more closely upon the self's nature and progress. At the same time the sequence is distinctively concrete, visual, and immediate in its experiences, intrinsically lyrical in character. The driving force, as might be expected, is appetite, a compulsive force, both creative and destructive, but the condition is time itself: acknowledging his initiation into vision, the character in the first song declares, "It is time" (*BF* 24). And indeed it *is* time that both impedes and makes possible such enlightenment, and it *is* time that brings failure and, through such failure, whatever triumph humans may achieve. The illustration in the Peppercanister edition (*SPysche* cover, 19) is of an ornament made of glass and enamel, now in the National Museum and reproduced in P. W. Joyce's *Smaller Social History of Ancient Ireland*. (Kinsella also uses Joyce's reproductions in other Peppercanisters, in *Her Vertical Smile* and *Out of Ireland*.) The ornament captures an organic and vital action, of a multiplicity radiating outward from a dark center, thereby suitably illustrating Kinsella's distinctive vision of the psyche's development. At the same time Joyce comments upon the art involved in the creation of such an ornament, "an art requiring long training and much delicate manipulative skill."[11] It is a comment that directs Kinsella's reader to another major center in the sequence: the creativity of the self and the artistic act.

While no firm "plot" is provided, the thirteen "Songs of the Psyche" that constitute the sequence's central section cohere through their several, often apparently unrelated, statements. Indeed, Kinsella is disinclined to draw upon any of them for a poetry reading because he believes they should be read together as one. Moreover, the absence of clear narrative line or plot does not detract from the sequence's explicitly fictive nature established at the outset, in which the distinctness of the "character, indistinct" emerges in the course of the expression of his songs. The sequence takes on the nature of a dramatic performance, sometimes lyrical, sometimes narrative, with the whole serving to define the self and its path to understanding:

> A character, indistinct, entered,
> looked about him, and began:
>
> Why had I to wait until I am graceless,
> unsightly, and a little nervous of stooping
> until I could see
>
> through these clear eyes I had once?
> It is time. And I am
> shivering as in stupid youth.
>
> Who have stood where I was born
> and snapped my bitten fingers!
>
> (*BF* 24)

11. Ibid., 294.

As previously in Kinsella's work, clarity of vision depends upon purgatorial suffering. His "character" here does not rage, like Yeats's wild wicked old men, against age and physical decrepitude; indeed, like the poet himself, he is only middle-aged (Poem V suggests a life of fifty years) and more resembles Eliot's Prufrock in his self-characterization as "graceless, / unsightly, and a little nervous of stooping." Yet, like Yeats's personae, what he sees depends upon time and appetite and his endurance of both. The subsequent songs constitute experiences that contribute to the self's growth toward fulfillment by enabling him to piece both them and himself together in a unity. By the time of the final song, Poem XIII, interpretation, albeit of an inconclusive kind, is offered. That inconclusiveness is caught in the poem's conflicting openings, as the character stumbles into self-expression:

> *I woke suffocating,*
> *slipped through a fault*
> *into total dark.*
>
> No.
>
> *I came to myself*
> *in the middle of a dark wood,*
> *electric with hope.*
>
> Please . . .
>
> (31)

The first version, offering only negative vision, is rejected in favor of the second, more hopeful one, with its Dantean imagery suggesting the opening lines of the *Inferno*. The appeal ("Please . . ."), however, reminds us that while much good in Kinsella's system is drawn from the exercise of difficult choice, another factor is chance, where self must accept forces beyond its control. What remains clear, nevertheless, is that

> . . . it *is*
> a matter of
> negative release:
>
> of being thrown
> up out of a state of storm
> into a state of peace

or sleep,
    or a dream,
or a system of dreams.
(31)

Such a search for peace has long formed Kinsella's purpose—"states of peace, nursed out of wreckage," as he put it earlier (*NLD* 56)—and is to be completed by descent into the unconscious dark self. Kinsella describes the process in what is by now familiar imagery: self and shadow, light and darkness, intellect and appetite, all caught in their spiraling dance toward the vertical, in a primordial process that is the source of creation and all psychic life:

By normal process
    organic darkness,
in potentia all things,

would summon
    Self firstly into being,
a Shadow *in actu*,

an upright on a flat plain,
    a bone stirs
in first clay

and a beam of light struck
    and snaked glittering across a surface
in multi-meanings and vanishes.
(31)

The Jungian nature of Kinsella's account is once more qualified by other versions upon which people have drawn in their search for meaning. Such qualification is less the product of doubt than of the poet's openness, his unwillingness to be constricted by a system. Structure can be positive only when it reveals rather than imposes order, and so the sequence's structure remains suitably open-ended. To reinforce such disinclination to close and so limit meaning, three of the thirteen songs lack final punctuation (Poems VI, VIII, and IX), as do "A New Beginning" (33) and "Self Scrutiny" (37), while some lack punctuation entirely (Poems VI and IX, and "A New Beginning"). The most dramatic lack occurs in the sixth song, where only one comma is supplied and where even nouns and verbs take on a deliberately ambiguous character. The poem ostensibly describes foxes in the night, but its larger concern is with the self and its symbiotic relation with its shadow:

> Night foxes
> body masks
>
> tilted up, eyes
> a city of lights
>
> a cistern hiss
> in their erect ears
>
> they are dreaming
> one another
> (28)

The Jungian shadow, to be found in the personal unconscious, is "the primitive, uncontrolled, and animal part of ourselves," "the natural, i.e. instinctive man."[12] It "personifies everything that the subject refuses to acknowledge about himself"; it is "that hidden, repressed, for the most part inferior and guilt-laden personality whose ultimate ramifications reach back into the realm of our animal ancestors and so comprise the whole historical aspect of the unconscious." At the same time, far from being simply evil, the shadow "displays a number of good qualities," including "creative impulses."[13]

If time is the medium, then appetite proves the driving force. Sometimes the reference to eating is explicit (for example, the "bitten fingers" of Poem I, the imperative to "Chew nine times" in Poem II, and the compulsion to eat in Poem III). At other times the character's response goes beyond ordinary sensory experience: "I smelled at a crack in the door" (Poem II); "I have kissed the inner earth / and the grin of stone upon stone" (Poem VI). Such experiences disrupt and displace reality, and demand restructuring in order to become meaningful. The unfolding psychic drama requires the persona's reassessment of his self and world:

> What a thing it is
> to know a thing
> full fifty years

12. Fordham, *An Introduction to Jung's Psychology*, 49, 50.

13. Jung, *The Archetypes and the Collective Unconscious*, quoted in the glossary to *Memories, Dreams, Reflections*, ed. Jaffé, 398–99.

with kindness as of one thing
for another
of only its kind.

A monster bore me
and I bear
a monster with me.

(26)

Even that Yeatsian image for transcendent love—the two trees grown into a single trunk, last seen in "Wormwood" (*N* 30)—now takes on a sinister, serpentine aspect: "The leaves reached out past us / and hissed: *We were so fond of you!*" (27). Likewise, the eleventh song begins in traditional lyrical fashion and language, with the idyllicism reinforced by Kinsella's imagery of the transcendent or "crystal" ("Come with me / o'er the crystal stream / where eyelids dart / in the dappled shadows"). But by the song's conclusion the persona experiences an *aisling* of a different and horrific kind, in which "leeches wrinkle / black in the water, / willow leaves / that have fed on blood" (30). The descent into a death-in-life is analogous to the knight's experience in Keats's "La Belle Dame Sans Merci" and that of other romantic exemplars. Irish writing and English romanticism fuse here without difficulty. At the same time such depths of darkness, whether in self or world, need to be explored. The antitheses remain in perpetual interdependence: light is gained only through experiencing darkness; the self struggles to become upright through descent into its land of the dead. And one experience particularly assumes symbolic significance as, once more, the reader is given a nocturnal vision of psychic wholeness in the form of a full moon accompanied by "a great moth of prey":

A great delicate self
approached her cold face

toward the window,
cheek wide and glowing,

afloat, bright, an O
stopped,

a whole mind
blind overhead.

Pegged to a rafter, bathed in smoke,
splayed in flight,

a great moth of prey,
flat, with excavated breast,

come from nowhere,
stared back.

(29)

Moon and moth complement each other, the one whole, bright but blind, the other epitomizing appetite and incompleteness, emerging from "nowhere" and staring back. The effect upon the persona is to cause him to writhe like "A silk maggot" at the memory: the image nicely captures the appropriate combination of delicateness, preciousness, and transformation in the self's progress toward wholeness, a transformation, nevertheless, that feeds, like the maggot, on decay. The penultimate song (Poem XII) is thus able to announce further commitment to time and the advent of "first light."

Given the driving force of appetite in Kinsella's world, it is hardly surprising that in "A New Beginning," the first of eight poems collected as "Notes" to *Songs of the Psyche*, his version of Creation sees the divine "*I am*" as an "ache" (33). Creation, like the poem also, remains thus unpunctuated, open-ended, in a state of perpetual flux and development. Kinsella has described the eight poems as "notes on matters of love, friendship and the self."[14] It is surely a measure of his achievement that both these and the "Songs of the Psyche" section bear comparison with the late poems of Yeats, for they too offer analysis of the self's intricacies in its experience of love and friendship, and exhibit the same Yeatsian gnomic expression and powerful conviction. Kinsella's "Opposites," for example, in itself a Yeatsian subject, achieves a haiku-like clarity and precision of a kind reminiscent of Yeats's Ribh:

Love is refreshment
in the recognition of pattern.

Grudging memory is its opposite:
it is revealed in the lips.

Our mouths locked in privacy.
The shadow pattern shifted.

(33)

14. Peppercanister 1985 flyer and price list.

Lips and mouths take on a near-separate existence, like Kinsella's hand, eye, jaw, belly, and other anatomical parts that give his work the appearance of pathological dissection. Here love is related to pattern and set off against memory, and "The shadow pattern" is affected by the lovers' privacy. That same sense of antithesis repeats Kinsella's version of Creation in "A New Beginning," where God needs to "lean Himself / over the motherly pit" and, met with a mouth to kiss, can declare "Let there be."

The light Kinsella sheds climaxes in the three concluding poems about the self, moving from "Self Scrutiny," to "Self Release," to "Self Renewal." The reader becomes aware as "The threadbare body" in "Self Scrutiny" is made "conscious / of its composite parts": eyes, ear, tongue, brain, mouth, thumbs, and digits, all on their "thunder-drive to Hell" (37). Kinsella's obsolete spelling of "mutabilitie" (37) reinforces the age-old nature of such a process. "Self Release" confronts those—including the poet's own critics—who would take issue with his vision of darkness:

> Possibly you would rather I stopped
> —uttering guttural Christ curses
> and destroying my nails down the wall
> or dashing myself to pieces once and for all
> in a fury beside your head?
>
> (38)

Release of self is gained, in fact, more by self-expression and acknowledgment of darkness than by the alternative posed with heavy irony by the poet-persona: radical crude surgery that brings release in the form of "glaze and numbness."

The most successful of the three concluding poems, however, is the last, "Self Renewal," where the persona places himself, in that quintessential Kinsella position, before a triptych of mirrors while engaging in earnest self-scrutiny. The revelation—and the religious sense is heightened by the opening adverb "Reverently," by the triptych image, and by the implied reference to the triple-faced Great Goddess—depends upon another recurrent Kinsella feature, the conjunction of wounding and wholeness. The forehead lines are thus like "two ragged cuts" and the "eyes hurt and full":

> Reverently I swung open
> the two side mirrors to reveal

everywhere, on a white brow crossed,
two ragged cuts; a wet mouth
held shut; eyes hurt and full.

(39)

The revelation that follows, however, has more to do with the business of living and the self's necessary accommodation with time than with any transcendently numinous experience. For what renewal the persona gains lies in learning the secrets of the lonely, as he comes to terms with humanity's essential aloneness and need for security, love, and reassurance. Such compassion has in fact proved a central motivation in the poet's persistent willingness to enter the land of the dead:

I peered into these
and their velvet stirred
with the pale secrets of all
the lonely that had ever sat
by their lonely mirrors

studying the lonely shame
that had brought them there to sit
and kiss the icy glass
and recover themselves a little
with icy brow on brow

and one eye cocked at itself
until they felt more able
to slip off about their business
with head held a little higher
and the glass clouding over

the memory of a couple
of fading eye diagrams.

(39)

In another sense, the persona's kiss upon the mirror's "icy glass" epitomizes the conjunction of self and anima that marks the self's recovery. Compassion is thus accompanied by affirmation, with both qualities reflecting the positive element of Kinsella's work. The persona is left with sufficient self-renewal to be "more able / to slip off about [his] business." The tone, however, is deliberately ironic and mildly deflationary: any triumph is misconceived or short-lived. At the same time the poet appreciates the strength gained as head is "held a little higher," even if the mirror clouds and the eye fades.

III

While the coherent pattern revealed in *Songs of the Psyche* was achieved through short lyrics, *Her Vertical Smile* (1985), with its three sections of short three-line unrhymed stanzas, possesses a more clearly defined narrative. Kinsella's epigraph provides the reader with the essential clue he or she needs, drawn in familiar fashion from his own previous work. In this instance the source is his prose commentary on the Ó Riada elegies in *Fifteen Dead*, where he describes his relationship with the composer and their shared taste in music. Ó Riada (Reidy) enabled one more initiation, here into the music of Gustav Mahler, in one more crucial room (Reidy's flat on Lower Mount Street):

> I remember the elaborate, opulent close of *Der Rosenkavalier* filling the mean little space: the unmade single bed, the dusty electric fire glowing in the grate, spattered with butts, Reidy's narrow unfocussed face intent in the dark like an animal. I heard Mahler there for the first time. . . . (*FD* 65; *BF* 42)

The initiation is in part one into the work of a composer Kinsella had previously not known but it also involves the replacement of Richard Strauss's "opulent" romanticism with the starker vision of Gustav Mahler. And indeed Mahler, together with another European master and exemplar, Thomas Mann, joins Ó Riada to constitute the central figures in *Her Vertical Smile*.

Music dominates the work, providing both narrative material and technique. The poem draws heavily upon events in Mahler's musical career to illustrate Kinsella's major concerns, while the division into "Overture," two movements separated by an "Intermezzo," and a concluding "Coda" is supplemented further by the musical interweaving of themes and analogies. The technique is not new; Kinsella has over the years perfected such contrapuntal development, which he learned from Joyce and Pound. The achievement in *Her Vertical Smile* enables him to comment further and with increased force and conviction upon those issues that have long concerned him: war, death, grief, and tragedy. In Kinsella's own terms, the poem is "on a theme of violence, order and music."[15] Certainly *Her Vertical Smile* embraces both the personal and the universal, Ó Riada as well as Mann and Mahler, and concludes in positive, even witty, affirmation.

15. Ibid.

The reader is prepared for the poet's descent once more into primordial darkness, partly by his description of Ó Riada and partly through the reference to Mahler. The room where Kinsella found Ó Riada in 1951 was, in his words, "a dark rat-trap" (*FD* 65); this description takes on added resonance in the light of previous references to rats and of the image of Ó Riada's face "intent in the dark like an animal." Animal and darkness combine with intellect and light to define the boundaries of both human nature and the world. A similar definition is achieved through the reference to Mahler and the work identified in the Commentary, *Das Lied von der Erde (The Song of the Earth)* which "Reidy played . . . again and again" (*FD* 65). In that work the Earth Mother—in yet another appearance of Kinsella's archetypal female—sings of darkness, farewell, and death. The sequence opens with "Das Trinklied von Jammer der Erde" ("The Drinking Song of the Earth's Misery," which Kinsella used previously in *Vertical Man*, Commentary, *FD* 72–73), with its bleak refrain, "Dark is life; dark is death"; it closes with the Earth Mother's final song, "Der Abschied" ("The Farewell"), a song which, while acknowledging the death of a beloved friend, concludes movingly by affirming Earth's future regeneration in the spring.

Kinsella's scene moves from Ó Riada to the Earth Mother, from the mean little Dublin room to the "luxuriant heavens" outside (*BF* 43), from Mahler's music to the Irish astrological diagram of an eclipse, with sun, earth, and earth's shadow projected onto the stars.[16] The diagram is comprehensible in Jungian terms, as one more instance of "the shadow" that man must ultimately confront and understand, but the volume's title depends upon a further source, W. H. Auden. When Kinsella entitled one of his earlier Ó Riada elegies *Vertical Man*, he was echoing the title of one of Ó Riada's recordings for Claddagh Records, a title which in turn depends upon Auden's poem to Christopher Isherwood in *Poems* (1930):

> Let us honour if we can
> The vertical man
> Though we value none
> But the horizontal one.
> (*FD* 74)

16. The diagram is taken from Joyce's *Smaller Social History of Ireland*, and shows a medieval astronomical diagram in the Royal Irish Academy; Kinsella, endnote to *Her Vertical Smile*, Peppercanister 10 (1985).

The vertical man represents the heroic quester, the self struggling to stand upright against insurmountable odds, learning from life in suitable Kinsella fashion, while the world values only the horizontal, the literally or the spiritually dead.[17] We remember also in the final poem in the "Songs of the Psyche" section that the emergence of the self is imaged as some ancient Celtic standing stone, "an upright on a flat plain" (*BF* 31), and also that "the shadow" is associated with the nocturnal underside of things. (The same use of "uprights" may be seen in "Finistère," in the lovely prayer to the Great Mother "in whose yearning shadow / we erect our great uprights / and settle fulfilled" [*One* 13], and in the poet's description of father and grandfather, upright, mending the family's shoes [*BF* 13]). In *Her Vertical Smile* the Earth Mother's shadow is a reflection of darkness and death —including those of Ó Riada, Mahler, and Mann—but constitutes also her vertical smile, at once an accommodation, a triumphant defiance, even joy, in the face of death. Her song, then, is sung for Ó Riada, "her beloved son / pale against the chilly fireplace," just as Bernadette Greevy sang at his funeral in 1971 (*FD* 25). Moreover, it was also *Das Lied von der Erde* that called up Ó Riada's presence before Kinsella in Philadelphia on the first anniversary of his death, just as the poet's experience, as we have seen, parallels remarkably the final song, "Der Abschied," of Mahler's work: "Ó Riada's presence was in the room; for an extraordinary moment we drank together. Then the presence went off into the darkness. It was a definite farewell" (*FD* 72).

In one sense, the volume serves as a further elegy to the poet's dead friend, but its prime purpose is to place that death in its larger universal context. For while the "Overture" opens with explicit reference to the poignant conclusion to *Das Lied von der Erde*, with its nine repetitions of "Ewig . . . Ewig" ("For ever . . . for ever"), that reference becomes immediately overladen with the reference, suppressed from the poem's epigraph, to Ó Riada's playing the Mahler "over and over again." Moreover, once more the question of divine judgment and apocalypse is raised and once more answered by appetite: in *Songs of the Psyche* appetite took early form in the child's sucking on his

17. In *transition* (1932), Samuel Beckett, with Hans Arp, Eugene Jolas, Thomas MacGreevy, and others, signed a surrealist manifesto, "Poetry Is Vertical," which is reprinted in Thomas MacGreevy, *Collected Poems*, ed. Thomas Dillon Redshaw (1971; Dublin: Raven Arts Press and New Writers Press, 1983), 73–74.

pen's nib; here it is caught by the embryonic "talent" of the two young men, their cigarette butts no longer flaring down onto the street below (as in "Baggot Street Deserta") but no less symbolic for all that. For the two men are engaged in a similarly creative endeavor and, "devouring an echo out of nothing" (*BF* 43), seek to transform nothingness into its positive antithesis, into a vision of the Quincunx or whole.

The poem shifts in its first movement from *Das Lied von der Erde* to the first performance of another Mahler work, his monumental Eighth Symphony, conducted by the composer in Vienna on 12 September 1910, less than a year before his own death. Kinsella's description captures Mahler exactly:[18] his age, his physique, his conducting style, his renowned tyranny over audiences, and above all his will (the last always crucial on Kinsella's path to understanding):

> He sports a little paunch
>   but this, in its boxy waistcoat,
> merely emphasises the force of will
>
> we find everywhere
>   in his strange work:
> the readiness to embrace risk,
>
> tedium, the ignoble,
>   to try anything ten times
> if so the excessive matter can be settled.
>
> (44)

"Ten times" is surely an acknowledgment of the Mahler canon of ten symphonies, the tenth remaining incomplete at the time of his death, for Kinsella's terms are anything but casual: even the clichéd "pregnant hush" takes its place within the sexual imagery developed here, of Mahler's baton exploring the Muse-Mother's "core of peace." Yet Mahler's triumph, as both the composer and the poet understand, does not settle "the excessive matter." Mortality and death may be

18. According to Bruno Walter, "His every appearance in the orchestra pit was preceded by the tenseness with which one looks forward to a sensation. The house grew silent when, with quick, firm step, he made for the desk. If a whisper would arise or an embarrassed latecomer sneak in, Mahler would turn around and a dead silence would reign over the intimidated audience . . . everybody was under his spell." Cf. Alma Mahler's description of the reception of the Eighth Symphony. Both are quoted in Egon Gartenberg, *Mahler: The Man and His Music* (London: Cassell, 1978), 83, 321.

confronted, disorder may be overcome, will may gain the self's survival, but, in terms reminiscent of his earlier *Wormwood* manifesto, the poet asks:

> Was there ever one chasm closed
>   but another opened
> on our case
>
>   —however the medium,
>   blood-bearing in itself,
> might seem temperate and good?
>
> Or our Music Master
>   fold the terms of the curse
> back upon itself
>
> in sensible figures in the air
>   so the blood might beat at our temples
> with the pulse of order . . .
>
> (47)

Instead of Mahler's sublime vision of a world interpenetrated by the Creator Spirit and man drawn heavenward by the Eternal Feminine, "Das Ewig-Weibliche" ("the ever-womanly"), "it's off to the mutton-chop slaughter," as Kinsella describes World War I, where "there are great iron entities / afloat like towns erect on the water / with new murderous skills" (46), and where deadly techniques of tank warfare reflect the self's endless capacity for inflicting pain:

>   iron animals clamber
> in staggered series
>
> up out of the creases and folds
>   in our spirits onto dry land
> and turn it to mud under us,
>
> and drums burst in ditches at our feet
>   and the ghosts of pikes
> stutter all around us
>
> and bannerets of our own selves
>   dangle on wires along
> irregular rivers of our own making, . . .
>
> (49)

Kinsella's emphasis is clear: the forces of destruction are within, they emerge "out of the creases and folds / in our spirits." Newly developed weaponry merges all too naturally with superseded drums and pikes, and all in turn reflect "our own selves" and a being "of our own making." Mahler performs his music "at the heart of old Vienna," but that heart proves spiritually dead as the Austrian Empire collapses at the outbreak of World War I. Kinsella's sketched details of "white gloves," "decorated bellies," "mirrored halls," and endless dances quickly give way before the disharmony and disorder of mass slaughter. Mahler's distinctive "withheld double dark beat" (48) proves the more accurate rhythm and music. It may be that in folding "the terms of the curse / back upon itself" Mahler might provide a unity that constitutes "a happy ending." The matriarchal revelation at the climax of his Eighth Symphony is established through the tenor "Doctor Marianus" jubilantly concluding with a prayer, "Virgin, Mother, Queen, Goddess, remain merciful" ("Jungfrau, Mutter, Königen, Göttin, bleibe gnädig"), and the Gloria. That matriarchal "happy ending," complete with Dantean-Yeatsian "blazing heart," however, is set off against Michelangelo's patriarchal version of the Creation on the Sistine Chapel ceiling: "a languid and burly young man // with everything limply on show, / and a little out of condition, / finger to finger with God the Father" (48). Yet no matter which account, "Patriarch-Mother /—ending or beginning," Kinsella argues, "it was only in the excesses of our minds and art / that we need to undergo / the outrage we appear to find essential." Consciousness, like art, requires "outrage," the fall and redemption of the self, the shaping into coherence and order. Hence the atrocities of World War I are "of our own making," for humanity's propensity for evil, like its creative imagination, appears endless.

> There are photographs
>   of the sudden peace:
> the late enemies together like family groups
>
> half leaning against one another.
>   There is a heavy boot in one
> actually standing on a fallen hand.
>
> (49)

The final grotesque detail takes on added significance in the light of Kinsella's recurrent imagery of hands. And the biblical echo—"For what shall it profit . . ." (Mark 8:36)—serves only to underline the spiritual death involved in such war making and its absurd outcome—"so that upon a fixed hour / a long horn will honk / and the field is his or another's. . . ." Yet Mahler's "double dark beat" captures the systole and diastole of both heart and world. Blood once again proves the medium of damnation and salvation, just as time both kills and saves.

The Intermezzo shifts attention from Mahler to Thomas Mann, whose letter to Richard Dehmel Kinsella versifies here.[19] Such versification in itself reflects a deliberate Mann technique and is Kinsella's acknowledgment of concerns shared by Irish poet and German novelist.[20] The letter expresses Mann's conservative, nationalist view of World War I, a view that provoked sharp reaction among liberals and which Mann himself repudiated later. As such, the letter is one more expression of humanity's fallen nature and potential for evil. For, setting his mind "to the service of the German cause," Mann ennobles war, revealing attitudes that are dangerously naive, ignorant, and wrong-headed, attitudes that pervert his search for meaning. Instead of the transformation Mann envisaged, Germany two decades later experienced the collapse of the Weimar Republic and the emergence of Adolf Hitler and Nazi barbarism.

> For I believe it is important
>   to articulate and ennoble these happenings
> and give them meaning.
>
> How will it all end?
>   The anxiety, the curiosity,
> are immense. But is there not
>
> a joy in the curiosity?
>   That all things will be made new
> by this profound and powerful event
>
> and the German people emerge from it
>   stronger and prouder,
> freer and happier?
>
> (50)

Kinsella may use Mann's letter with obvious heavy irony, but in many other ways the novelist proved an early and powerful attraction.

19. Letter dated Munich, 14 December 1914, in *The Letters of Thomas Mann, 1889–1955*, trans. Richard Winston and Clara Winston (Harmondsworth, U.K.: Penguin, 1975), 69.

20. In a letter to Theodor W. Adorno (30 December 1945) Mann described his montage technique "which peculiarly and perhaps outrageously runs through this entire book [*Dr. Faustus*] without any attempt at concealment"; see *Letters of Thomas Mann*, ed. Winston and Winston, 361.

He was drawn to Mann, he has said, "for the comprehensiveness and reach of his ideas, his minute control over detail."[21] Certainly he has concerned himself similarly with large issues: the fulfillment of the self, the relationship between the artist and society, the connections between art and life. Like Mann, he has been interested in alchemy and numerology, imaging the artist as a Faustian magician. Indeed, they share a fascination with Hermes-Mercury, that mythic conductor of souls to the underworld whom Mann called his "favourite divinity."[22] They both admire the principles of reason and order and both have been drawn to the example of the French Enlightenment. They both are "adept at literary music-making,"[23] depend upon musical analogies, and use montage techniques. It is tempting also to see parallels between Mann's composer Adrian Leverkuhn in *Dr Faustus* experimenting upon a name (Esmeralda) and Ó Riada's atonal experiment upon a name (Hercules, Duke of Ferrara) in *Hercules Dux Ferrariae*, a work influenced in turn by Mahler. Indeed, Mann was an ardent admirer of Mahler and was present at the première of the Eighth Symphony described in the poem's first movement.[24] We might even note that Mann's letter to Dehmel was written from Munich, the city where *Das Lied von der Erde* was first performed, since such coincidences Kinsella would be quick to appreciate. Coincidence, after all, constitutes that chance which, following Yeats, Kinsella sets in perpetual antithesis to choice. Above all, however, in its ennoblement of war Mann's letter serves as a counterpoint to Kinsella's own theme, and it was Mahler who insisted that "[t]here is no harmony—only counterpoint."[25]

The second movement returns to the première of Mahler's Eight Symphony and employs familiar Kinsella imagery: the baton fall becomes "A timed excision" while the speaker asks the rhetorical but quintessentially Kinsella question, "Is there anything quite like / get-

21. O'Driscoll, "Interview," 58.

22. Letter to Karl Kerényi, 24 March 1934, in *Mythology and Humanism: The Correspondence of Thomas Mann and Karl Kerényi*, trans. Alexander Gelley (Ithaca, N.Y.: Cornell University Press, 1975), 48.

23. Mann's description to Adorno; see *Letters of Thomas Mann*, ed. Winston and Winston, 362.

24. The day after the première Mann declared: "[Mahler] seems to me to embody the most serious and sacred artistic purpose of our time"; quoted in Gartenberg, *Mahler*, 366.

25. Quoted in Geoffrey Crankshaw, sleeve note to Mahler, Symphony No. 8, Chicago Symphony Orchestra, dir. Georg Solti. London/Decca OSA 1295.

ting to the root?" And for Mahler-Kinsella, getting to the root involves bringing back notes—signs, information, or musical sounds—from the land of the dead:

> He is summoning
> the ghost of a double beat,
>
> a felt weight on the ear,
> fishchill,
> a remote stink
>
> from the depths,
> news ascending
> speechless from a lower cold
>
> where the senses have no function.
> (51–52)

The self emerging to declare its existence—"*I am! I am!*" (52)—is defined in part by Yeatsian terminology ("It is a brute bobbin // throwing a hard shade"). But that terminology is quickly subsumed under a more distinctively Kinsellan description of the self's evolution, "teeming everywhere / with your aches and needs // along our bloody passageways, / knocking against one another / in never ending fuss" (52). Moreover, in place of God's finger reaching out to touch Adam's finger in Michelangelo's version of the Creation story, Mahler-Kinsella wags an alternative finger and offers a rather different music, ironically termed "a gavotte":

> I wag this pale finger
> down among you
> in promise
>
> (fuss
> propped upon promise
> implying purpose,
>
> waste
> a part of the process,
> implying life):
>
> that there is an outer carrion
> bone-walking in a dream bedlam,
> half lit, idling

in foul units,
  circling our furthest reach
with a refusing snarl,

and that from even this matter
  (as of man's head rammed against stone
and woman a mad animal)

we might yet make a gavotte
  to feed
that everlasting Ear.

(53)

The definition the music provides contradicts orthodox religious accounts: teleology ("purpose") is subject to doubt just as "waste" is "part of the process," while physical man is severely discredited ("an outer carrion / bone-walking in a dream bedlam"). In contradistinction, the poet offers a picture of Gustav and Alma Mahler "taking the air / by the sea side" in a world "absolutely Heavenly," like "the very first morning." Ocean and earth touch in a union that reflects the conjunction of male and female in an epiphany. Kinsella used the same imagery in an early uncollected poem, *The Starlit Eye* (1952), and again in the Sandycove section of "Nightwalker." "All the strings are agreed," Kinsella notes here in a parodic reversal of Auden's elegy on Yeats ("O all the instruments agree / The day of his death was a dark cold day"). Composer and wife, artist and muse, experience a temporary, but nonetheless real, suspension of time, a numinous moment as Alma-muse is seen "coupling her attentive shadow with his" (54). As the final movement begins its conclusion, the poet announces the moment not of Creation but of the Fall and the inevitable dialectic at work:

Let the Fall begin,
  the whole wide
landscape descend gently

—the open air
  a single throat
thrown wide

in a gasp of
  alarm and praise—
and a portal close.

(54)

Likewise, recognizing that "Good man-made matter // is best for our design," Kinsella turns not to the sublime transcendence of Mahler's Eighth Symphony but to that "double beat" or dialectical organic process that the sequence has followed and celebrated, and to the corresponding need to embrace the contraries. It is a direction paralleled more particularly in Mahler's own conclusion to *Das Lied von der Erde*, scenes from the final song of which Kinsella details explicitly here:

> forest murmurs; a tired horseman
> drinking in friendship and farewell;
>
> voices blurred in longing;
> renewal in Beauty;
> Earth's pale flowers blossoming
>
> in a distance turning to pure light
> shining blue
> for ever and for ever.
>
> (55)

Mahler's final song, "Der Abschied," likewise ends with a moving affirmation of eternal renewal, the "Ewig . . . Ewig . . ." poignantly repeated nine times to resurface in Kinsella's own song ("for ever and for ever"). Just as the singer's "single throat" is "thrown wide // in a gasp of / alarm and praise," so too "central to the Song's force" is "an awareness . . . of her two nutrient smiles" (55). Such duality constitutes an affirmation by both Austrian composer and Irish poet of the contrary nature of the world and the regeneration that counterpoint makes possible.

It may legitimately be asked whether Kinsella is justified in placing himself and Ó Riada in a context that embraces Mahler and Mann and a century of barbarism. Of Ó Riada's significance Kinsella has no doubt—"he was Ireland's foremost composer and musician" (*FD* 59)—while all three have profound significance for Kinsella personally. Indeed, they have enabled him to comment upon the nature of the self, its dark forces making for evil, and the need to face that reality and its ultimate conclusion. Kinsella concludes more modestly, however, with a coda with a partly deflationary purpose: the coda enables him to avoid Yeatsian heroics, but it also reminds his readers, in an absurd parody of the Fall pictured as the falling down of one's trousers, that failure is not only likely but necessary. For failure is inevitable in a world in which chance constantly undermines choice and in which the self, while persisting in its spiritual journey toward completeness, at the same time understands that such completeness within time is unattainable. Moreover, chance or "Luck" is not only among "the enabling elements"; it is "the greatest of these," an acknowledgment by Kinsella of both human frailty and Darwinian accident in a world where change occurs through coincidence as much as through choice:

> Nine are the enabling elements
> in the higher crafts
> and the greatest of these is Luck.
>
> I lift my
> baton and my
> trousers fall.
>
> (*BF* 56)

IV

The sequence's two concluding works, *Out of Ireland* and *St. Catherine's Clock*, were issued simultaneously in 1987 and bring *Blood and Family* to an impressive close. Once more we return to Ireland, to Ó Riada, and to Kinsella's family. The first title echoes the late Yeats poem "Remorse for Intemperate Speech": "Out of Ireland have we come. / Great hatred, little room, / Maimed us at the start. / I carry from my mother's womb / A fanatic heart" (*Collected Poems* 288). The lines serve Kinsella well, a fact that illustrates how he has successfully managed to emerge from Yeats's great shadow. For Yeats is now subsumed within Kinsella's own work and preoccupations so as to enable him to comment upon Ireland, origins, process and evolution, and the maiming that leads to understanding. Far from cramping the younger poet, Yeats has now become—Kinsella's previous assessment to the contrary—another fertile precursor in the dual Irish tradition.

Time as well as place prove central to these two works, and, as has been Kinsella's practice for at least the last twenty years, the moment in time includes all time, bringing together past and present in a numinous moment. His personae have long been engaged in psychic expeditions through time and space; in *Out of Ireland* the poet adds the new figure of the ninth-century Irish philosopher, Johannes Scotus Eriugena,[26] who is well qualified to serve the contemporary audience, not the least in his role of peregrinator. Kinsella's vision, like his technique, radiates outward, accumulating significance as figures, events, places, and experiences combine in rich and fruitful embrace. That both Kinsella's vision and technique are defined superbly by way of that archcritic of the Irish, Giraldus Cambrensis (Gerald of Wales), is yet one more characteristic irony. For Giraldus's description of the distinctive nature of Irish music is used to illustrate both Eriugena's philosophical system and Kinsella's own poetic practice. Such dazzling contrapuntal patterns, however, do more than illustrate; they also substantiate by embodying the very process by which the poet reaches his inclusive vision. Kinsella had used La Tène spirals and coils to similar, although not so extended, effect in earlier poems. But, as the epigraph from Giraldus indicates, the reader must recognize Kinsella's considerable irony: the poet uses the epigraph to instruct the reader how to read his poem, just as Giraldus lectures the audience on how to listen to early Irish music (the only feature of Irish life he, as a Norman Welsh invader, found fit to praise). Both the twelfth-century commentator and the twentieth-century poet answer criticism by noting the limitations of their audiences. At the same time appearance and reality are wryly turned inside out: "what appears but confused and disordered noise" is in reality supremely harmonious and perfected art. In Giraldus's words, such art lies in

> concealing it, as if "it were the better for being hidden. An art revealed brings shame." Hence it happens that the very things that afford unspeakable delight to the minds of those who have a fine perception and can penetrate carefully to the secrets of the art, bore, rather than delight, those who have no such perception—who look without seeing, and hear without being able to understand. When the audience is unsympathetic they succeed only in causing boredom with what appears to be but confused and disordered noise. . . . (*BF* 58)

26. Joyce praised Eriugena both in his 1907 Trieste lecture, "Ireland, Island of Saints and Sages," and in the *Wake*; see Kearney, "Introduction" to *The Irish Mind*, ed. Kearney, 27–28. John J. O'Meara has described Eriugena as "the most considerable philosopher in the Western world between Augustine and Thomas Aquinas and the greatest Irish philosopher (with the possible exception of Berkeley) ever. He was the brightest ornament of Ireland's much vaunted group of saints and scholars." See John J. O'Meara, *Eriugena*, in *Irish Life and Culture*, vol. 17 (Cork: Mercier Press, 1969), vii.

Once more the poet approaches a definition of his art while at the same time upholding art's essential mystery; in so doing he also achieves his necessary accommodation with time and the nature of things.

Repetition has proved a constant feature of Kinsella's work for the past twenty years: he has returned to places and experiences; recognized the persistence of a process reaching back into the past, even to the first invasions of Ireland; and explored both his origins and the nature of origin itself. "Is there anything quite like / getting to the root?" (51), Mahler-Kinsella asks. In *Out of Ireland* the poet returns to a location that provoked crucial and numinous experiences almost two decades earlier: the graveyard of St. Gobnait's Church, Ballyvourney, Co. Cork, where his friend Seán Ó Riada is buried. Already Giraldus's comments on Irish music take on added relevance and poignancy. And presiding over the scene once more are the familiar, sinister black crows, for they too constitute part of the native wisdom or folklore and myth. Repetition too is furthered by Kinsella's incorporation of lines from earlier poems in his canon: as his "Precedents and Notes" accompanying the sequence make explicit, he quotes from himself, using lines from A *Selected Life*, and from "Nightwalker" and "Phoenix Park" *(N)*. The practice, serves to extend the lines' original meaning. The process pursues a direction analogous to that recurrent Kinsella motif inherited from La Tène and early Irish decoration, the coil or spiral, and paralleled in Joyce and Beckett. The Giraldus Cambrensis epigraph once more provides useful commentary by reminding the reader of the poet's intricate interweaving of themes, images, and experiences. But, as with the spiral and as with Yeats's winding stair, the repetition goes beyond simple restatement of previous positions. The spiral or winding stair includes all previous positions in a new, superior (because more comprehensive) synthesis. "Without contraries is no progression," as William Blake affirmed in *The Marriage of Heaven and Hell.* A dialectic provides for progress along the self's labyrinthine path. Kinsella's self-quotations serve a function in part analogous to his quotations from Yeats or Joyce or Ó Rathaille: the poet can both draw upon and diverge from his literary ancestors. In quoting from himself, however, the fragments take on the expression of old selves or skins shed in previous stages of his development. They are acts of "dramatic borrowing," to use his own description:

> "Out of Ireland" makes use of bits and pieces from previous love poems in an act of dramatic borrowing, with the speaker of the earlier statement a character in the later. It is a love sequence, with the effect metaphysical and dramatic. . . .[27]

Such emphasis upon drama is significant since it draws attention away from plain self-expression and grants the poet vital distance: it must be conceded that the experiences are rooted, after all, in autobiography and self, in his relations with his wife and Ó Riada. However, Kinsella has given a deliberately fabricated quality to the endeavor, seeing the poems as a psychic drama with characters and settings. Ó Riada, for example, becomes "our forgotten young hero" (63), as much a symbolic figure as Eriugena. Similarly, the poet's shuttling back and forth in time places that drama in a context larger than Ballyvourney or Ireland, in a universal context where Giraldus and Eriugena play their parts as naturally as the poet and his wife, St. Gobnait, the Black Robber, the *sheela-na-gig*, and "Seamus of the Smart Suit" (61). The title *Out of Ireland* thus refers to the tracing of origins but also, in another sense, to extension beyond Ireland, to include, indeed, the exile Eriugena and generations of Irish have undergone and their drawing upon and contributing to the European cultural tradition.

Yet the reader is made aware at the outset of the sequence of one further context in which the poem operates, one other coil included in the intricate spiraling, that of tradition or community. Blood and family once more combine to define the self in the context of history and culture. The way in to the sequence is via the poem "Entrance" (59), which leads the reader through and then out of the churchyard, and ultimately to understanding. The path is guarded, as archetypal mythic paths are, by symbolic beasts, the Morrigan crows overhead. Following naturally from that acknowledgment of symbolic myth is the poet's simple statement: "Two languages interchanged." For while *Out of Ireland* may be subtitled, at least in the Peppercanister edition, "A metaphysical love sequence," it has ramifications also for Ireland and those cultural issues still troubling the living stream: its two languages, one dying, the other not just alien but imposed by the colonizer, and the effect of that linguistic-cultural-political duality upon the living Irish poet; and its tradition, torn similarly along linguistic and political lines. The point is dramatically illustrated in the final

27. Deane, "A Conversation," 89.

poem, "Exit," which incorporates the title of an early seventeenth-century Irish air, "Tabhair dom do lámh." In the Peppercanister edition Kinsella quotes the title in its original Irish; in the Oxford collection, *Blood and Family*, he gives it in English, "Give me your hand," and relegates the Irish to the Notes. To add to the rich linguistic mixture, he points out in his note that the title is often given in the Latin, "Da mihi manum" (89). Far from mere pedantry, the point illustrates exactly thc larger context, European and universal, which the poem maintains, together with the ravages of time upon linguistic inheritance: Irish, like Latin before it, is no longer a thriving language. Furthermore, it may be that among the "half-certainties" the poet affirms, in lines from "Phoenix Park," is "*that love is / to clasp simply, / question fiercely*," but the poem proceeds to place that affirmation less in the context of love than of "The artistic act." The original poem, "Phoenix Park," after all, embraced both love and the creative imagination; the poet's love was both wife and muse, and, as he acknowledges in that poem, her wisdom was known bodily, unlike his own inferior experience ("mental, in my fever—mere idea" [*N* 79]). Once more, however, the process proves deathly, as this first poem, "Entrance," concludes with oblique advance notice of Eriugena and his tragic, almost absurd, death at the hands of his own students whom he taught to question fiercely. For his death came through the pen, the artist's very instrument of creation—a calculated marriage of contraries—just as love itself is both to "*clasp*" and to "*question*."

"Native Wisdom" follows naturally from the initiation into the mystery that Kinsella offers in the opening poem and provides a similarly contrary position staked out by way of its different voices. Kinsella's work is not only more dramatic but more concrete than his critics have appreciated. Here the poem becomes another arena for conflicting voices, again much in the manner of late Yeats. The purging in the earlier work of the older poet's ghost now enables Kinsella to call upon him as a productive influence. This is so not necessarily because he agrees with Yeats, but because the older poet no longer constitutes a threat and represents, after all, a powerful expression of "native wisdom." If the dialectic in "Entrance" includes physical and intellectual experience, here that dialectic takes another form, of masculine and feminine, Black Robber *(an gadaidhe dubh)* and *sheela-na-gig*, both transfixed in stone in the walls of the church, both set off against the saint whose church this is and whose holy well is located in the churchyard.[28] Moreover, saint and *sheela* also offer antithetical native wisdom: it may be that St. Gobnait is associated with bees and sweetness (as Seamus Murphy's modern statue at Ballyvourney illustrates), but her name too means "sweet mouth" and is set off against her dark opposite, the *sheela* offering an alternative appetite and mouth. The gravestones, however, remind us that appetite, whether masculine or feminine, has bearing also upon articulation and therefore upon the artist: "A flat root of stone / lay like a tongue / in the coarse grass." And over all is the ubiquitous and omniscient crow, the archsurvivor:

> A crow scuffled in the hedge
> and floated out with a dark groan
> toward the church tower,
>
> and flapped onto
> the parapet:
> *I am native born in this place.*
>
> *I have knowledge*
> *of flesh and blood.*
> *Come and buy.*
>
> (*BF* 59–60)

Each subsequent voice makes a similar sales pitch, in ironic echo, as Kinsella's note quoting Riché makes plain, of the Irish scholars (or Scoti) at the Carolingian court: "The Irish were astonishing, sometimes even scandalous, because of their free speech, worldly science,

28. "The Black Robber" (in Irish, *an gadaidhe dubh*) is the local name given to a stone carving of a human head in the wall above the chancel arch at Ballyvourney. The *sheela-na-gig*, to be found on the south wall, is a medieval stone carving of a naked female grotesquely displaying her genitalia. The figure, of which there are numerous instances in Ireland, was previously supposed to originate in pre-Christian fertility cults. Recent scholarship regards them as representing the sin of lust to the Christian faithful. For both *sheela* and Black Robber figures, see Françoise Henry, "The Decorated Stones at Ballyvourney, Co. Cork," *Journal of the Cork Historical and Archaeological Society* 47 (January–June 1952): 41–42 and plates VII, VIII. For the *sheela*, see Anthony Weir and James Jerman, *Images of Lust: Sexual Carvings on Medieval Churches* (London: Batsford, 1986); Stella Cherry, *A Guide to Sheela-na-Gigs* (Dublin: National Museum of Ireland, 1992); and Jørgen Andersen, *The Witch on the Wall: Medieval Erotic Sculpture in the British Isles* (Copenhagen: Rosenkilde and Bagger/London: Allen and Unwin, 1977). Andersen commented at length upon the Ballyvourney *sheela* and the practice of pilgrims in the 1930s performing their "pattern," having to reach up to touch the *sheela*, "not with the bare hand, however, but with a handkerchief" (24–25).

and intellectual audacity. These were incomparably learned men. They cried out to a crowd of customers, 'If anyone desires wisdom, let him come to us and receive it, for we are here to sell it' " (87). The irony, however, is played off against present-day Ireland, as Kinsella's historical allusions constantly do, since the medieval intellectual vitality and certain worldview have given way to doubt and confusion, at best the "half-certainties" of "Entrance." The Black Robber ("a grotesque head in the tower wall" [86]) offers an equally dark wisdom, "*native born,*" as he claims, "*in your foul deeds*"; "*Good and evil*" each "*come and buy.*" The *sheela*, predictably, epitomizes sexual appetite, set off against the concluding voice from the "mouth" of a grave: "*I am born again in the spirit. / So shall you be. Love is all / or nothing. Come and buy.*" The voice may be the poem's concluding one but to infer that it therefore speaks for Kinsella would be to misread his vision and world. The Christian spiritual wisdom is one of several conflicting voices, and out of that conflict or dissonance the poet creates not so much harmony as polyphony. Indeed, Kinsella provides the necessary gloss in his Notes to the volume, quoting from an account by the twentieth-century historian Ludwig Bieler of the ninth-century Eriugena's musical analogy—one more instance of polyphony and intricate interweaving, as Bieler is played off against both Eriugena and Giraldus Cambrensis. And once more Kinsella goes back to the root, to *Musica Enchiriadis*, possibly the work of an Irishman and "the earliest treatise on polyphony" (Bieler, *BF* 87):

> For as instrumental music is composed of notes of different length and quality (pitch), which, heard in isolation, differ considerably according to tension, but if they are combined variously in certain relations according to the rules of musical theory result in sounds of a natural sweetness, so also the unity of the universe is made up of the parts, dissonant from one another when considered separately, yet of one all-embracing nature. (*Musica Enchiriadis*, iii, 6; *BF* 87–88)

Kinsella may not subscribe to such a worldview, but he recognizes that understanding may be gained from a similar polyphony of intellectual positions. Precisely such a polyphony he practices himself in this poem. And in his juxtaposition of Irish traditional music, as rearticulated by Ó Riada, and Eriugena's musical analogy to prove the world's divine unity, Kinsella is suggesting a continuity and inheritance the value of which persists and transcends the conflicting linguistic claims of Irish and English.

The function of Kinsella's polyphonic technique is to define all the more clearly the nature of his own experiences. In drawing upon Eriugena he does not need to subscribe to the medieval vision. Indeed, while he marks their common images of fire and melting down, he is quick to point out the limitations of his own vision: his terms are, with nice irony, "half-baked" (*BF* 62) but also, notice, intrinsically physical ("Bodily"). As Kinsella, quoting John J. O'Meara, makes plain in his note (88–89), "The Return" for Eriugena involves the ascent of "the deified" which includes physical as well as spiritual resurrection since "God will be all in all. . . . In this return the substance of things does not perish, but moves upwards to the better. . . . The intelligible body does not cease in the higher, as molten iron does not cease in fire, or air in light; but it is further on the way of return. . . ." Likewise, "the division into sexes was in punishment of man's perverse will. . . ." Both medieval philosopher and modern poet ache for what the latter calls "a containing Shape" (62); their wills are "*designing*," an image that unites purposeful, scheming, even crafty aspiration with the shaping spirit of the imagination, seeking designs in the craft of poetry. Kinsella's recurrent search for structure or "containing Shape" is made all the more dynamic now with polyphony replacing the static and cold crystal of earlier poems. Such a structure may reveal order and meaning in a world appearing to lack both. But, as "The Furnace" makes clear, the epiphany that comes through love is experienced but not sustained within time. Again, with deliberate irony, it is an epiphany that defies articulation, that renders one "speechless." Likewise, in further acknowledgment of his own inadequacy, the kiss he bestows on his wife at the poem's close is "dry" in contrast to her "rain-wet hair." As the poet-lover expresses it, he

> . . . will turn again toward the same furnace
> that melted the union of our will
> to ineffable zero
>
> how many times in its radiant clasp
> (a cancellation
> certainly speechless for a minute or two)
>
> in token of the Union and the Light.
> Until gender returned
> and we were made two again

Male and Female
in punishment for Man's will
and reminded of our Fall.

In token of which
I plant this dry kiss
in your rain-wet hair.

(62)

His kiss is thus a "token" that acknowledges the Fall, is indeed a product of that "punishment for Man's will," and is set off against the other "token of the Union and the Light." It may be that Kinsella cannot subscribe to Eriugena's faith but the medieval is used to define the contemporary, to highlight not just the differences but also the fundamental continuities. In Eriugena, the soul's return to union with God is achieved through remarkably Kinsellan means: "the return of all things to the One is brought about by man when he purifies his self-understanding and 'reverts' upon himself and upon his cause (i.e. God) in the right manner. Self-knowledge then is the lynch-pin of the entire system." More remarkably, "God is always the unknown darkness above the world," a One hidden not in light but in darkness and to whom man must return by way of his "intellectual journey."[29] Or again: "the most high Wisdom itself is very often signified by the word 'darkness.' "[30]

Kinsella has been preoccupied since at least *Downstream* with the fearful potentialities within the self, and in both the title poem of that volume and in "Old Harry" he explored the question of evil. In Eriugena he found confirmation that "hell is a state of mind which the sinful bring about in themselves of their own doing."[31] Similarly, "the seeds or principles of all things are contained in the human mind,"[32] and humanity's fall into separation from God is not only willful but enables it, through self-knowledge, to return to God.

A sinister parallel, less compatible than Eriugena, is pursued in Kinsella's Notes to the sequence, where he quotes from the Spandau diaries of the jailed Nazi minister for munitions Albert Speer. Speer

29. Dermot Moran, "Nature, Man, and God in the Philosophy of John Scottus Eriugena," in *The Irish Mind*, ed. Kearney, 101, 103–4.

30. Eriugena, *Periphyseon*, quoted in John J. O'Meara, *Eriugena* (Oxford: Clarendon Press, 1988), 113.

31. Moran, "Nature, Man, and God," 92.

32. Ibid., 103.

too writes of polyphony, as he notes his listening to a recording of Gregorian chants, music that evidences not only medieval piety but the people's "unspoiled capacity for emotion. In the painting of the age, also, small gestures sufficed to express drama. Stronger stimuli were not needed. And recently I read that people fainted when they first heard early polyphony. Thus progress can also be understood as impoverishment" (*BF* 88). The quotation provides multiple ironies to which the reader must attend: not just the evolutionary dialectic of Speer's conclusion (progress that is also impoverishment) but, as another commentary upon Kinsella's own technique, the recognition that "small gestures" can "express drama." His own work since *Notes from the Land of the Dead* has provided ample proof of the effectiveness of such "small gestures" as the long narrative-meditative poem ("Downstream," "Nightwalker," "Phoenix Park") has given way to the short lyric (*A Technical Supplement* and *Songs of the Pysche*). The most striking irony, however, points to the poet's persistent awareness of human frailty and capacity for evil. It is not simply a question of the frequently noted conjunction of Nazi barbarism with cultural refinement—the appreciation of music by people capable of the most inhuman and bestial behavior—but the savage irony Kinsella gains from the implied conjunction of Eriugena's furnace, his own imagery of flames, the furnaces of Speer's manufacturing war effort, and—most hideous of all—the gas furnaces of the concentration camps. The poet has shown on numerous occasions since *Downstream* his preoccupation with the Holocaust, although Kinsella keeps these last instances of polyphony out of "The Furnace," and relegated to the Notes.

"The Dance" brings the reader back to "our forgotten young hero," Ó Riada, whose burial place this is, and to "his high-spirited doings." The imagery of the dance, prominent in earlier sequences, and the poet's description of Ó Riada's spirit combine to counter the preceding bleak native wisdom. Yet, as in the earlier elegies to his friend, Kinsella again sees Ó Riada as a sacrifice to the world's appetite, a psychic quester who suffered the ultimate purgation, and it is his "*terrible new capabilities*"—as effective an oxymoron as Yeats's "terrible beauty"—which the reader is now offered:

> His spirit, in one piece still
> (just for a little while,
> and only just)

is cavorting in answer
all brains and bare feet
along the scruffy skyline,

stepping the parish boundary
in goodbye
and beckoning with a comical thumb

up over the edge:
Come and buy
my terrible new capabilities . . .

(63)

It may be the "breeze" that Kinsella detects is "out of the Next Testament"—some future revelation inspiring us with epiphanies born out of further polyphony—but he resists attributing such characteristics to his friend. There will be "no sign"; the religious term is quite explicit. Instead, Kinsella's imagery, while referring back to Ó Riada's pioneer work with Ceoltóirí Chualann in Irish traditional music, is also calculatedly reminiscent of Yeats's *Purgatory*, the late play which, like *Blood and Family*, focuses upon continuities, inheritance, appetite, and tragedy.

And there would be no sign
if we tried to follow
his shifting rhythms,

the throaty piping,
the dry taps fractured on the drum skin,
the delicate new hooves

on approval, slithering to the beat
down out of sight
into the stony places.

(64)

The poem is Kinsella's "final farewell"[33] to his friend.

The sequence's penultimate poem, "The Land of Loss" (64), thus brings the reader back to the crucial Kinsella issue of choice. He may describe temporal existence in terms both reminiscent of and bleaker than those of Matthew Arnold's "Dover Beach": "it grows dark and we stumble / in gathering ignorance / in a land of loss / and unfulfillable desire"; he may also note the fearful irony of Eriugena's death, stabbed

33. Deane, "A Conversation," 87.

by his students with their pens "because he made them think." He may not be able to share Eriugena's faith, but one certainty remains in the form of responsibility: "Nothing certain of this world, / Johannes teaches, / except for certain impediments / we might carry with ourselves." The poet, making his exit from both churchyard and sequence, thus takes up that responsibility, arming himself with the only "weapon" he has—the same instrument, the pen, which proved fatal to Eriugena—and accepting, like Eriugena, the burden of making us think. Since at least the formal commitment in "Wormwood" (N 28) to draining the ordeal cup, Kinsella has continually stressed the persistence and endurance his psychic adventurers must possess. He accepts no less here. While the poet's craft involves battle and wounding, Kinsella suggests no other way forward. The "outstuck tongue" of the gravestone in Ballyvourney thus mocks as well as articulates and consumes. The poet's irony, like Ó Riada's cavorting spirit, offers "*terrible new capabilities.*" For, at the same time, the eternal dance of process—whether of life and death, choice and chance, or the poetic process itself—continues, and the concluding poem, "Exit," commits the poet, despite the sequence's bleakness, to continuing participation in that "dance." Indeed, the poem itself reads more positively than Kinsella's own gloss: "the gesture at the end of the sequence—a turning away from love, the human and everything else."[34] For both "hand" (relationship and love) and "weapon" (poetry) make the existential dance a cause for affirmation rather than nihilistic rejection, despite the graveyard dead awaiting the Day of Judgment and the finality of the poet's gesture ("once and for all"). In Kinsella's world things are never that closed:

> Lidless, lipless, opensocketed
> and dumb with suspended understanding,
> waiting for the Day,
>
> our best evidence
> is aligned all about under us,
> their figures finished.
>
> The dance is at our own feet.
> *Give me your hand.*
> A careful step

34. Ibid., 89.

together over that outstuck
tongue, and shut this gate
in God's name

behind us, once and for all.
And reach me my weapon
in the goat-grey light.

(65)

V

The final work in the collection, *St. Catherine's Clock*, returns to Dublin and the poet's inheritance through family and Irish history. Readers of the Peppercanister edition are made immediately aware, through the cover and title-page illustration of the clock's hands dripping blood, of the familiar Kinsella conjunction of time and wounding or death. Mortality has been a central theme from the very beginning and the poet's "instruments" have included knife, probe, and pen, as well as organic pot. Hands, however, like mouth, can lead to destruction as well as creation. The inheritance here—that which is "handed down"—is bloody and mortal. The cover for the collected volume *Blood and Family* reprints James Malton's 1792 engraving of St. Catherine's Church, an engraving that serves as the subject of one poem, "1792—*Jas. Malton, del.*" The Dublin landmark provides firm evidence of the confluence of blood and family. As one of Kinsella's many landing places or crossroads, Malton's scene relates past and present: the engraver captures a fine eighteenth-century classical façade against which Robert Emmet's blood was later shed, located in a neighborhood full of memories of the 1803 rebellion, including Lord Kilwarden's assassination, but memories also of the poet's own childhood and of his grandparents. And the whole is set, in one of those fortuitous coincidences to which Kinsella, like Joyce, is prone, on Thomas Street.

The introductory untitled poem sets the scene, as the poet, "divining the energies of the prowler," gains understanding of contemporary Dublin. Set off against the poet's vision—"I see"—is the alternative and disturbing visionary experience sought by the drug addict, in another lonely Kinsella room, injecting himself. The addict's needle thus joins, ironically, with the poet's pen, the clock's "gilded point" (70), and the earlier knife or dissecting probe of *A Technical Supple-*

ment as one more means by which the self seeks understanding. Addiction, obliterating awareness, becomes one more instance of Ireland's deathly inheritance, of a contemporary underworld or land of the dead to be explored.

The whole terrace
slammed shut.
I inhaled the granite lamplight
divining the energies of the prowler.

A window opposite, close up.
In a corner, a half stooped image
focused on the intimacy
of the flesh of the left arm.

The fingers of the right hand are set
in a scribal act on the skin:
a gloss, simple and swift as thought,
is planted there.

The point uplifted,
wet with understanding,
he leans his head a moment
against the glass.

I see.

(69)

The rest of the sequence may thus be regarded as the consequence of such vision, much as *Songs of the Psyche* define the "character" emerging in its first song. The sequence is shaped, by way of a dramatic succession of short lyrics, into a polyphony, a unified whole which by this time Kinsella's readers have come to expect. The scene in this opening poem thus serves as "a gloss," in the sense of a commentary upon the entire sequence, but also, with overtones of the medieval Irish scribe's gloss poems, offering a bleak picture of the present in sharp contrast to the freshness and spontaneity caught in the early Irish lyric. The "skin" likewise reflects polyphonic or multiple meaning: it is at the same time the particular focus of the addict's attention, the medieval scribal parchment, and the very medium by which the modern poet gains understanding. Such "a scribal act on the skin" parallels that of Joyce's Shem the Penman who writes over "the only foolscap available, his own body" (*FW* 185). Kinsella's pen, like the earlier dissecting knife and, in its way, the addict's needle, is poised to reveal "understanding." The pun, another form of polyphony,[35] is not unintentional: we see the point, both literally and figuratively.

The centrality of time to this sequence may be judged in several ways: by the sequence's title; by those brief poems that serve in the manner of stage directions ("Thomas Street at the first hour," "Grand Canal Place / at the second hour," "About the third hour"); but also by the fact that while some poems remain untitled, others are assigned dates for titles ("1803," "1792," "1938," "1740"). The last instance, like the whole sequence, indicates Kinsella's historical sense which persistently reveals the confluence within time of past and present. Moreover, the historical events taking place on the larger national stage serve no less to define the nature of Kinsella's family inheritance. We have learnt on previous occasions of the family's contribution to the 1798 rising, when they hid the Croppies on their retreat from Wexford ("His Father's Hands," *One* 25) and of his father's alignment with Connolly's socialism and nationalism (*BF* 13). It follows naturally from the poet's attention to the engraver James Malton that two of the historical poems should focus upon prints: "1803" (71–72) places a George Cruikshank engraving against a "non-contemporary nationalist artist's impression," in a pair of contrary political perspectives. Cruikshank's picture presents the Dublin mob as "a pack of hatted simians" with "snouted malice" set off against the prim English lord and "two coachmen / picked, like his horses, from a finer breed."[36] The nationalist's engraving draws upon familiar rhetoric, not just T. D. Sullivan's "God Save Ireland" ("on the scaffold high") but Emmet's famous "Speech from the Dock."[37] Kinsella's irony establishes the complexity of his response: the two prints illustrating the 1803 rising go beyond simple approval or disapproval from a nationalist perspective. As Maurice Harmon has noted, Kinsella's style is "both echoing and mocking the emotion of Emmet's speech from the dock and the patriotic flourishes of those who inflated his signifi-

35. For early Celtic punning, see Rees and Rees, *Celtic Heritage*, 340–49.

36. Lyons commented upon nineteenth-century descriptions (by Thomas Carlyle, Charles Kingsley, and J. A. Froude) and cartoons, both of which portray the Irish as possessing "simian or porcine features"; see *Culture and Anarchy*, 12, 14.

37. "I am going to my cold and silent grave; my lamp of life is nearly extinguished; my race is run; the grave opens to receive me and I sink into its bosom. I have but one request to ask at my departure from this world; it is—THE CHARITY OF ITS SILENCE"; see Robert Emmet, "Speech from the Dock" (Dublin: Kilmainham Jail Historical Society, 1978), 7.

cance."[38] The shock with which the poem ends lies less with the beheading and more with the artist's impression of "The pasty head," a description borne out by nineteenth-century portraits. And indeed Kinsella recognizes the politically motivated distortions in both perspectives. Investigation of blood lines must also entail revision of the myths by which one has lived.

The Malton print that provides the cover for the Oxford *Blood and Family* is the subject of the last engraving poem, "1792." The version Kinsella describes is in fact a variant upon that reproduced on the cover, and while all the other details (with the exception of the redcoat) remain constant, one variant detail serves Kinsella well. The version Kinsella works from replaces the wooden-legged man with a stick toiling across Thomas Street with that quintessentially Kinsellan and Irish figure of the hag, the *cailleach*, ancestor of the poet's grandmother and all the other threatening and forbidding old women inhabiting his work:

> Centre, barefoot,
> bowed in aged rags to the earth,
> a hag
>
> toils across the street
> on her battered business,
> a drained backside
>
> turned toward St Catherine;
> everybody, even those
> most near, turned away.
>
> (73)

The relationship between the Dublin population and the hag has a relevance both political and aesthetic: Gaelic Ireland (represented by the bowed old woman "in aged rags") stands in sharp contrast to Georgian Dublin (reflected in the verticals of the church's classical façade to which she offers irreverently "a drained backside"). The political persists, moreover, with the inclusion of the redcoat, standing to one side and "handling the entire matter." The vista, too, "beyond St James's Gate" toward "Bow Lane / and Basin Lane" includes the poet, with oblique acknowledgment of the future employment of grandfather and father at Guinness and the poet's childhood experi-

38. Harmon, "Nutrient Waters," 21.

ences of his grandmother's house in Bow Lane. Appropriately enough, the only figure in apparent anticipation of the hag is the dark shape with a cart and whip in the right foreground, called, significantly, "a shade." Notes from the land of the dead, indeed.

What Kinsella has shown very effectively since the 1972 *Notes from the Land of the Dead* is that such an archetypal underworld is not to be relegated to some primordial existence in a distant past, but instead is a psychic state persistently renewed, drawn upon, and in need of constant reinvestigation. Georgian Dublin thus gives way in "1938" (74–79) to the poet's own working-class experience of the land of the dead, populated now by aunts, uncles, cousins, and the formidable grandmother whose effect upon the young boy has been indicated in other poems. Furthermore, while the poet is concerned with tracing lines of inheritance—psychic evolution as much as genetic or familial or cultural evolution—the ground over which such evolution takes place is given in precise naturalistic detail:

> Two red-and-black matched silky-decorated
> tin boxes out of India
> fit beside each other behind her
> up on the tea shelf, behind her head.
>
> The shoulders of the black iron-flowered
> weighing-scales on the counter
> balance, embossed, across the socket-top of the stand.
> The brass plates hang, equal, in their chains.
>
> Round ounce weights
> and multiples and little
> black fractions nestle
> on one another against the base.
>
> (74)

At the same time, in the portrait of the grandmother whose Bow Lane shop this is, Kinsella need now only sketch in a few suggestive details to recall for the reader her previously established symbolic status. Similarly, the epiphany to which she leads depends once more upon the child's experience of an egg, the zero of being, and once more the prize, like other such prizes in the archetypal mythic narrative, is offered by the grandmother-protectress of the underworld and indicates initiation into experience and meaning:

She had a fat sugar sack,
with the twiny neck rolled back,

tucked in against her high stool
and the black boot laced up
under her skirt and the black beads
hanging down over her brown apron.

In on a dark shelf
on the way into the back
she had the goose eggs from down the country,
green and big, the fill of your palm.

(74)

The child remembers the egg through touch, as much "a scribal act on the skin" as the addict's injection or the poet's writing his poem, and, involving his persistent hand imagery, leading to understanding.

Various other childhood experiences flood in—of aunts and uncles, family feuds, visits to "our best cousins, // older, handsome boys, all with fine teeth," looking for fish in the river, ruthless games in the dark skipping "around in wickedness / with no mercy to the weak or the fat / or the witless or the half blind." That image of the dance is central, whether to the merging of experiences and the subsequent polyphony within the self or to the larger evolutionary dance in the world outside. We have seen the same image in the previous work, *Out of Ireland*, and in the waltz "with Disaster" that serves as prelude to World War I *(Her Vertical Smile)*. The image pursues the same evolutionary pattern as the spiral or coil of earlier sequences and evidences the same torsion. As legitimately as Yeats in "Among School Children," Kinsella can pose the question, "How can we know the dancer from the dance?" Whether an internal or an external dance, blood and family play their part, contributing to the endless appetitive dialectic and leading to one more epiphany where the mother offers both comfort and temptation, another instance of the world's dialectic:

I have struggled, hand
over hand,
in the savage dance.

I have lain inert, the flesh in nightmare,
eating and eaten,
with eyes wide open.

The balm of a clouded breast . . .
The musk of a stocking rolled down
over her pale knee beside the fire-place.
(77)

The child learning "the security of love" thus dreams of a golden self, imaged appropriately enough as evolving from the status of "shade" to being "upright in beauty" and possessing "pinions," like some embryonic Hermes. That golden state, however, remains a dream. On falling back into consciousness, the child knows only "love's hatred" and alienation, "a brutal nail nagging out of nowhere." Such self-examination brings the dividend of self-definition, whether in relation to the mother or the brother, to the larger world outside the family, or, above all, to the lines of inheritance that the poem itself, like the whole sequence, has been charting. Indeed, Kinsella's lines read like a latter-day negative of Amergin's famous *rosc:* no large affirmation of the power of the imagination granted by a *Magna mater*, but working-class decency and respectability practiced in Inchicore according to his mother's standards. The lines again remind Kinsella's reader that, for all his assimilation of Yeats, it is Joyce with whom he has the larger affinity and whose Dublin accents he shares here:[39]

Sometimes it sounded like she was giving out
but she was really minding us.

I know I was not bold
even if I did terrible things.

I was not a barefaced liar
or a thick-ah or a go-boy, or a pup.

I never went with the cur next door
or those gets down the street.

I was always properly dressed,
and minded my brother.

39. I am indebted to Richard Wall's research into Irish idiom and slang for "thick-ah" (meaning "stupid," the suffix "-ah" adding emphasis) and "go-boy" (from "go-by-the-wall," meaning "a sly person" or "hypocrite"); letter to Brian John, 26 March 1992. "Gets" is British-Irish pejorative for "children"; see Eric Partridge, *A Dictionary of Historical Slang*, abridged by Jacqueline Simpson (Harmondsworth, U.K.: Penguin, 1972), 369.

> One night we scrounged up together
> and felt the little eggs in each other.
>
> And I always remembered
> who and what I am.
>
> (79)

The young boys' growing sexual awareness parallels the initiation into meaning by way of the goose egg at the poem's beginning. Likewise, familiar parental moral exhortation ("remember who you are") thus naturally translates into blood lines and identity: "I always remembered / who and what I am." Such translation is at the center of the sequence, establishing continuity and revealing meaning.

The striking of the second hour by St Catherine's clock, however, leads to further uncertainty and self-examination (81–82), and to the questioning of the poet's legitimacy—whether by neighbors or by family remains unclear. Writing of his own conception in the first sequence, *The Messenger* (*BF* 11), Kinsella referred to "a woman and her secret husband"; here, in the final sequence, he refers to family dissension suggesting similar impropriety: "Not fifty yards from here / she took the certificate / and slapped it down on the table. / It took that to shut them up." Certainly, the father, like the poet, speaks of lines of inheritance, blood, and family:

> His voice, empty and old,
> came around to it more than once:
> something about the family
> he had to tell me sometime.
>
> A dead voice now
> in my ear: You can be certain
> from your own cold certainties
> that you are a son of hers.
>
> (81)

But the "dead voice" offers further commentary, as befits the role of the father-Hermes as messenger of the gods, carrying news from the underworld to his Orpheus-poet son. Blood and family go beyond the "passing kind of doggedness" the father acknowledges as the inheritance passed on to the son. Instead, he directs the son to the son's shadow self ("closer than a brother"), to forces within the unconscious, but he also leaves certain things untold:

> Closer than a brother
> (born of the same woman,
> face down face up to her fondness,
> and a quiet brutal other
>
> closer than a brother)
> look for the dimpled smile
> empty of understanding
> that will tell you the rest of it.
>
> I leave you a few faint questions
> and good and bad example
> and things I have not told you,
> and who and what you are.
> (81–82)

In contrast to such emptiness of understanding and sinister "dimpled smile" Kinsella poses his Aunt Bridie, elevated, appropriately, in view of the poet's analogy of music and understanding, as "the musical one of the family" and possessed of a "schoolteacher's smile," for she too is part of the poet's inheritance: "the pair of us so alike, / everybody agreed, / wherever we got our brains."

From the intimacy of such self-examination and family history the poet moves outward, to Thomas Street and "As far as we can reach" (83). That boundary is of Irish history, more particularly of Robert Emmet's hanging and beheading and subsequent influence upon the independence movement. Hence the "modest bloody little trickle" becomes the source of political renewal, as handkerchiefs are dipped in the martyr's blood, as the legendary "second-last letter" is found years later, and leading, like "a river / coiling its potent flood," to "the far-off / impossible magnificat" (the Easter Rising and eventual independence from Britain). Once more the lines of inheritance are anything but simple: Kinsella brings the reader back to St. Catherine's clock, to time and history but also to acknowledgment of the complexities and tension within Irish history. For we are reminded of the Protestant contribution to Ireland's inheritance, to Emmet and to St. Catherine's itself, and to the reversal in time, as Northern Protestants insist, contrary to Emmet, Wolfe Tone, and Parnell, upon maintaining the British connection. The wheel's "tooth" reminds us of the appetite that is the driving force in time, in history, and in the individual self.

The final poem of both the sequence and the volume, "1740" (85), takes place at the third hour, the pitch of night, where the marketplace setting indicates both appetite and shambles, for the neighborhood, among the oldest in Dublin, has a long association with slaughterhouses and related crafts and trades. The emerging figure of Jonathan Swift, however, suggests another form of shambles, as the poem's title also indicates. In 1740 Swift wrote his will; left money for the founding of St. Patrick's, popularly known as Swift's Hospital; and thereafter underwent rapid physical and mental decline. The year signifies mind and body brought to extremity, with Swift, his clerical black suitably reflecting the darkness within and without, and, above all, "reading the ground." The ancient Irish form of *dinnseanchas* (by which a place's significance is communicated and sustained through the Gaelic place name and the myth, folklore, and history associated with the place) is thus brought up to date and practiced here by one more distinguished representative of the Protestant Anglo-Irish tradition. Moreover, in the dark Dean Swift's black clerical dress, together with his obsessive movements, makes him appear "like a madwoman"—a suitable and dark analogue to the hag figure in "1792," both indicating a self dispossessed, whether of status or reason, respect or health. Swift has acquired symbolic status, much as he did in the late poems of Yeats. The lines of tradition and inheritance Kinsella has drawn, though not necessarily embraced, thus encompass Catholic and Protestant, nationalist and unionist, Irish and Anglo-Irish. For these converge at the crossroads on the cultural map and parallel the contrary forces at work, in time and history, nation and community, and therefore impinge upon both family and self.

Kinsella's scope extends backward in time, downward into the self, and outward to include the cultural family of Ireland itself. Like Swift, he has constantly "read the ground" and undertaken, despite the severe demands involved, to understand himself and his world. Above all, we would seriously misread him if, in "1740," despite the scene's ominousness, the essentially affirmative nature of the experience were overlooked. Certainly Kinsella's figures have never lived a comfortable, unharried existence; his vision remains founded in hurt and wounding, suffering to be endured and built upon, an appetite that ravages ceaselessly. At the same time, that appetite not only destroys but creates, and the evolutionary principle, whether of self or existence, takes force and direction from such dialectical progression. For all his darkness of vision Kinsella can still celebrate and affirm the will to go on, and as a poet, through increasingly rich polyphony, bring together disparate experiences in new and creative wholes. In doing so, he has pursued a formidable and sustained exploration of who and what he is; he has traced his ancestral blood lines—familial, racial, and literary—and he may be said now, without exaggeration, to have come into his inheritance.

Conclusion

With work so dynamically "in progress," it is inevitable that the latest complete volume, *From Centre City* (1994), collecting the previous five Peppercanister sequences—*One Fond Embrace* (1988), *Personal Places* and *Poems from Centre City* (both 1990), *Madonna* and *Open Court* (both 1991)—should reveal Kinsella setting forth on further journeys, with new departures leading to new beginnings. He has returned to Ireland, for example, to full-time writing, living first in Dublin and next Co. Wicklow. As the poet himself has noted, "The business has begun again."[1] Indeed, the "business" will go on, by definition, without end: the quest for understanding in a world of process and perpetual dialectical tension can never be final nor can the possession of understanding be absolute. The "data" accumulate and never remain static, and thus structures require constant refining and rearranging. Likewise, Kinsella's protagonist persistently investigates his self, his family and ancestral ghosts, and both his present and ancient primordial history, and such investigations in turn bear closely upon the discipline of the artist and his literary inheritance. The search for structure to encompass meaning, whether within the self,

1. O'Driscoll, "Interview," 65.

the world of time and space, or the creative act itself, is compelling and necessary, even if, in the last resort, it must remain incomplete. Moreover, that search, while leading to understanding, also involves suffering and loss and demands sober self-scrutiny and unflinching integrity. In "At the Head Table" Kinsella offers through the familiar figure of the craftsman one more defense of his poetic purpose and strategy:

> I have devoted
> my life, my entire career,
> to the avoidance of affectation,
> the way of entertainment
> or the specialist response.
> With always the same outcome.
> Dislike. Misunderstanding.
> But I will do what I can.
> (*FCC* 54)

No other contemporary poet, it may be said, has submitted himself to a stricter regimen nor been subject to so much misreading: Kinsella's comprehensive vision may be dark but it is not nihilistic; it may be grim but it is not negating. The poetry, while often making severe demands, requires a similar discipline on the part of the reader if the poet's "reading [of] the ground" is to be followed. That is not to say that he has always succeeded: of the two longer poems in *From Centre City*, "One Fond Embrace" suffers from "spleen," as the poet acknowledges in conclusion, despite his decision to delete the more personal references present in the 1988 version, while "Open Court" offers only disgust at and rejection of contemporary literary Dublin. It may be that Jonathan Swift, who brings *Blood and Family* to a close, is a major driving force in both poems; certainly Kinsella's *saeva indignatio* is at its most excoriating in them. However, he is indebted, in addition to Swift, to another eighteenth-century satirical master, this time from the Gaelic half of the Irish dual tradition: Brian Merriman. The 1988 version of "One Fond Embrace" (*OFE* 1988, 13) specifically alludes to Merriman's masterpiece, *The Midnight Court*; "Open Court" pursues the judicial analogue; and both longer poems in *From Centre City* seek to reproduce "the fierce individual energy" (*TNOBIV* xxvi) for which Kinsella has praised Merriman's poem. In "One Fond Embrace" he draws upon an even earlier Gaelic model, of medieval curse poetry, to condemn the developer-destroyers (a suitably paradoxical title) of Dublin's architectural heritage: "May their sewers blast under them!" (*FCC* 3). However, his own "modest proposal" to deal with Ireland's continuing partition is especially worthy of his ancestral exemplar, Swift:

> everything West of the Shannon,
>
> women and children included,
> to be declared fair game.
> Helicopters, rifles and night-glasses permitted.
>
> The natives to have explosive
> and ambush and man-trap privileges.
> Unparalleled sport
>
> *and in the tradition*
> —the contemporary manifestation
> of an evolving reality.
>
> (9)

Yet for all his mordant anatomizing of Irish hypocrisy and cant, his principled scourging of contemporary Ireland's lack of principle, "One Fond Embrace," like "Open Court," does not show Kinsella at his most impressive: his strengths have always been more clearly evident when anatomizing the self, although in the last resort private and public evil are inseparable.

While John Montague criticized Kinsella's early poetry for being insufficiently located in time and place, a criticism that I have argued is only partly valid, *From Centre City* illustrates how certainly Kinsella has made his Dublin neighborhood a fitting context for his continuing moral and aesthetic struggles to elicit order and meaning. Percy Lane, Haddington Road, and the Grand Canal serve to bring the poet's story up to date, with the volume concluding in his latest home in Co. Wicklow. Kinsella, like Joyce, has managed to trace journeys through a Dublin both exact in its geography and convincing in its symbolism. In Kinsella's case, the landscapes are also populated by the same collection of disparate anatomical parts which, from *A Technical Supplement* onward, the poetry has attended to—face, eyes, lips, mouth, throat, hands—as if the geographical might have its corresponding elements in human anatomy, with both needing some encompassing structure. Kinsella's readers have learnt from previous volumes his need to pursue such anatomizing, and expect to find the poet's scrupulous attention to what makes a thing work. By this time too such parts have acquired significance as the poet's symbolism has gained in strength and resonance. Furthermore, *From Centre City* continues the poet's practice of echo and allusion, whether in self-reflexive acts of intertextuality or in acknowledgment of past masters, so that his entire corpus might inform, clarify, and extend his present meaning and enable his distinctive drama to unfold in increasing complexity and comprehensiveness. Whether quoting from himself or from his ancestral literary mentors, Kinsella establishes important connections which, while sometimes broken or fragmented, nevertheless make possible an enabling structure. Such structures help to sustain and make sense of one's identity, constitute one's inheritance, and clarify one's participation in an organic process that has its origins in the very beginnings of time and space but that bears irrevocably upon the individual life.

Hence, in "At the Head Table," while addressing the woman-mother-muse figure—"the source of trouble," as Kinsella ironically puts it—the after-dinner speaker describes "the lovely beaker / with the slim amphibian handles" that he has made. In the manner of other Kinsella artists, the speaker, in describing the beaker, also captures the nature of the creative process itself: the cup has caused him "the greatest trouble," brought him "the craftsman's stoop," yet, reflecting perfection, amplitude, measure, precision, and plenitude, the artefact's "vital decoration" is

> in fact a web of order
> each mark accommodating
> the shapes of all the others
> with none at fault, or false;
>
> a system of living images
> making increased response
> to each increased demand
> in the eye of the beholder,
>
> with a final full response
> across the entire surface
> —a total theme—presented
> to a full intense regard:
>
> (55)

The decoration reflects Kinsella's purpose as a poet, his intent to weave "a web of order" and to construct "a system of living images" that require the reader's "full intense regard." With a sudden temporal shift, the poet brings his reader back once more to Amergin and the Sons of Mil, to the First People and the poet's own origins, in part because *The Book of Invasions* has provided such a "web of order," brought poet and reader "to a full intense regard," but also because the occasion is Amergin's famous first judgment in Ireland:

> Nine waves out, a ship
> lying low in the water,
> battered from a journey,
> the waves lapping around it
>
> marked with the faint detail
> of all the perils past.
> The first firm footprints
> emerging from the ocean . . .
>
> (55–56)

Hence, with familiar self-deflation, Kinsella has the muse-mother hand down a more contemporary judgment—at best "A smile, dry and lipless"—when, with "stern features" and "lean arms," she offers half-hearted acknowledgment of her poet-son's limited achievement and his own contrary toast to "the Father" (Amergin). Equally characteristic also is the dance in which the limping poet—a further self-deflation—participates with "everyone in turn": the phrase, as we have seen previously, denotes both inclusiveness and dynamic torsion or the "turn" in all things.

While Kinsella's vision gains in inclusiveness, an essential feature of the process is nevertheless waste, a consumption that makes consummation possible. Consequently, in "One Fond Embrace," those assembled around the protagonist's Last Supper, another celebratory dinner, are advised:

> Discern process. You know that,
> mangled by it. We are all participants
> in a process that requires waste.
>
> (6)

The "waste" involves suffering and loss and accounts for Kinsella's numerous wasted figures experiencing dispossession of identity or property or, more simply, having to enact rituals of departure. At times such waste seems simply negative—the hypocrisy, cant, deceit, begrudgery, selfishness, greed, conceit, common to public affairs and literary life. However, in "Night Conference, Wood Quay: 6 June 1979," a poem written during the occupation of the Viking Wood Quay site in which the poet himself took part,[2] the developers and the members of Dublin Corporation are described as "white-cuffed marauders" with "Visages of rapine," intent on destroying a priceless archaeological site. The irony is manifold: the latter-day marauders uncover a Viking past characterized by similar rapine and violence; and those defying the site's "development" possess only a "mental force" gained in part from their experience of evil, past and present, as they face the abyss revealed by the bulldozers: "The half-dug pits and night drains brimmed with matter" (25). At such times waste constitutes a considerable positive.

The dark abyss must be traversed and the waste confronted and endured as the individual self participates in or falls short of meaning and fulfillment. The recurrent mouths experience and share that appetite, just as the equally recurrent lips and throat enable the poet to articulate meaning. The woman-mother-wife figure continues her vital role as seductress, Terrible Mother, lover, and muse in everyday settings like the kitchen and the bedroom. Hence in "Madonna," the several scenes describing the wife figure climax in the cutting open of an orange and the making of a pot of tea, actions which in Kinsella's hands lead to epiphanies, illuminations into the nature of things made possible by the wife-muse:

> Cut and fold it open,
> the thick orange, honey-coarse.
> First blood: a saturated essence
> tasted between the teeth.
>
> I held the kettle out high
> and emptied it
> with a shrivelled hiss
> boiling into the scalded pot.
>
> A stubborn memory:
> her tender, deliberate incursions.
>
> (49)

2. An earlier version of the poem, entitled "Night Conference, 6 June 1979," appeared in the ephemeral news-sheet, *Wood Quay Occupation News*, no. 2 (12 June 1979). For an account of the dispute and of Kinsella's participation in it, see *Viking Dublin Exposed: The Wood Quay Saga*, ed. John Bradley (Dublin: O'Brien Press, 1984).

We are reminded not only of the boy's consumption of a pomegranate in "A Hand of Solo" (*NLD* 15) and the persistence of appetite in Kinsella's world, but of the conjunction of appetite, whether gustatory or sexual, and the muse-prowler with "her 'sudden and / peremptory incursions' " (A *Technical Supplement*, Poem XV, *One* 45).

From Centre City offers many such resonances not because the poet, imagination exhausted, recycles old experiences and poems, but because such echoes embody the very process he seeks to define and capture. His readers have previously been made aware of how relevant the practice of his intertextuality is to embodying his view of process. Moreover, it is such intertextuality that establishes continuity with the poet's past work, that serves to acknowledge past masters—Keats, Auden, Jung, Yeats, Ó Rathaille—and that in turn provides a defining and inclusive structure. In this respect the sensation of touch and the imagery of hands make possible in an explicitly physical way the connectedness of data. For "hands" indicate or signify; they touch, make contact, connect, confer, transfer, take in hand, and verify. Hands themselves embody intertextuality. In "The Back Lane," for example, the poet-protagonist abandons his writing, leaves his workroom, and walks through the night "into the world of waste." His distinctive prayer defines precisely the self's quest for meaning:

> Lord, grant us a local watchfulness.
>   Accept us into that minority
> driven toward a totality of response,
>
> and I will lower these arms and embrace what I find.
>   —Embarrassed. Encountering my brother figure.
> Startled likewise, in that posture
>
> of seeming shyness, then glaring,
>   lips set and dark, hands down and averted
> that have dipped in the same dish with mine.
>
> (38)

Hands and appetite come together in an act of near-sacramental relevance. Just as the prayer is quintessentially Kinsella, so too is the embarrassment, the undercutting with which the poem concludes as the "brother figure" (whom Yeats might more properly describe as his daimonic self) is both encountered and denied: "But it was no one I knew. . . ."

While he may seek through intertextual reference to structure his work into coherent wholes, Kinsella also recognizes past exemplars. Sometimes his recognition is oblique: in "Rituals of Departure" (18), Keats surfaces through Kinsella's rearrangement of the "Ode on Melancholy," in which Keats's "Joy, whose hand is ever at his lips / Bidding adieu" becomes "Melancholy, retiring with her finger to our lips." At other times, as in "Brothers in the Craft," he returns to his beginnings as a poet in the 1950s, to the shadow of Yeats, and to the general principle of literary exemplars: "In the creative generations there is often / a conspiracy of the mature and the brilliant young, / a taking in hand, in hopes of a handing on." Such inheritance is caught in imagery of the hand and, equally characteristically, the evolutionary process at work is of action and reaction, until "these settle in the medium in their turn." The "medium"—meaning both "balance" and the "medium" of poetry itself—is attained through a synthesis or marriage of opposites. But it is a synthesis that maintains its own dynamic, as the ambivalent phrase "in their turn" suggests: the phrase refers to an order achieved or a circuit completed, but implicit also is a further "turning" in which the medium will be unsettled by its own perpetual torsion, and the whole business (or dance, as it is imaged elsewhere) once more set in motion. In the latter half of the poem the youthful Kinsella while prowling in Inchicore, pursuing his own dynamic, models himself more after Thomas Mann than Yeats—an acknowledgment of the German novelist's early powerful influence—while the dead Irish poet's presence or "animus" (an ironic conjunction of "soul" and "animosity"), pictured as perched Sweeney-like on a tree, is more keenly felt by Clarke in Templeogue than by Kinsella himself. Indeed, the "brothers in the craft" engage in conflict just as fratricidal, if less fatal, as that which Kinsella condemned earlier in "A Country Walk":

> Again and again, in the Fifties, "we" attended
> Austin Clarke. He murmured in mild malice
> and directed his knife-glance curiously amongst us.
>
> Out in the dark, on a tree branch near the Bridge,
> the animus of Yeats perched.
> Another part of the City,
> Tonio Kroeger, malodorous, prowled Inchicore.
>
> (19)

Since the deaths of Yeats and Joyce (in 1939 and 1941, respectively), Irish poetry has had to come to terms with what Kinsella early identified as "the double shadow of Yeats and English verse." We have seen Kinsella, like many of his contemporaries, turn to Joyce as the more liberating "Father of Authors," finding Yeats's major poetic achievement too dominating and his Anglo-Irishness inappropriate. What is especially striking about Kinsella's latest work, however, is the reappearance of Yeats, now in the company of an exemplar whom Kinsella has long found more compatible: Aogán Ó Rathaille.

Kinsella had grouped the two poets together in a much earlier work, "The Irish Writer," his 1966 MLA address in New York, in which he sought to define the particular nature of the Irish tradition and his own broken inheritance: "Yeats is isolated to begin with, like Aogán Ó Rathaille, at a turning point in history—there is a notable similarity in the way these poets regard their times: turning away from a miserable present and a terrible future to lament and celebrate an old nobility at the end of the line."[3] Moreover, as his recent statements indicate, Kinsella continues to reassess Yeats's greatness as a poet and, as such, his place in and contribution to the dual Irish tradition.[4] Indeed, rather than reacting against the older poet, Kinsella now appears to be engaged in assimilating him, with the late poems of Yeats taking on a more distinctly Kinsellan coloring. From *Michael Robartes and the Dancer* (1921) onward, Kinsella argues, "there is an outbreak of understanding in the poetry of the place of violence and the random at the heart of vital processes"—an observation that might legitimately be applied to Kinsella's own work. Furthermore, he criticizes the debate over Yeats's rightwing, sometimes fascist, politics, not because he shares Yeats's views, but because it is "a trivialisation of great intellectual and imaginative activity" and "the avoidance of great poetry in the pursuit of argument." Rather, he sees in "Yeats's last books . . . a man at the approach of death finding the place of violence and meaninglessness in man's best efforts," a paradox again fundamental to Kinsella's own awareness of the real. As he has come to reevaluate Yeats's achievement, so too Kinsella has increasingly acknowledged the older poet's place in relation to his own work: his ancestry or inheritance, for all their essential differences, includes both Joyce and Yeats.

3. Kinsella, "The Irish Writer," 62.

4. "W. B. Yeats, the British Empire, James Joyce, and Mother Grogan," *Irish University Review* 22 (Spring-Summer 1992): 69–79. Subsequent quotations are from this article.

Kinsella praises the last poems of Yeats for, among other things, a "perspective of an Irish tradition, complete with murderous 'strangers.' " In Yeats's "The Curse of Cromwell," for example, Kinsella notes the presence of

> Cromwell in a line of murderous strangers; the levelling wind howling through the ruins of a tradition; and Aogán Ó Rathaille—the last major poet in Irish, a poet of the dispossessed, and a beggar in the time of Swift—vanishing with an echo out of his own last poem:
>
> *rachad 'na bhfasc le searc na laoch don chill,*
> *na flatha fá raibh mo shean roimh éag do Chríost.*
>
> And there is an old beggar wandering in his pride—
> His fathers served their fathers before Christ was crucified.[5]

Yeats and Ó Rathaille have come to constitute part of Kinsella's poetic inheritance, an inheritance that has proved from the outset a matter of crucial significance. As we have seen, he has persistently striven to know "who he is and where he comes from"[6]—questions that, as a poet, touch upon his relationship with the Irish tradition and the several exemplars to whom he has turned for enablement and liberation.

Yeats appears most prominently in conjunction with Ó Rathaille in "At the Western Ocean's Edge." Distinct as the two men might be, they arrive at similar experiences from different sources, both coming to an understanding of the heroic nature. The poem may open by proclaiming one definition—"Hero as liberator"—in which the echo of Daniel O'Connell's title suggests a public, political role, but it pursues a second, intrinsically tragic definition, of "the warrior marked by Fate," whose struggle is internal, with his self. Certainly, Kinsella's work has traced that same internal struggle to establish identity for himself and his people. One instance of such a hero is Cuchulain, who, Kinsella says in explicit reference to Yeats's poem "Cuchulain's Fight with the Sea," "finding the foe inside his head, / . . . turned the struggle outward, against the sea." In Cuchulain Yeats found an image of the conflict within himself and, in a battle Kinsella has himself continued in his own time, used the mythic hero "as a second shadow / in his own sour duel with the middle classes":

5. Ibid., 76.
6. Kinsella, "The Irish Writer," 57.

> Yeats discovered him through Lady Gregory
> and found him helpful as a second shadow
> in his own sour duel with the middle classes.
> He grew to know him well in his own right
> —mental strife, renewal in reverse,
> emotional response, the revelation.
>
> (26)

Yeats gives way once more, however, to another forebear, Aogán Ó Rathaille, a poet closer to Kinsella in both temperament and participation in the Irish tradition. Living in poverty in the Dingle Peninsula—"at the Western ocean's edge"—in geographical, physical, economic, and cultural extremity, Ó Rathaille is brought to a similar revelation, taking on the sea in much the same way as Cuchulain. What Kinsella, like Yeats, finds praiseworthy is heroic endurance in the face of chaos combined with a persistent, contrary rage for order; he believes that this combination is at the heart of understanding and of the poetic or creative process. Ó Rathaille thus becomes an ancestral familiar, an exemplar whose work elicits the contemporary poet's approval:

> Aogán Ó Rathaille felt their forces meeting
> at the Western ocean's edge
> —the energy of chaos and a shaping
> counter-energy in throes of balance;
> the gale wailing inland off the water
> arousing a voice responding in his head,
>
> storming back at the waves with their own force
> in a posture of refusal, beggar rags
> in tatters in a tempest of particulars.
> A battered figure.
> Any force remaining
> held in waves of threat inside the mind.
>
> As who can not confirm, that set his face
> beyond the ninth shadow, into dead calm.
> Dame Kindness, her bowels torn.
> The stranger waiting on the steel horizon.
>
> (26)

Ó Rathaille may be "A battered figure" (the *Personal Places* version read "wasted"): we know that in later years, dispossessed and living in internal exile, he suffered considerable poverty and hardship. At the same time we know, with Kinsella's worker in mirror, that "The process is elaborate, and wasteful" and that "out of its waste matter, / it [the "work in hand"] should emerge light and solid" (*NLD* 56). We might question why Kinsella replaced the original adjective, "wasted" —so quintessentially a Kinsellan quality—with the more Yeatsian "battered." It may be that the original, despite its precedents in Kinsella's work, could too easily be misread as "squandered," "spent," "ineffectual"; "battered" certainly reinforces the Yeatsian analogue. In any case, Ó Rathaille, like Cuchulain or Lear, confronts chaos and, in suffering waste or battering, embodies the very process he seeks to understand. It may be that Kinsella has turned Ó Rathaille into an image of himself, much as Yeats did with his own personae. It may be also that the figures in the concluding lines—man as a beggar, Dame Kindness, and the ominous stranger—are a fusion of *King Lear*, Yeats's tattered coat, and Auden's Dame Kind and Stranger, with the last suggesting more a Cromwellian murderousness than the Stuart Pretender's welcome return.[7] But the argument is distinctively Kinsella's. With all such exemplars, including Yeats, Kinsella has reached that degree of maturity in which he can assimilate without loss of identity.

Be that as it may, Joyce and others like Auden or Ó Rathaille remain more enabling voices, more compatible forebears than Yeats. It would be a misreading of Kinsella not to recognize that other exemplars have played a more explicitly positive and dominant role in his poetic development. At the same time, Kinsella's own disclaimers at the outset of his career, his subsequent statements about Yeats and his isolation in the Irish tradition, and his most recent discussion of Yeats's understanding of violence and the random, need to be put in the context of his own work, with its recurrent echoes of and parallels with the older poet. What is significant about these late poems, in addition to their intrinsic accomplishment, is that they show not only Kinsella's continuing reference back to Yeats—references which in fact he never entirely renounced—but his gradual assimilation, even appropriation, of Yeats as a recognizable brother in the craft with

7. *King Lear*, 3.4.28; W. B. Yeats, "Sailing to Byzantium"; W. H. Auden, "The Watershed" and "On This Island" (for "Stranger") and "Sext," "Dame Kind," and elsewhere (for "Dame Kindness"), *Collected Poems*, ed. Mendelson, 41, 112–13, 478, 503–4.

whose inheritance he can now live comfortably, without fear of being swamped or overshadowed. That appropriation, I suggest, is itself a measure of Kinsella's own poetic majority and achievement.

I have argued that Ó Rathaille comes to embody the very process he seeks to understand. Such embodiment is the heroic version of the aesthetic after which Kinsella as a poet strives. "I am looking," Kinsella has declared, "for totality of imaginative response with the merely linguistic characteristics deleted so that one is brought closer and closer to the data."[8] His technical development—from the early lyrical poems, through the narrative and meditative poems of *Downstream* and *Nightwalker*, to the dense, intertextual, polyphonic later poems—has proved necessary in order more adequately to articulate the data. A poem thus becomes, like Ó Rathaille in "At the Western Ocean's Edge," an embodiment, in which the data's "form and unity" and those of the poem itself most closely coincide. Samuel Beckett's comment on Joyce's *Work in Progress*—"His writing is not about something; it is that something itself."[9]—thus looks increasingly applicable to Kinsella. For much of his writing career, he has sought to exorcise the ghost of Yeats and, through the liberating example of Joyce, to evolve a style that accommodates the punishing integrity and inclusiveness of his vision. He has spoken out against "narrowness" of vision, whether that which "sees nothing beyond 'Anglo-Irish' " or that which abjures "the English element in the Irish inheritance."[10] It is fitting, therefore, to see Kinsella writing at the height of his powers; embracing not just his long-standing exemplar, Joyce, but his shadow, Yeats; and, through the figure of Aogán Ó Rathaille, resolving, at least to his own satisfaction, the dual nature of the Irish tradition.

Such resolution, however, should not be misread as implying any continuity between the English and the Gaelic halves of the Irish tradition. "Nothing could be less likely. Ireland's history discounts continuity of any kind," he has pronounced flatly.[11] Nevertheless, what Kinsella is drawn to and which he believed was exemplified in his edition, *The New Oxford Book of Irish Verse*, is that "there is a

8. O'Driscoll, "Interview," 65.

9. "Dante . . . Bruno, Vico . . . Joyce," in Samuel Beckett et al., *Our Exagmination Round His Factification for Incamination of Work in Progress* (Paris, 1929/London: Faber and Faber, 1961), 14.

10. Kinsella, "Another Country . . . ," 178.

11. O'Driscoll, "Interview," 64.

poetic response to the complex of experience and it exists in two languages. The two bodies of response interact among themselves in some extraordinary ways."[12] The same interaction occurs in Kinsella's bringing together of Yeats and Ó Rathaille, resulting in what he sought from the beginning: a poetry that can say and do anything, that responds in abundant, consummate, and convincing ways to modern experience. That in itself, I would suggest, is a major achievement and has made him an essential voice of our time.

12. Ibid., 64–65.

Works Cited

WORKS BY THOMAS KINSELLA

Books of Poems

Another September. Dublin: Dolmen Press, 1958.

Baggot Street Deserta. Advance proof copy of *Another September*. Freyer Collection, Trinity College, Dublin.

Blood and Family. Oxford: Oxford University Press, 1988.

Butcher's Dozen. Peppercanister 1, reissued. Dublin: Peppercanister, 1992.

Downstream. Dublin: Dolmen Press, 1962.

Fifteen Dead. Dublin: Dolmen Press/London: Oxford University Press, 1979.

From Centre City. Oxford: Oxford University Press, 1994.

Moralities. Dublin: Dolmen Press, 1960.

Nightwalker and Other Poems. Dublin: Dolmen Press, 1968.

Notes from the Land of the Dead. Dublin: Cuala Press, 1972.

Notes from the Land of the Dead and Other Poems. New York: Knopf, 1973.

One and Other Poems. Dublin: Dolmen Press/London: Oxford University Press, 1979.

One Fond Embrace. Peppercanister 13. Dublin: Dedalus Press, 1988.

Personal Places. Peppercanister 14. Dublin: Dedalus Press, 1990.

Poems. Glenageary, Co. Dublin: Dolmen Press, 1956.

Poems and Translations. New York: Athenaeum, 1961.

Selected Poems, 1956–1968. Dublin: Dolmen Press, 1973.

Songs of the Psyche. Peppercanister 9. Dublin: Peppercanister, 1985.

Three Legendary Sonnets. Drumcondra: Dolmen, 1952.
Wormwood. Dublin: Dolmen, 1966.

Editions

The New Oxford Book of Irish Verse. Edited and translated by Thomas Kinsella. Oxford: Oxford University Press, 1986.

Translations

An Duanaire, 1600–1900: Poems of the Dispossessed. Edited by Seán Ó Tuama. Dublin: Dolmen Press, 1981.
Longes Mac nUsnig: Being the Exile and Death of the Sons of Usnech. Dublin: Dolmen Press, 1954.
The Táin. Dublin: Dolmen Press/London: Oxford University Press, 1970.

Individual Poems

"Brothers in the Craft." *Quarry* 39 (Winter 1990): 83.
"Dick King." *University Review* 2, no. 12 (1961): 10–11.
"Downstream." *Massachusetts Review* 5 (Winter 1964): 323–25.
"Dusk Music." *Irish Writing* 24 (September 1953): 66–68.
"Night Conference, 6 June 1979." *Wood Quay Occupation News* 2 (12 June 1979): np.
"Old Harry." *Studies* 50 (Summer 1961): 186–89.
"The Poet Egan O'Rahilly, Homesick in Old Age." *Dublin Magazine* 5 (Summer 1966): 23.
"The Secret Garden." In *Fifteen Poems for William Shakespeare*, edited by Eric W. White. Stratford-upon-Avon, U.K.: Shakespeare Trust, 1964.

Essays and Notes

"Another Country. . . ." In *The Pleasures of Gaelic Poetry*, edited by Seán Mac Réamoinn, 175–82. London: Allen Lane, 1982.
"A Background to Modern Irish Painting." *National Student*, ns, 110 (January 1951): 14–22.
"The Divided Mind." In *Irish Poets in English*, edited by Seán Lucy, 208–18. Cork: Mercier Press, 1972.
"From *The Dual Tradition*." *Krino* 14 (Winter 1993): 30–32.
"The Irish Writer." In *Davis, Mangan, Ferguson?: Tradition and the Irish Writer. Writings by W. B. Yeats and Thomas Kinsella*, edited by Roger McHugh, 57–70. Chester Springs, Pa.: Dufour Editions, 1970.
Note on *Another September*. *Poetry Book Society Bulletin* 17 (March 1958).
Note on *Downstream*. *Poetry Book Society Bulletin* 34 (September 1962).
Note on *Nightwalker*. *Poetry Book Society Bulletin* 55 (December 1967).
"W. B. Yeats, the British Empire, James Joyce, and Mother Grogan." *Irish University Review* 22 (Spring–Summer 1992): 69–79.

Reviews

Review of Richard Murphy, *The Archaeology of Love*. *Irish Writing* 33 (December 1955), 62–63.
"Art of Austin Clarke." *Irish Times*, 10 March 1956, p. 6.

"Auden and Achilles." *Irish Press*, 18 February 1956, p. 4.
Review of Louis MacNeice, *Autumn Sequel*. *Irish Writing* 29 (December 1954): 65–67.
"A Gathering of Poets." *Irish Press*, 16 June 1956, p. 4.
"Here Are the Poets." *Irish Press*, 14 December 1957, p. 4.
"The Hundred Cantos of Ezra Pound." *Irish Press*, 26 October 1957, p. 4.
"Major American Poet." *Irish Press*, 23 June 1956, p. 4.
"New Found Land." *Irish Writing* 36 (Autumn–Winter 1956–1957): 184–86.
"A Poet's Minor Miracle." *Irish Press*, 5 November 1955, p. 4.
"Poetry Must Be Human." *Irish Press*, 19 November 1955, p. 4.
"Prim American Poet." *Irish Press*, 16 February 1957, p. 4.
"Song at Fifty." *Irish Times*, 9 July 1959, p. 8.
"Words from Three Poets." *Irish Press*, 22 February 1958, p. 4.
"The World of the Poets." *Irish Press*, 1 December 1956, p. 4.

SECONDARY SOURCES

Andersen, Jørgen. *The Witch on the Wall: Medieval Erotic Sculpture in the British Isles*. Copenhagen: Rosenkilde and Bagger/London: Allen and Unwin, 1977.
Auden, W. H. *Collected Poems*. Edited by Edward Mendelson. London: Faber and Faber, 1977.
———. *The English Auden: Poems, Essays, and Dramatic Writings, 1927–1939*. Edited by Edward Mendelson. London: Faber and Faber, 1977.
Beckett, Samuel, et al. *Our Exagmination Round His Factification for Incamination of Work in Progress*. London: Faber and Faber, 1961.
———. *Three Novels: "Molloy," "Malone Dies," "The Unnamable."* New York: Grove Press, 1965.
Bradley, John, ed. *Viking Dublin Exposed: The Wood Quay Saga*. Dublin: O'Brien Press, 1984.
Broder, Peggy. "Breaking the Shell of Solitude: Some Poems of Thomas Kinsella." *Eire-Ireland* 14 (Summer 1979): 80–92.
———. "Images of the Feminine in the Poetry of Thomas Kinsella." *Canadian Journal of Irish Studies* 5 (June 1979): 87–99.
Broderick, Edna. Review of *Another September* and *Downstream*. *Icarus* 38 (December 1962): 40–42.
Brown, Terence. *Ireland: A Social and Cultural History, 1922–1979*. Glasgow: Collins, 1981.
Browne, Noel. *Against the Tide*. Dublin: Gill and Macmillan, 1986.
Campbell, Joseph. *The Hero with a Thousand Faces*. New York: World, 1969.
Carson, Julia, ed. *Banned in Ireland: Censorship and the Irish Writer*. Athens: University of Georgia Press, 1990.
Cherry, Stella. *A Guide to Sheela-na-Gigs*. Dublin: National Museum of Ireland, 1992.
Clarke, Austin. *Poems, 1955–1966*. Edited by Liam Miller. Dublin: Dolmen Press, 1974.

———. *Selected Poems*. Edited by Thomas Kinsella. Dublin: Dolmen Press, 1976.

Coleridge, S. T. *Biographia Literaria*. 2 vols. Edited by J. Shawcross. London: Oxford University Press, 1967.

Crankshaw, Geoffrey. Album backcover notes to Gustav Mahler, *Symphony no. 8*, Chicago Symphony Orchestra, dir. Georg Solti, London/Decca OSA 1295.

Crashaw, Richard. *The Poems, English, Latin, and Greek, of Richard Crashaw*. Edited by L. C. Martin. Oxford: Clarendon Press, 1957.

Culler, Jonathan. *The Pursuit of Signs: Semiotics, Literature, Deconstruction*. London: Routledge and Kegan Paul, 1981.

Danaher, Kevin. *The Year in Ireland*. Cork: Mercier Press, 1972.

Dash, Samuel. *Justice Denied: A Challenge to Lord Widgery's Report on "Bloody Sunday."* New York: Defence and Education Fund of the International League for the Rights of Man and the National Council for Civil Liberties, 1972.

Davie, Donald. "First Fruits: The Poetry of Thomas Kinsella." *Irish Writing* 37 (Autumn 1957): 47–49.

Deane, Seamus. "The Appetites of Gravity: Contemporary Irish Poetry." *Sewanee Review* 84 (Winter 1976): 199–208.

———. *Celtic Revivals: Essays in Modern Irish Literature, 1880–1980*. London: Faber and Faber, 1985.

———. *History Lessons*. Dublin: Gallery Books, 1983.

———. "The Music of Kinsella's Poetry." *Irish Literary Supplement* 7 (Fall 1988): 34, 38.

de Paor, Liam. *The Peoples of Ireland: From Prehistory to Modern Times*. London: Hutchinson/Notre Dame, Ind.: University of Notre Dame Press, 1986.

de Tolnay, Charles. *Hieronymus Bosch*. N.p.: Reynal, 1966.

Donoghue, Denis. "Irish Writing." *Month*, ns, 17 (March 1957): 180–85.

———. *We Irish: Essays on Irish Literature and Society*. New York: Knopf, 1986.

Eliot, T. S. *Four Quartets*. London: Faber and Faber, 1944.

Elliott, David L. "An Interview with W. S. Merwin." *Contemporary Literature* 29 (Spring 1988): 1–25.

Emmet, Robert. *Speech from the Dock*. Dublin: Kilmainham Jail Historical Society, 1978.

Evans, E. Estyn. *Irish Folk Ways*. London: Routledge and Kegan Paul, 1979.

Fallon, Padraic. "Synge to Kinsella: Half-a-Century of Poetic Change." *Irish Times*, 20 October 1962, pp. 9, 12.

Fauchereau, Serge. "La génération d'après-guerre." *Les Lettres Nouvelles*, special issue: *Écrivains irlandais d'aujourd'hui*, March 1973, pp. 99–104.

Fordham, Frieda. *An Introduction to Jung's Psychology*. Harmondsworth, U.K.: Penguin, 1970.

Fraser, G. S., ed. *Poetry Now*. London: Faber and Faber, 1956.

Garratt, Robert F. "Fragilities and Structures: Poetic Strategy in Thomas Kinsella's 'Nightwalker' and 'Phoenix Park.' " *Irish University Review* 13 (Spring 1983): 88–102.

———. *Modern Irish Poetry: Tradition and Continuity from Yeats to Heaney*. Berkeley and Los Angeles: University of California Press, 1986.

Gartenberg, Egon. *Mahler: The Man and His Music*. London: Cassell, 1978.

Graves, Robert. *The White Goddess: A Historical Grammar of Poetic Myth*. New York: Vintage, 1948.

Greacen, Robert. "The Two Voices." *Irish Writing* 3 (November 1947): 82–91.

Haffenden, John, ed. *Viewpoints: Poets in Conversation*. London: Faber and Faber, 1981.

Harmon, Maurice. "The Era of Inhibitions: Irish Literature, 1926–60." *Emory University Quarterly* 22 (Spring 1966): 18–28.

———. "Nutrient Waters." *Poetry Ireland Review* 21 (Spring 1988): 20–24.

———. *The Poetry of Thomas Kinsella: "With darkness for a nest."* Dublin: Wolfhound Press, 1974.

Hartnett, Michael. *A Farewell to English*. Enlarged ed. Edited by Peter Fallon. Dublin: Gallery Books, 1978.

———. *Inchicore in Haiku*. Dublin: Raven Arts Press, 1985.

Heaney, Seamus. "Earning a Rhyme." *Poetry Ireland Review* 25 (Spring 1989): 95–100.

———. *The Government of the Tongue*. London: Faber and Faber, 1988.

———. *An Open Letter*. Derry: Field Day Theatre Company, 1983.

———. *Preoccupations: Selected Prose, 1968–1978*. London: Faber and Faber, 1980.

Henry, Françoise. "The Decorated Stones at Ballyvourney, Co. Cork." *Journal of the Cork Historical and Archaeological Society* 57 (January-June 1952): 41–42.

Hewitt, John. "Recent Verse by Irish Poets." *Threshold* 2 (Summer 1958): 70–75.

Hutcheon, Linda. *A Theory of Parody: The Teachings of Twentieth-Century Art Forms*. London: Methuen, 1985.

John, Brian. "Contemporary Irish Poetry and the Matter of Ireland: Thomas Kinsella, John Montague, and Seamus Heaney." In *Medieval and Modern Ireland*, edited by Richard Wall, 34–59. Gerrards Cross, U.K.: Colin Smythe, 1988.

———. " 'To Hunger Fiercely after Truth' ": Daimonic Man and Yeats's Insatiable Appetite." *Eire-Ireland* 11 (Spring 1974): 90–103.

Johnston, Dillon. *Irish Poetry after Joyce*. Notre Dame, Ind.: University of Notre Dame Press/Mountrath: Dolmen Press, 1985.

Jordan, John. "Irish Poetry, 1939–1972." In *Irish Poetry Now*, catalogue of the Projects Arts Centre Exhibition, 29 February–11 March 1972, Dublin, pp. 5–13.

Joyce, James. *Finnegans Wake*. London: Faber and Faber, 1950.

———. *A Portrait of the Artist as a Young Man*. New York: Viking, 1960.

———. *Ulysses*. London: Bodley Head, 1955.

Joyce, P. W. *A Smaller Social History of Ancient Ireland*. 2d ed. London: Longman, Green/Dublin: M. H. Gill, 1908.

Jung. C. G. *Memories, Dreams, Reflections*. Rev. ed. Edited by Aniela Jaffé.

Translated by Richard Winston and Clara Winston. New York: Pantheon Books, 1973.

———. *Psyche and Symbol: A Selection from the Writings of C. G. Jung.* Edited by Violet de Laszlo. New York: Doubleday, 1958.

———. *Symbols of Transformation: An Analysis of the Prelude to a Case of Schizophrenia.* Translated by R. F. C. Hull. In *The Collected Works of C. G. Jung,* vol. 5, edited by Herbert Read et al., Bollingen Series no. 20. Princeton, N.J.: Princeton University Press, 1967.

Kavanagh, Patrick. "Diary." *Envoy,* June 1950, pp. 85–90.

———. *Lough Derg: A Poem.* London: Martin Brian and O'Keeffe, 1978.

Kearney, Richard, ed. *The Irish Mind: Exploring Intellectual Traditions.* Dublin: Wolfhound Press, 1985.

———. "Poetry and Myth: Kinsella, Montague, Kennelly." In *Myth, History, and Literary Tradition,* 18–23. Dundalk: Dundalk Arts Publications, 1989.

———. *Traditions: Narratives in Modern Irish Culture.* Manchester, U.K.: Manchester University Press, 1988.

Keats, John. *The Poems of John Keats.* Edited by Jack Stillinger. Cambridge, Mass.: Harvard University Press, 1978.

Kelly, John C. Review of *Another September* and *Downstream. Studies* 51 (Winter 1962): 545–50.

Kelly, Rita. "Darwin and Mr. Kinsella." *Belle* 1 (Autumn 1978): 64–69.

Kenner, Hugh. "Thomas Kinsella: An Anecdote and Some Reflections." In *The Genres of the Irish Literary Revival,* edited by Ronald Schliefer, 179–87. Norman, Okla.: Pilgrim Books/Dublin: Wolfhound Press, 1980.

Kiberd, Declan. "Irish Literature and Irish History." In *The Oxford Illustrated History of Ireland,* edited by R. F. Foster, 275–337. Oxford: Oxford University Press, 1989.

Kilroy, Thomas. "Thomas Kinsella: *Out of Ireland* and *St. Catherine's Clock.*" *Krino* 5 (Spring 1988): 157–59.

Kinsella's Oversight: A Reply to "The Butcher's Dozen." Belfast: British and Irish Communist Organisation, [1973].

Larkin, Philip. *The North Ship.* London: Faber and Faber, 1966.

———. *Required Writing: Miscellaneous Pieces, 1955–1982.* London: Faber and Faber, 1983.

———. "Speaking of Writing." (London) *Times,* 20 February 1964, p. 13.

Lebor Gabála Érenn: The Book of the Taking of Ireland. 5 vols. Edited and translated by R. A. Stewart Macalister. Dublin: Irish Texts Society, 1938–1956.

Liddy, James. "A Difficult, Scrupulous Art." *Kilkenny Magazine* 8 (Autumn–Winter 1962): 45–48.

Longley, Edna. "The Heroic Agenda: The Poetry of Thomas Kinsella." *Dublin Magazine* 5 (Summer 1966): 61–78.

———. *Poetry in the Wars.* Newcastle upon Tyne, U.K.: Bloodaxe, 1986.

———. "Spinning through the Void." (London) *Times Literary Supplement,* 19 December 1980, p. 1446.

Lucy, Seán, ed. *Irish Poets in English.* Cork: Mercier Press, 1973.

Lyons, F. S. L. *Culture and Anarchy in Ireland, 1890–1939*. Oxford: Oxford University Press, 1982.

———. *Ireland since the Famine*. London: Fontana, 1973.

McGreevy, Thomas. *Collected Poems*. Edited by Thomas Dillon Redshaw. Dublin: Raven Arts Press and New Writers Press, 1983.

McGuinness, Arthur E. " 'Bright Quincunx Newly Risen': Thomas Kinsella's Inward 'I.' " *Eire-Ireland* 15 (Winter 1980): 106–25.

MacNeice, Louis. *Collected Poems*. London: Faber and Faber, 1977.

Mac Réamoinn, Seán, ed. *The Pleasures of Gaelic Poetry*. London: Allen Lane, 1982.

Mahon, Derek. "Poetry in Northern Ireland." *Twentieth-Century Studies* 4 (November 1970): 89–93.

Mann, Thomas. *The Letters of Thomas Mann, 1889–1955*. Edited and translated by Richard Winston and Clara Winston. Harmondsworth, U.K.: Penguin, 1975.

———. *Mythology and Humanism: The Correspondence of Thomas Mann and Karl Kerényi*. Translated by Alexander Gelley. Ithaca, N.Y.: Cornell University Press, 1975.

Marcus, David, ed. *New Irish Writing: An Anthology from "The Irish Press" Series*. Dublin: Dolmen Press, 1970.

Miller, Liam. *Dolmen XXV: An Illustrated Bibliography of the Dolmen Press, 1951–1976*. Dublin: Dolmen Press, 1976.

Montague, John, ed. *Bitter Harvest: An Anthology of Contemporary Irish Verse*. New York: Charles Scribner's Sons, 1989.

———. *A Chosen Light*. London: MacGibbon and Kee, 1967.

———. *The Figure in the Cave and Other Essays*. Edited by Antoinette Quinn. Syracuse, N.Y.: Syracuse University Press, 1989.

———. "Living for Ireland." In *16 on 16: Irish Writers on the Easter Rising. Letters from the New Island*, edited by Dermot Bolger, 7: 17–19. Dublin: Raven Arts Press, 1988.

———. *Mount Eagle*. Loughcrew, Co. Meath: Gallery Books, 1988.

———. "The Painting of Barrie Cooke." *Dubliner* 3 (Spring 1964): 38–41.

———. Review of *Another September*. "Strife in Darkness." *Irish Times*, 26 April 1958, p. 6.

———. "Thomas Kinsella." In *Contemporary Writers of the English Language: Contemporary Poetry*, edited by James Vinson, 834–36. London: St. James Press, 1975.

Montague, John, and Liam Miller, ed. *A Tribute to Austin Clarke on His Seventieth Birthday, 9 May 1966*. Dublin: Dolmen Press, 1966.

Morley, John Viscount. *Diderot and the Encyclopaedists*. 2 vols. London: Chapman and Hall, 1878.

Moynahan, Julian. "The Battle of Aughrim: A Commentary." *Irish University Review* 13 (Spring 1983): 103–13.

Murphy, Richard. *The Battle of Aughrim*. New York: Knopf, 1968.

Neumann, Erich. *The Great Mother: An Analysis of the Archetype*. Translated by Ralph Manheim. Bollingen series, no. 46. Princeton, N.J.: Princeton University Press, 1970.

———. *The Origins and History of Consciousness.* Translated by R. F. C. Hull. Bollingen series, no. 42. Princeton, N. J.: Princeton University Press, 1954.

New Larousse Encyclopedia of Mythology. London: Prometheus Press, 1963.

O'Driscoll, Dennis. "An Interview with John Montague." *Irish University Review* 19 (Spring 1989): 58–72.

———. "Interview with Thomas Kinsella." *Poetry Ireland Review* 25 (Spring 1989): 57–65.

———. "Remembering the Past (Reply to John Hill)." *Crane Bag* 3 (1979): 88–91.

O'Hara, Daniel. Review of *Song of the Night* and *The Messenger. Eire-Ireland* 14 (Spring 1979): 131–35.

O'Meara, John J. *Eriugena.* Oxford: Clarendon Press, 1988.

———. *Eriugena.* In *Irish Life and Culture,* vol. 17. Cork: Mercier Press, 1969.

Orr, Peter, ed. *The Poet Speaks: Interviews with Contemporary Poets.* London: Routledge and Kegan Paul, 1966.

Ó Tuama, Seán. "Gaelic Culture in Crisis: The Literary Response, 1600–1850." In *Irish Studies: A General Introduction,* edited by Thomas Bartlett, Chris Curtin, Riana O'Dwyer, and Gearóid Ó Tuathaigh, 28–43. Dublin: Gill and Macmillan/Totowa, N.J.: Barnes and Noble, 1988.

Partridge, Eric. *A Dictionary of Historical Slang.* Abridged ed. Edited by Jacqueline Simpson. Harmondsworth, U.K.: Penguin, 1972.

Percy, Thomas. *Reliques of Ancient English Poetry.* 4 vols. 6th ed. London: Richards, 1823.

Plato. *The Laws of Plato.* Translated by A. E. Taylor. London: Dent, 1934.

Redshaw, Thomas Dillon. "The Wormwood Revisions." *Eire-Ireland* 6 (Summer 1971): 111–56.

Rees, Alwyn, and Brinley Rees. *Celtic Heritage: Ancient Tradition in Ireland and Wales.* London: Thames and Hudson, 1961.

Rideau, Émile. *Teilhard de Chardin: A Guide to His Thought.* Translated by René Hague. London: Collins, 1967.

Ross, Anne. *Pagan Celtic Britain: Studies in Iconography and Tradition.* London: Routledge and Kegan Paul/New York: Columbia University Press, 1967.

Skelton, Robin. "The Poetry of Thomas Kinsella." *Eire-Ireland* 4 (Spring 1969): 86–108.

Simmons, James. Review of *The New Oxford Book of Irish Verse. Linen Hall Review* 3 (Autumn 1986): 7–9.

Smyth, Darragh. *A Guide to Irish Mythology.* Blackrock, Co. Dublin: Irish Academic Press, 1988.

Teilhard de Chardin, Pierre. *The Future of Man.* Translated by Norman Denny. London: Collins, 1964.

Thwaite, Anthony. *Poetry Today,* 1960–1973. Harlow, U.K.: Longman/British Council, 1973.

Tracks. Special Thomas Kinsella Issue. Edited by John F. Deane 7 (1987).

Weir, Anthony, and James Jerman. *Images of Lust: Sexual Carvings on Medieval Churches.* London: Batsford, 1986.

Woods, Macdara. "John Jordan, 1930–1988." *Poetry Ireland Review* 25 (Spring 1989): 15–30.
———. Review of *Fifteen Dead* and *One*. *Cyphers* 11 (Winter 1979): 52–53.
Yeats, W. B. *Collected Plays*. London: Macmillan, 1953.
———. *Collected Poems*. London: Macmillan, 1955.
———. *A Vision*. London: Macmillan, 1937.

Index

Reading the Ground: The Poetry of Thomas Kinsella was composed in 10/12 Electra with Hiroshige Sans Black display type by dix!, Syracuse, New York; printed on 60-pound Glatfelter Supple Opaque Recycled and bound by Thomson-Shore, Dexter, Michigan; and designed and produced by Kachergis Book Design, Pittsboro, North Carolina.